Uneasy Partnerships

SHORENSTEIN
APARC
STANFORD

THE WALTER H. SHORENSTEIN
ASIA-PACIFIC RESEARCH CENTER

Studies of the Walter H. Shorenstein Asia-Pacific Research Center

Andrew G. Walder, General Editor

The Walter H. Shorenstein Asia-Pacific Research Center in the Freeman Spogli Institute for International Studies at Stanford University sponsors interdisciplinary research on the politics, economies, and societies of contemporary Asia. This monograph series features academic and policy-oriented research by Stanford faculty and other scholars associated with the Center.

Uneasy Partnerships

CHINA'S ENGAGEMENT WITH JAPAN,
THE KOREAS, AND RUSSIA
IN THE ERA OF REFORM

Edited by Thomas Fingar

Stanford University Press
Stanford, California

Stanford University Press
Stanford, California

Printed in the United States of America on acid-free, archival-quality paper

Library of Congress Cataloging-in-Publication Data

Names: Fingar, Thomas, editor.
Title: Uneasy partnerships : China's engagement with Japan, the Koreas, and Russia in the era of reform / edited by Thomas Fingar.
Other titles: Studies of the Walter H. Shorenstein Asia-Pacific Research Center.
Description: Stanford, California : Stanford University Press, 2017. | Series: Studies of the Walter H. Shorenstein Asia-Pacific Research Center | Includes bibliographical references and index.
Identifiers: LCCN 2016043165 (print) | LCCN 2016044486 (ebook) | ISBN 9781503601413 (cloth : alk. paper) | ISBN 9781503601963 (pbk. : alk. paper) | ISBN 9781503601970 (ebook) | ISBN 9781503601970 (ebook)
Subjects: LCSH: China—Foreign relations—1976– | China—Foreign relations—Japan. | Japan—Foreign relations—China. | China—Foreign relations—Korea. | Korea—Foreign relations—China. | China—Foreign relations—Russia (Federation) | Russia (Federation)—Foreign relations—China.
Classification: LCC DS779.27 .U63 2017 (print) | LCC DS779.27 (ebook) | DDC 327.51—dc23
LC record available at https://lccn.loc.gov/2016043165

Typeset by Newgen in 11/14 Garamond

Contents

Preface

When everything comes together, the challenges of producing an edited volume are more than compensated for by the increased understanding of complex problems that results from interaction among the contributors and insights that emerge from the juxtaposition of independently authored analyses. Most of the patterns and trends that become apparent when comparing and aggregating the interpretations in this volume were not anticipated when we began this project in 2012 or predicted by any of the participants when we discussed alternative ways to explore and explain interactions among China and the countries of Northeast Asia. The decision to focus on specific dyads and multistate groupings without attempting to fit the analysis to a predetermined framework, model, or theory proved fruitful. We all learned new and important things about China's engagement and about changes within the countries of Northeast Asia. I hope—and expect—that our readers will also discover new insights and deepen their understanding of China's perceptions, priorities, and policies and that they will gain similar insight into the ways in which regional states responded to perceived opportunities and risks resulting from China's rise and greater activism on the regional stage.

As director of the Shorenstein Asia-Pacific Research Center, I am pleased that the center was able to support the project and proud to include this volume in our series published by Stanford University Press. It is the second in a planned series that will examine China's interactions with other regions of the world and, we hope, reveal additional trends and patterns transcending individual regions and strengthen confidence in our judgments about how and why those patterns exist. Neither this volume nor others in the series attempt to predict the future, but the identification of trends, what drives them, and their implications for the countries involved provide a useful starting point for anticipating how events may unfold.

Tom Fingar's acknowledgment section properly cites the contributions of the many people who helped transform an interesting idea into a scholarly contribution to our understanding of China's objectives, how other countries perceive them, and how China's increased engagement with other parts of the world is changing both regional and global interactions. Many people contributed, but the genesis of the project was his observation, based on decades of experience as a State Department and intelligence community analyst, that all nations formulate foreign policy goals and strategies on the basis of their perception of perils and opportunities and that no nation ever achieves all that it hopes to achieve in the international arena.

What actually happens, he observed, almost always results from the interaction of multiple actors pursuing independent agendas with varying amounts of skill and resources. China's rise, he argued, makes it a more formidable player, but China does not and cannot have the ability to ignore the actions and aspirations of prospective partners and interested third parties. He translated this insight into a proposal and the proposal into a plan. His observation and argument made sense but remained to be subjected to rigorous empirical analysis. My Shorenstein APARC colleagues and I decided to fund the project because it appeared both possible and important to learn whether, or to what extent, his observations were correct and to discover the most important directions and drivers of China's global engagement. This book more than justifies the confidence we had in both Fingar and the project. More important, its publication makes the research of the contributors and the insights from the project available to students, scholars, and government officials seeking to understand and to influence developments in the global arena.

Gi-Wook Shin
Director
Walter H. Shorenstein Asia-Pacific Research Center

Acknowledgments

This volume, like all successful endeavors, has many "parents." Each contributed in a unique way, but all contributions were essential. No individual scholar could have produced the insightful analyses of so many and so diverse dyadic and multiparty interactions, and any attempt to identify and explain spatial and temporal patterns, trends, and linkages would perforce be severely limited without high-quality case studies. This was a team effort, and I acknowledge, albeit inadequately, the important contributions of each member of the team.

The genesis of the project was an invitation from the Shorenstein Asia-Pacific Research Center's (APARC) director, Gi-Wook Shin, to propose new ways to examine changing relationships in Asia and between Asian countries and other portions of the globe. His invitation spurred me to write down a number of observations about China's increasing engagement with other regions, dissatisfaction with existing explanations of what was happening and where it was headed, and an initial list of questions for empirical research. Over the following few months, Gi-Wook, Shorenstein APARC associate director for research Dan Sneider, and APARC colleagues Mike Armacost, David Straub, Karl Eikenberry, Harry Rowen, and Don Emmerson critiqued and commented on successive drafts with the shared goal of developing a research strategy that, if successful, would significantly enhance our understanding of China's role and limitations in the global order. I am deeply grateful for their insights, suggestions, and frank and sincere criticism.

The project would have remained just an idea without the funding from APARC that made it possible to commission papers and convene meetings to talk through what we hoped to accomplish and to begin integrating the results of the research and synthesis undertaken by each of the contributors. Without funding, even the best research proposal is simply an interesting idea. Thanks to Gi-Wook, Dan, and Shorenstein APARC, this idea became a reality.

Before commissioning papers, we decided to hold a "proof of concept" workshop to explore the utility of tentative hypotheses about drivers and shapers of China's policies toward countries in different regions and at different stages of development. Although we intended to focus on China's interactions with countries in Northeast Asia, we wanted to ensure that we developed a framework that would also be appropriate for other regions of the world. To do so, we included scholars and policy practitioners from Southeast Asia, Russia, and the United States. The approach worked, thanks to the substantive engagement and insights of all participants and fabulous logistical support from Shorenstein APARC staff and the Stanford Center at Peking University.

Only a few of the Beijing workshop participants eventually wrote chapters for this book, but all contributed to our understanding of the dynamics at work and to development of the analytic framework used in this and other volumes in the series. Those who attended the workshop and subsequent exchanges on specific issues were Liru Cui, Shen Dingli, Wang Jisi, Yang Xiyu, and Yu Tiejun (China); Christine Susanna Tjhin (Indonesia); Kokubun Ryuosei and Seiichiro Takagi (Japan); Chung Jae Ho and Myung-Hwan Yu (Republic of Korea); Victor L. Larin (Russia); Li Mingjiang (Singapore); Michael H. Armacost, Robert Carlin, Gi-Wook Shin, Daniel C. Sneider, and David Straub (United States); Nguyen Hung Son and Ninh Ton-Nu-Thi (Vietnam); and Chulacheeb Chinwanno (Thailand).

Those who authored chapters for this volume were, of course, indispensable for its success. Their backgrounds and affiliations are given at the beginning of the book, but I would be remiss not to list their names in this section as well. Thanks go to the contributors, without whom we could not have produced this book: Liru Cui, Suisheng Zhao, Seiichiro Takagi, Myung-Hwan Yu, David Straub, and Artyom Lukin. Their patience and willingness to rework their chapters to ensure better integration and clearer exposition of similarities and differences were invaluable to the project.

APARC colleagues Debbie Warren, Irene Bryant, and Wena Rosario were indispensible and indefatigable in managing correspondence and meeting arrangements, as was Tracy Hill, my incredible assistant based in the Center for International Security and Cooperation. Jean Oi, Andy Andreasen, and Victoria Kwong provided invaluable assistance during the workshop in Beijing, and APARC editor George Krompacky saved me repeatedly from computer errors that threatened to destroy large chunks of text and helped with formatting and other issues. Thank you all.

Shepherding the book through the editorial process required and benefited from the efforts of APARC series editor Andy Walder, Stanford University Press editor Jenny Gavacs, and Stanford University Press editorial assistant James Holt. It was a pleasure working with them, and I appreciate their confidence in the project.

The contributions of all were essential, but I alone am responsible for the generalizations in Chapters 1 and 10. Others may, and I trust do, share many of the judgments expressed there, but they do not share responsibility for them and are not culpable for any errors that may remain. Finding and fixing them was my responsibility, and if any remain, I apologize.

Thomas Fingar
February 2017

Contributors

Liru Cui is a senior adviser to China Institutes of Contemporary International Relations (CICIR), a think tank in China known for its comprehensive studies on current international affairs and prominent role in providing consulting services to the Chinese government. He served as the president of CICIR from 2005 to 2013. He concurrently teaches at three universities in China. His research covers US foreign policy, US-China relations, international security issues, and Chinese foreign policy. Professor Cui is a member of the Committee of Foreign Affairs of the Chinese Peoples' Political Consultative Conference and also serves as a member of the Foreign Policy Consulting Committee of the Ministry of Foreign Affairs. He is vice president of China National Association for International Studies and serves as senior adviser to multiple institutions for the study of national security and foreign relations.

Thomas Fingar is a Shorenstein Distinguished Fellow in the Shorenstein Asia-Pacific Research Center at Stanford University. From May 2005 through December 2008, he served as the first deputy director of national intelligence for analysis and, concurrently, as chairman of the National Intelligence Council. He served previously as assistant secretary of the State Department's Bureau of Intelligence and Research (2004–2005), principal deputy assistant secretary (2001–2003), deputy assistant secretary for analysis (1994–2000), director of the Office of Analysis for East Asia and the Pacific (1989–1994), and chief of the China Division (1986–1989). Fingar is a graduate of Cornell University (AB in government and history, 1968) and

Stanford University (MA, 1969, and PhD, 1977, both in political science). His most recent book (editor) is *The New Great Game: China's Relations with South and Central Asia in the Era of Reform* (2016).

Artyom Lukin is deputy director for research and associate professor of international relations at the School of Regional and International Studies, Far Eastern Federal University (Vladivostok, Russia). He was a public relations officer in the Vladivostok city administration (1998–2002) and at the largest energy utility in the Russian Far East (2002–2007). He earned his PhD in political science from Far Eastern State University in 2002 and has authored numerous chapters and articles on Russia's engagement with Asia and international politics in the Asia-Pacific region. His most recent book, coauthored with Rensselaer Lee, is *Russia's Far East: New Dynamics in Asia Pacific and Beyond* (2015).

David Straub is an independent researcher, educator, and commentator on current Korean Peninsula affairs. From 2008 to 2016, he was associate director of the Korea Program in Stanford University's Walter H. Shorenstein Asia-Pacific Research Center. Previously, he served a thirty-year career as a US Foreign Service officer focused on Northeast Asia, including as director of the offices of Korean and Japanese affairs at the Department of State. Straub is the author of the book *Anti-Americanism in Democratizing South Korea*, published in 2015, as well as of numerous chapters, papers, and op-eds on the North Korea problem and the US–South Korea alliance.

Seiichiro Takagi is a senior associate fellow at the Japan Institute of International Affairs. From 2003 to 2011, he taught in the School of International Politics, Economics, and Communication, Aoyama-Gakuin University, and from 1999 to 2003, he served as director of the Second Research Department, National Institute of Defense Studies. He taught previously at the National Graduate Institute for Policy Studies (1997–1999) and its predecessor, the Graduate School of Policy Science, Saitama University (1978–1997). He is a specialist on Chinese foreign policy and Asia-Pacific security issues. Takagi is a graduate of the Tokyo University (BA in international relations, 1965) and Stanford University (MA, 1969, and PhD, 1977, both in political science).

Myung-Hwan Yu is currently a senior adviser of Kim & Chang Law Office in Seoul, Korea. At the same time he also works as chairman of the Board of

Trustees, Sejong University. He served under the Lee Myung-bak adminis-tration from February 2008 to September 2010 as minister of foreign affairs and trade. As a career diplomat, he served as ambassador to Japan (2007–2008), the Philippines (2004–2005), and Israel (2002–2004), respectively. He also served as vice-minister of foreign affairs and trade from 2005 to 2006. During his thirty-seven-year diplomatic career, he also served in the United States (1988–1991, 1998–2001) and the United Nations (1994–1995). He graduated from Seoul National University, College of Law, in 1970. He was a visiting scholar at the Shorenstein Asia-Pacific Research Center at Stanford University in 2010–2011.

Suisheng Zhao is professor and director of the Center for China-US Co-operation at the Josef Korbel School of International Studies, University of Denver, and founder and editor of *Journal of Contemporary China*. His previous positions include associate professor of political science and inter-national studies at Washington College in Maryland, Campbell National Fellow at Hoover Institution of Stanford University, associate professor of government and East Asian politics at Colby College, and visiting assis-tant professor at the Graduate School of International Relations and Pacific Studies (IR/PS) at University of California–San Diego. He received his PhD in political science from the University of California–San Diego, MA in sociology from the University of Missouri, and BA and MA in economics from Peking University.

Note on Names

Most Chinese names are rendered using the Pinyin system of Romanization. Family names are listed first, followed by the given name or names written as a single word (Zhou Enlai). This convention is not used for names that are more often rendered with other forms of transliteration (Chiang Kai-shek instead of Jiang Jieshi), or when authors in this volume use the Western order of last name last (Liru Cui). Japanese names list given name first and family name last (Shinzo Abe). Korean names are generally given in the order of family name first (Park Geun-hye). Exceptions are made for the names of authors who prefer the reverse order (Myung-Hwan Yu). The names of South Koreans use the convention of separating first and middle given names with a hyphen (Park Geun-hye); North Korean names are rendered without hyphens (Kim Il Sung).

ONE

Uneasy Partnerships

Thomas Fingar

China's rise and increasing activism in the world during the past two decades have produced admiration, anxiety, and an avalanche of academic and journalistic analysis and speculation about China's goals, actions, and intentions. Despite the large volume, amount of detail, and interesting insights produced by foreign and Chinese observers, the number of empirically based comparisons is small, and the cases examined are often so diverse that it is difficult to determine what is being compared and how to interpret their findings.[1] The net result is a collection of inconsistent judgments that call to mind the conclusions of the six blind men who touched different parts of the elephant. For example, depending on the study consulted, one learns that China has a grand strategy and a rather detailed plan that guide its foreign interactions or that it addresses problems and opportunities in an ad hoc and pragmatic way.[2] Other studies reach different judgments on the extent to which China acts as a status quo power or is determined to change the international order,[3] has coherent and tightly coordinated policies or increasingly acts in ways reflecting the divergent interests of competing actors,[4] or manifests a new-type foreign policy to achieve win-win and mutually beneficial outcomes or ruthlessly pursues its own objectives with little regard for the interests of others.[5] Another dichotomy is that between analyses that emphasize historical continuities—the so-called Middle Kingdom syndrome—and those that focus on China's communist authoritarianism and efforts to maintain party rule.[6]

Evidence can be found to support all these—and other—interpretations, but many of them are contradictory, and not all of them can be correct.

More important, it is not obvious whether a particular course of action was intended to capitalize on a transient opportunity, ameliorate especially salient problems, restore China's preeminence, or maintain communist rule. In short, the generalizations are not very helpful.

One reason for the disparate findings and generalizations about China's international behavior is that analysts approach the subject using different perspectives and expertise. The different perspectives can be summarized as those that deduce and explain the actions of China and other countries from the laws and lessons of international relations (IR) theory, China-centric interpretations that focus on China's goals and actions toward one or a few specific countries, and those that examine and interpret China's actions from the perspective of the target or partner country.

International relations–based analyses and predictions of China's goals and behavior focus on the nature and dynamics of regional and global systems. Most who write in this genre are IR specialists who do not claim to have deep knowledge of China or its policy-making processes. Their lack of deep knowledge about China is not regarded as a serious impediment because their system-dominant approach treats China as a generic rising power or, in more refined versions, as a rising power "with Chinese characteristics."[7] In this approach, the modalities of decision making in China (and elsewhere) are much less important than the dynamics of the international or regional system in which it operates. Objectives and behaviors associated with rising states, such as a tendency to perceive the actions of others as intended to constrain or thwart the rising state's ascension to its "rightful" place in the regional or global order, are imputed to China, and Chinese actions are interpreted as evidence that it is behaving as a stereotypical rising power.[8]

The system-level analysis category can be further divided into "realist" and "liberal internationalist" subdivisions. Realists, like John Mearsheimer and Aaron Friedberg, generally interpret—and predict—China's behavior as intended to regain supremacy in Asia and, ultimately, to challenge the United States for global leadership.[9] Liberal internationalists like John Ikenberry, Bruce Jones, and Joseph Nye, in contrast, place greater emphasis on China's increasing integration into the US-led global order and growing dependence on that order for the attainment of its developmental and political objectives.[10]

IR theorists and others who focus on the international system tend to assess China's actions primarily in terms of its relationship with the United

States and a small number of other major powers, and to interpret China's interactions with other countries as extensions or manifestations of Beijing's goals vis-à-vis the United States, India, or—in the first half of the period examined here—the United States and the Soviet Union.[11]

A second genre of work on China's global engagement is more China-centric and tends to explain Chinese policy and behavior in terms of the country's history, culture, political system, domestic situation, and security calculus. Unsurprisingly, most who employ this approach are China specialists who build on their detailed understanding of the country.[12] In contrast to system-dominant analyses that emphasize universal factors, those by China specialists tend to focus on factors that are China-specific (although not necessarily unique to China), such as the nature of the political system, the importance of historical memory (and mythology) of China's past greatness and "century of humiliation," and increasing economic capabilities and requirements.[13]

[margin note: First & Second approach]

China-centric analyses of China's actions on the world stage assign different importance to specific factors shaping Chinese perceptions and policies but generally focus on what China is attempting to do, and why it is attempting to do it, more than on the objectives and actions of the countries that are the target of China's attention. Implicitly, if not explicitly, China's aspirations and actions are treated as independent variables, and the reactions of other nations are assessed as dependent variables. The result is often an unbalanced assessment that gives inadequate attention to the goals, strategies, and second- and third-order consequences of a country's interaction with China.

The third and much smaller category of works on China's engagement with the world consists of those written from the perspective of other countries or regions.[14] For a China specialist, most of these works provide unsatisfactory descriptions and explanations of China's objectives and policy calculus. However, and more important, they provide useful insights into the way the countries in question perceive China and its actions and what the other countries do to capitalize on opportunities resulting from China's rise and to mitigate adverse consequences for their own interests.[15]

[margin note: Third approach]

The chapters in this book attempt to redress this imbalance, in part by demonstrating that the countries that interact with China do not simply respond to challenges and opportunities from the People's Republic. They have objectives of their own, sometimes leverage their relationship with

China to entice or counterbalance third countries, and often seek to take advantage of spillover effects of engagement with China.

Thesis This volume builds on the insights of others who have examined foreign-policy dimensions of China's rise by employing empirical approaches to discover, describe, and explain China's interactions with key states in Northeast Asia during the period of "reform and opening" that began in 1979. Contributors to the volume have eschewed single-issue focuses, diplomatic history, detailed chronologies, archival research, interview-based approaches, and other methodologies in favor of approaches that synthesize insights from their own and others' research to assess and explain what they regard as the most important drivers, characteristics, and trajectories of interactions between China and Japan, the Republic of Korea (ROK), the Democratic People's Republic of Korea (DPRK), and the Soviet Union/ Russia. The contributors do not explicitly assess or apply the approaches and findings of others or develop broad generalizations, theoretical models, or detailed predictions of how events will unfold in the future. Instead, they focus on three questions that, to the extent they can be answered, provide a basis for comparisons within and among regions, over time, and across issue areas. Those questions are:

- What happened?
- Why did it happen that way?
- What impact have China's interactions with the countries studied had on China, the other countries, and the global system?

Taken together, the chapters provide the basis for addressing two additional questions:

- What patterns, trends, and trajectories can be discerned when comparing the findings of the individual chapters?
- Do the findings of the book suggest or support predictions about future actions and interactions?

The framework developed here is based on two key judgments about China's priorities. One is that national security always has the highest priority even if it is not always identified as such. As used here, and in China, security is a compound and elastic concept that comprises the country's ability to deter or in other ways manage actual and imputed threats from abroad, threats to internal stability, and at least some of the time, threats to continued rule by the Chinese Communist Party.[16] Without security, in the analysis of Chinese officials, it is impossible to pursue other objectives.

The second-highest priority is rapid and sustained development. Development, or modernization, has been a Chinese priority for more than a century, but its elevation to the second position dates from the late 1970s. Modernization is seen as critical to the achievement of the prosperity and power necessary to ensure security, stability, and continued legitimacy of the regime. This implies that one of the principal considerations when Chinese leaders make foreign-policy decisions is whether a particular course of action or form of engagement with another country will assist or impede the quest for modernization.

This way of conceptualizing the Chinese calculus of decision posits that when thinking about whether, when, and how to engage with particular countries, two of the principal considerations are the nature and magnitude of the threat that they pose to China's security (or what they can do to mitigate the threat from others) and whether a country can provide what is most needed at a particular time to sustain a high rate of growth and acquisition of advanced technologies. This might be summarized as consideration of what they can do *to* China and what they can do *for* China.

Geopolitics is a strong determinant of both the nature of the threat to China and the potential to assist China's drive for development in specific ways. Thus, for example, countries located far from China generally pose less significant threats and have fewer historical issues with China than do countries located closer to China. The obvious and important exceptions are the United States and, particularly during the Soviet era, the Soviet Union. Similarly, the wealthiest and most advanced countries (in North America, Europe, and Northeast Asia) have the greatest ability to provide markets, capital, technology, and training. Nations in other regions have greater capacity to provide oil, timber, minerals, or other inputs to China's economy.

Rationale for Focusing on a Single Region

Northeast Asia has been the most dynamic region of the world for four decades. Oft-cited indicators include sustained high rates of economic growth, increasing intraregional trade, and production and supply chains involving multiple firms and nations. Japan led the way, demonstrating what could be accomplished through participation in the rules-based economic and security order led by the United States. Taiwan, Hong Kong, and South Korea adapted Japan's strategy to their own situations and achieved comparably impressive results. China learned from their experiences, capitalized on their achievements, and eventually became, by many indicators, the largest economy in the world. It also became a more integral, influential, and assertive player on the regional stage, rekindling historical concerns about China's leverage, ambitions, and intentions.

The story of how Northeast Asia became the region of superlatives and, in many respects, the poster child for export-led growth, transitions from authoritarianism to more responsive and responsible political systems, and economic integration despite deep and often antagonistic historical memories is both instructive and important, but that is not the focus of this book. This is a book about the evolution of relations between China and its most important neighbors—specifically Japan, the two Koreas, and the Soviet Union/Russia—during the era of reform and opening that began in 1979.[17] More specifically, the book examines how China's quest for security and economic development; shared history; the capabilities, concerns, and objectives of China's neighbors; and developments in the broader international system shaped perceptions and policy choices in each of the countries studied here.

China and the other countries discussed here have interacted with one another for thousands of years. They "know" one another very well, but familiarity is a source of distrust, dislike, and disdain. Natural and developmental complementarities create opportunities for cooperation and mutual benefit, but divided memories, different priorities, and deep suspicions shape and constrain interactions. Geographic proximity facilitates trade, cultural interaction, political influence, and armed conflict. People in all countries in the region are cognizant of their shared past but often focus on different aspects of their history, and sometimes remember events very differently.[18] The extent to which history facilitates or impedes particular forms of interaction is a function of contemporary perceptions and priorities. Thus, for example, when Japan and China accorded high priority to increasing their economic ties, both emphasized cultural similarities and the advantages of proximity. But when either acted in ways that impinged on the other's interests, the aggrieved party was quick to cite negative examples from the past.[19] History and proximity influence but do not determine perceptions or the way each country prioritizes and pursues its interests.

Geography, history, and influences such as factor endowment and perceptions of what is possible shape but do not determine national interests and priorities. Interests are defined and prioritized by people. During the first three decades of the People's Republic of China (PRC), Mao Zedong was the principal arbiter of the country's priorities and the policies to pursue them. His choices proved disruptive, divisive, and detrimental to the attainment of declared security and developmental objectives.[20] After Mao died in 1976, Deng Xiaoping and other "veteran cadres" determined that it was both possible and imperative to adopt a very different strategy to enhance China's security and achieve the long-aspired goals of wealth and power.[21]

An important part of the new strategy was designed to address the so-called bad emperor problem by making it far more difficult for any individual to hijack the system as Mao had done repeatedly during the first three decades of PRC history. Chinese communist ideology had always espoused collective leadership, but Mao so dominated the system he led that doctrinal constraints proved totally inadequate. Although party leaders and documents eschew use of the term, what they sought and appear to have achieved was a more effective system of checks and balances.[22] They also appear to have altered procedures in ways designed to impede dramatic policy shifts of the kind that characterized the Maoist era, when no policy remained in place long enough to make informed judgments about how well it worked or which adjustments were needed to enhance performance. The new system was designed to facilitate minor adjustments but impede wholesale changes. The third element of the new strategy was to adopt and adapt approaches that had proved effective in other Confucian culture states.

China's new strategy, announced in December 1978 and immediately sloganized as "Reform and Opening to the Outside World" (or "Reform and Opening"), was actually an old—and proven—strategy pioneered by Japan and adapted successfully by Taiwan, South Korea, and others who became known as the "Asian tigers."[23] The countries that had employed this strategy successfully were different in many ways, but all, like China, had been Confucian cultures, and all but Singapore were in Northeast Asia.[24] If countries that had been strongly influenced by Chinese culture could apply this strategy successfully, China could expect to do likewise. Moreover, the culturally similar and proximate countries that had already achieved success could, if given the right incentives, help China to succeed. One strand of analysis in this book traces the evolution of PRC efforts to engage its neighbors in ways that would contribute to China's quest for rapid modernization and economic growth.

China's quest for sustained development was—and is—Beijing's highest national priority, but it was not the only determinant of how events transpired in Northeast Asia. As important, albeit somewhat more susceptible to redefinition and interpretation, are security considerations. During the era of reform and opening, China has perceived other nations and potential interactions through lenses colored by a deep sense of insecurity and victimhood attributed to real and imagined enemies. The sense of victimhood is reinforced by officially inculcated memories of how the country suffered during the "century of humiliation" from 1840 to 1949.[25] The quest for wealth and power through modernization and economic growth is driven, in part, by conviction than China must have advanced science and technology to support modern military capabilities, and that possessing a modern military is essential to deterring and defeating hostile intent imputed to Japan, the United States, and other historical or potential rivals.[26]

As used here—and by Chinese officials—security is a multifaceted concept that subsumes direct and indirect military threats; threats to global or regional stability with the potential to affect adversely China's access to markets, technologies, and particular commodities; and internal threats to stability, sustained growth, and regime legitimacy.[27] All three dimensions are relevant to China's perceptions and policies in Northeast Asia. Party-controlled media and official statements try to strike a balance between reaffirming Deng Xiaoping's judgment that war with the imperialist powers is inevitable but not imminent and can be delayed through diplomacy and deterrence, and reminding citizens of putative threats from the United States, Japan, and (until its demise) the Soviet Union. These direct threats are compounded by the US-Japan and US-ROK alliances that Chinese officials characterize as "remnants of the Cold War," inherently detrimental to China's security.[28]

As Chinese leaders regularly assert, their developmental strategy requires a stable and peaceful international environment. Sustained growth requires ensured access to increasing volumes and varieties of commodity imports (e.g., oil, iron ore, agricultural products) and stable markets for Chinese goods. Success has enabled the Chinese government and firms to invest in "developing markets" on all continents, and growing requirements for inputs from abroad have made China increasingly vulnerable to supply disruptions in distant locales. Forty years ago, Beijing could be indifferent toward, or even supportive of, political unrest in the Middle East, for example. Heavy reliance on oil from the region changed that in ways that made the danger of instability there and elsewhere a matter of grave concern to Beijing and softened its once-rigid position on sovereignty, noninterference, and United Nations–sponsored peacekeeping operations.[29]

The prospect of regional instability is also a concern with respect to Northeast Asia because of the number of situations with the potential to increase political tensions sufficiently to affect important economic relationships and, in the worst case, to escalate into military confrontation (e.g., cross-strait relations between China and Taiwan, tensions between the ROK and the DPRK and the North's history of provocations, and the Diaoyu/Senkaku territorial dispute between China and Japan). Managing these situations has been a continuing challenge for Chinese diplomats and decision makers.

Threats to internal stability also have both direct and indirect, and global and Northeast Asia–specific, manifestations. All have potency because the two primary pillars of regime legitimacy are performance (i.e., meeting the needs and expectations of ever-more-demanding citizens) and nationalism. Anything that threatens the ability of the country to continue to grow at high rates is perceived as threatening the willingness of China's increasingly well-informed, well-educated, and well-connected middle-class urban citizens to tolerate the downsides of Chinese-style modernization (e.g., corruption, inequality, air and water pollution, unsafe food, costly health care, many other quality-of-life conditions). As China attained upper-middle-income status, the challenges of sustaining high rates of growth and meeting public expectations became more difficult, and this translated into a sense of increased regime vulnerability, which required stronger measures to deter and suppress dissent. It also required increased diligence in managing relations with key economic partners, especially the United States, Japan, the ROK, and Taiwan.

Management of these and other crucial economic and developmental relationships is made more problematic by the fact that key partners have also been characterized as posing significant security threats to the PRC. Downplaying the imputed threat helps to preserve important economic ties but risks appearing to compromise China's security and/or sovereignty, and that, in turn, jeopardizes regime legitimacy. Adopting a tough line in disputes with key economic partners plays the nationalism card to preserve legitimacy but risks diminution of investment, market access, and technology transfers. The situation of Chinese leaders is further complicated by the fact that public demonstrations in support of government positions defending China's territorial claims or protesting military developments that could affect China's security carry an inherent risk of morphing into demonstrations protesting government inaction on the myriad downsides of development already noted. The challenges of managing relations in Northeast Asia are exceptionally difficult because of historical memories and animosities, and the critical importance of China's economic links to countries that are aligned with the United States and perceived as posing potential or actual threats to China's security.

Chinese perceptions and priorities are not the only factors determining the character of relations among states in the region. Each of the other actors has concerns and objectives with respect to China, sees dangers and opportunities in China's rise, and has relationships with third parties that expand and/or restrain their options for dealing with the PRC.[30] Moreover, the perceptions, priorities, and policies of the other actors in the region have changed over time in response to changes in the international system, changing concerns and possibilities linked to China's economic success and military buildup, and changes in their own internal situations (e.g., Japan's prolonged economic downturn, democratic transitions in the ROK and Taiwan, DPRK acquisition of nuclear weapons, and successive changes in Soviet/Russian politics and priorities).

Changes in the International Situation

In the era of globalization, the "international system" is more than an analytic construct, because what happens in any part of the system can have significant consequences and implications for actors across the increasingly integrated and interdependent network of relationships. Three developments in the international system had significant impacts on relationships between China and the other countries in Northeast Asia during the period examined in this volume: the normalization of relations between the United States and China in 1979; the demise of the Soviet Union in December 1991; and the consequences of "globalization" made possible by the computer revolution, the end of the Cold War, and the rules-based liberal international order.

China was a proactive actor in only one of these developments, namely, the normalization of relations with the United States that opened the door to China's participation in the US-led system known at the time as the "free world." In the other two cases, China—and other countries—had to adjust its policies in response to developments it had not initiated. Globalization has proved very beneficial to Beijing's drive for modernization, sustained economic growth, and international influence, but it has also constrained China's freedom of action by making it increasingly dependent on the global system into which it has been integrated. Opportunities and constraints resulting from greater interdependence and the nature of China's economic and technical relationships with Japan and the ROK are a central part of the evolutionary story examined in this volume.

Later chapters examine specific consequences of US-China normalization in greater detail, but it is worthwhile to note a number of them here in order to illustrate the cascade effects of decisions taken for relatively narrow reasons. When Beijing determined that Mao's quest for a self-reliant path to modernity had caused the PRC to fall increasingly far behind countries it considered potential threats to China's security, and that it was prudent to abandon experimentation in favor of adapting a strategy that had proved effective in other Confucian culture states, it did so recognizing that this required closer relations with Washington than the "enemy of my enemy is my friend" relationship established by Mao and Nixon. To secure American support for Chinese participation in the system previously limited to members of the "free world," Beijing determined that it must normalize relations and that this, in turn, required abandoning China's long-held position on resolution of Taiwan-related issues. That cleared the way for the establishment of diplomatic relations between the United States and China, which arguably reduced the military threat from the United States and its allies and made it possible for China to shift resources from the military to economic construction.[31] These developments facilitated China's rise, but that was not the only consequence.

The decision of the Carter administration to assist China's drive to modernize via the reform and opening strategy provided direct and substantive benefits to China in the security and the developmental arenas. Symbolically, it signified that the United States did not regard China as an enemy and would provide access to American training and technology. Substantively, it ended the US Mutual Defense Treaty with the Republic of China and relaxed export controls and other impediments to economic cooperation in ways that both responded to China's announced priorities and helped Beijing to prioritize on the basis of what was immediately accessible.[32] But it also brought critical indirect benefits by making clear to US allies in the region and beyond that Washington would not object if they too improved ties and deepened their relationships with China. Tokyo took steps to do so almost immediately after Nixon's 1972 trip to China, but Seoul was not ready to begin exploring possibilities for economic cooperation until the late 1980s.

The most immediate and tangible of the indirect benefits came from Japan. Negotiations between Tokyo and Beijing to conclude a treaty of peace and friendship had stalled until Jimmy Carter's national security adviser Zbigniew Brzezinski urged Japan to conclude the treaty after visiting Beijing in May 1978.[33] Japan had been eager to expand economic ties with China but was reluctant to do so without clear indication of approval from the United States.[34] As noted by Seiichiro Takagi in Chapter 5, normalization of relations between the United States and China cleared the way for aid, trade, and investment from Japan, arguably the country with greatest knowledge of what was needed to jump-start China's economy.

The normalization of relations between the United States and China did not have the same immediate impact on either South or North Korea because China was not yet willing to put distance between itself and the DPRK, the ROK did not have what China most needed to modernize quickly, and Seoul was consumed by its own internal political turmoil.[35] The changed relationship between Washington and Beijing paved the way for later changes in China's perception of and policies toward the ROK and the DPRK, but conditions were not ripe for (or did not require) substantive change until China made progress toward modernization and economic engagement, ROK political and economic evolution made it more able and willing to engage with China, and DPRK actions forced Beijing to respond. The chapters by Yu, Fingar, and Fingar and Straub examine key parts of this evolutionary tale.

The rapprochement initiated by Nixon and Mao was intended to catch the attention of the Soviet Union, and as demonstrated in the chapter by Artyom Lukin, it did. So did the derivative improvement in Sino-Japanese relations described by Seiichiro Takagi, which was interpreted in Moscow as evidence of a US-led effort to forge a US-PRC-Japan united front to contain and threaten the Soviet Union. Moscow responded by increasing its military deployments along China's northern border and, later, attempting to improve its own relationship with Beijing.

Changes in Soviet priorities and policies during the Gorbachev era had a more immediate impact on relations in Northeast Asia than did the demise of the Soviet Union and end of the Cold War. Gorbachev's decision to reduce the number of Soviet troops deployed along China's northern border and other steps to improve long-frosty relations with Beijing reduced the threat to China's security in ways that validated Deng's contention that China had a window of opportunity to pursue modernization because the external threat could be managed through deterrence and diplomacy. Moscow's efforts to jump-start its own economy and improve relations with the West caused it to move away from the DPRK and toward the ROK. This triggered developments that led to the admission of both Koreas to the United Nations in 1991 and cleared the way for Beijing to recognize the ROK the following year.[36]

Formal demise of the Soviet Union ended the Cold War at the global level but it did not lead to collapse of the DPRK, reunification of Korea, or immediate changes in relations across the Taiwan Strait. It did, however, remove the primary rationale for rapprochement between the United States and China, and for the US-Japan alliance. It was not immediately obvious or certain that the broader interests and ties that had developed in the US-China relationship would be sufficient to withstand the loss of a common enemy, especially in the aftermath of the 1989 Tiananmen incident. Beijing appears to have decided that it was prudent to be more attentive to US concerns, especially on transnational issues.[37] Nor was it immediately clear whether or how the US-Japan alliance should be changed, or what should be done to prevent the appearance or reality of transforming it into an anti-China alliance.[38] This issue still has not been fully resolved, and China frequently condemns the alliance as an outmoded remnant of the Cold War, but Japan's immediate response to the changed circumstances was to press ahead with efforts to assist China's modernization and to demonstrate to Beijing that it had not become hostile because the common enemy had ceased to exist.[39]

Russia under Boris Yeltsin had begun to distance itself from the DPRK, depriving Pyongyang of its traditional means to counterbalance China at a time when China's strategy of development was beginning to produce impressive results. In response, Kim Il Sung, and later Kim Jong Il, began to explore possibilities for better relations with the United States, Japan, and even the ROK.[40] China, in turn, had to adjust to the now much more fluid situation on its border.

A third international development affecting China's relations with its neighbors in the region was the process of globalization. Japanese companies were among the first to build multinational production and supply chains and were looking for new locales when China adopted the strategy of reform and opening. Proximity, cultural similarities, and natural complementarities made cooperation between Japan and China an attractive option despite historical legacies and deep animosity. As demonstrated in the chapter by Seiichiro Takagi, the Japanese felt both confident of their own economic prowess and a responsibility to make amends for the actions of imperial Japan. The chapter by Suisheng Zhao demonstrates that Chinese were willing to cooperate with Japanese firms for analogous reasons.

South Korea's economic takeoff and readiness to participate more fully in globalization lagged those of Japan by approximately a decade, but by the late 1980s, Korean firms were eager to expand into China, in part to remain competitive with Japanese firms. This created new opportunities for China that proved attractive enough to change long-standing PRC policies toward both the ROK and the DPRK (described in Chapter 6). Although they are not examined in this volume, similar evolutions in the economies of Taiwan and China led to the establishment of economic ties that both required and facilitated changes in political relations.[41]

Interdependence is inherently a two-way street, and developments that made China increasingly dependent on Japan and the ROK also made the latter countries increasingly dependent on China. Actors on both sides of the dyads perceived the resultant situation as a source of both leverage and concern.[42] Ambivalence about the consequences of economic interdependence increased after the financial crisis of 2007–2008. The direct financial consequences in Asia were considerably less than they were in North America and Europe, but their indirect and psychological impacts were significant. China was not affected immediately or directly because it had not participated in the practices that led to and exacerbated the banking collapse elsewhere. Many in and outside of China interpreted this to mean that China's political economy and economic policies were demonstrably superior to those of the United States and the West more generally, and as another indicator that China was about to—or had already—displaced the United States as leader of the global system.[43] At a minimum, it increased Chinese confidence that they were on the right track.[44]

The resultant and extended slowdown in the world's two largest markets (the European Union and the United States) inhibited Japan's recovery from its own prolonged recession. This compounded the psychological blow of losing its status as the world's number-two economy to China, but it also underscored Japan's growing economic dependence on China and concerns about Beijing's ability to exploit economic leverage for political benefit.[45] But the economic relationship between China and Japan is interdependent, not unidirectional. With the slowdown in China's other principal markets, it is more dependent on Japan, and this, in turn, constrains what either Beijing or Tokyo is willing to do in the dispute over the Diaoyu/Senkaku Islands.[46] The slowdown in the United States and Europe also increased the importance of the Chinese market to South Korea.[47]

Changes Linked to China's Rise

The success of China's reform and opening policies has transformed the country from impoverished regional laggard into the world's second-largest economy. Almost four decades of high growth and its place in multinational production chains have made it the largest importer of many commodities, the largest exporter, and the world's largest trading nation. It is, by almost any measure, a very important economic power and, by volume and value, the most important trading partner of Japan and both of the Koreas. Success bolstered Chinese confidence in their strategy and their country. The chapter by Liru Cui illustrates well the interplay of success, confidence, and conviction that China was following a trajectory unlike that of any previous modernizer or rising power. I argue (in Chapter 2) that China's approach and trajectory are less unique than Cui considers them to be.

As other chapters in this volume demonstrate, the extent of their perceived economic dependence on China is worrisome to all of its regional partners. Political leaders and ordinary citizens in these countries recognize that their own prosperity is tied to that of China and are troubled, especially so in the ROK, by Beijing's efforts to exploit economic interdependence to achieve political goals.[48] Russians, as Lukin demonstrates, were initially condescending toward China's reform and opening policy and saw no immediate opportunities for their country to contribute to or benefit from the PRC's quest for modernity. Russians' perceptions changed, however, as China demonstrated success, needed more of what Russia had to offer, and threatened to undercut or overwhelm their own country's drive to modernize. China now looms as an economic challenger—or threat—to Russia.

Exactly how much influence Beijing gains from its economic strength is impossible to determine, but it seems reasonable to conclude that it is less than many in China assume and more than many in Japan, the ROK, and the DPRK want it to be. Indeed, an oft-heard lament in discussions about the evolving situation in the region is that allies of the United States feel caught between their most important security partner, the United States, and their most important economic partner, the PRC.[49]

The concern is understandable as a theoretical problem but seems difficult to reconcile with reality for two reasons. One is that it seems premised on the assumption that clashes, even conflict, between China and the United States are inevitable. Many commentators treat this assumption (or prediction), which derives from realist theories of international relations, as an accurate depiction of current reality despite the fact that the United States has arguably done more to assist China's rise than any other nation and has pursued a policy of engagement through eight administrations.[50] The second reason is that China is not the final destination for most of the products shipped there by Japan, the ROK, or Taiwan. The "huge" China market remains more latent than realized, except for commodities and certain producer goods. The most important ultimate markets remain those in North America, Europe, and Japan. The large volume of goods shipped to China from the other economies in the region includes components and intermediate goods for assembly in China and delivery to the ultimate consuming nations. In other words, China's apparent economic strength and importance to the region is substantially the result of its place in global supply chains and decisions made in boardrooms far removed from the PRC.

Despite China's $10.4 trillion gross domestic product (GDP), however, it is still a middle-income country with per capita GDP of only $7,593, because its population is so large. Comparable per capita GDP figures for Japan and the ROK are $36,194 and $27,970, respectively.[51] China can and will become a larger market for consumer and other goods, and it could well become a more important engine of growth elsewhere. But it has not yet achieved that status, and to do so, it must manage successfully the many challenges of escaping the "middle-income trap."[52] I write this not to gain-say China's achievements but to underscore that there is still a considerable gap between what China is and what it could become. Nevertheless, its neighbors, and many around the globe, sometimes seem to perceive China as having already achieved that to which it aspires. Even if they do not phrase the matter in this way, they hedge against the possibility that China will be more important to their economic fate in the future by acting as if it had already achieved greater importance than it has.

On one dimension of China's rise, however, there is no question about China's "arrival" as a major player. That dimension is military power. After deferring military modernization and equipment acquisitions for many years, China embarked on a program of double-digit military growth (measured in budgetary terms) that has now lasted for two decades.[53] The cumulative effect of this growth has changed the actual and perceived strategic situation in Northeast Asia. Other governments in the region did not react for many years but eventually concluded that they must do something to reassure citizens and hedge against the possibility that China intended to use its military capacity for more than deterrence. China has exaggerated and misconstrued the actions of Japan, South Korea, and the United States as unprovoked and anti-China. As of now, what has transpired can be characterized as prudent hedging, but there is real danger that hedging could morph into a classic security dilemma and arms race that no one in the region wants to happen.

Internal Changes Affecting Perceptions and Policies

China and all of its neighbors are very different today from how they were at the outset of reform and opening in 1979. China's population has increased by more than 375 million, providing a considerable "demographic dividend" in the quest for economic growth but restricting per capita gains. The dividend is over, but the additional people will require food, water, and services for many decades. Two generations of the "one child per family" policy have kept population growth lower than it otherwise would have been, but at the expense of producing a society with few siblings, cousins, aunts, or uncles able to provide support when impersonal institutions prove inadequate. Moreover, approximately half of the population consists of single children raised as "little emperors and empresses" who have lived their entire lives in the period of extraordinary growth. More than half the population now lives in cities, where they need and expect more from the government than their rural forebears. They expect and demand more from officials and are at least as impatient as young people elsewhere.

These and other demographic changes in China have increased the need for and importance of quantitative and qualitative growth to meet rising expectations, making it imperative to maintain access to the markets, technologies, and training necessary for sustained development. The legitimacy of the regime depends heavily on its ability to satisfy the rising expectations of younger generations and the parents and grandparents each couple must support in retirement. This is a formidable challenge that will compel leaders to continue to accord high priority to doing what is necessary to sustain high rates of growth, including the management of China's relations with the countries in and outside the region that are most important to PRC growth and stability.[54]

Meeting performance expectations of the increasingly well-informed and well-connected populace will become more difficult as China struggles with the challenges of middle-income status and faces increased competition from the dozens of countries that adopted the Asian tiger model of development after China did. Unless Beijing modifies the political system in ways that provide safety valves in the form of greater accountability and citizen participation, it seems likely to rely more heavily on the nationalist pillar of legitimacy. Doing so may conflict with the imperative of maintaining good relations with neighboring countries critical to China's economic success. The chapters by Zhao and Takagi illustrate how this has played out in recent years.

The net result of the analysis summarized here is that it is likely to become more difficult for Beijing to manage relations with Japan, the Koreas, the United States, Russia, and others at precisely the time that doing so becomes more important to economic performance and regime legitimacy. The problem is made more difficult by the perceived imperative to build China's military capacity as a hedge against uncertainty and the imputed hostile intent of the United States and its allies.

Domestic developments in Japan and the Koreas are also changing perceptions and calculations. As noted in the chapter by Seiichiro Takagi, the lenses through which Japanese officials and the public view China and Chinese actions have changed over the decades of reform and opening in China. Developments contributing to the changes include the economic collapse in the early 1990s that ushered in a prolonged recession and loss of confidence, generational change that diminished the role and influence of persons with extensive experience in China and contrition for Japanese actions during the war and occupation, and the gradual erosion of support for leftist parties and policies on a host of issues, including relations with China.[55] These, and other, domestic developments changed the way Japanese people and politicians viewed China and Chinese actions, what Japan was willing and able to do vis-à-vis China, and the efficacy of Chinese policy toward Japan.

Changes in the Republic of Korea were as significant as those in Japan. The chapter by Myung-Hwan Yu reflects the impact of some of these changes, the most important of which were the transitions from authoritarianism to democracy, and from middle-income to advanced-economy status. Political change made it necessary for politicians to be more attentive to public sentiment about China, the DPRK, Japan, and the United States.[56] Truly competitive politics and the highly polarized character of the Korean electorate led to frequent and substantial changes in policy, especially policies toward the DPRK and, both directly and indirectly, the PRC and the United States.[57]

The growth and maturation of South Korea's economy also had a profound effect on Korean perceptions of China and Chinese perceptions of the ROK. When Deng launched the policy of reform and opening in 1979, the ROK had much less to contribute to China's quest for modernity than did the United States, Japan, or Western Europe, and Korean firms were not yet looking to expand overseas. That changed, and by the last decade of the twentieth century, Korean companies were eager to invest in countries with more and cheaper labor and a proven ability to meet tight deadlines. At roughly the same time, China became an attractive location because, after a decade of reform and experience gained by working with firms from other countries, China was ready for the jobs and technologies Korean companies could provide. Changed possibilities contributed to changes in ROK foreign policy vis-à-vis the PRC.[58] Chapters 6 and 7 examine the impact these developments had on both sides of the PRC-ROK relationship.

North Korea's acquisition of nuclear weapons was a very different type of domestic change.[59] The chapter by Fingar and Straub describes Pyongyang's two-pronged strategy to enhance DPRK security (pursuit of nuclear weapons and use of diplomatic means to counterbalance and defuse perceived threats). Despite partial successes on the diplomatic front, it proved easier to acquire the bomb than to normalize relations with the United

States, Japan, and the ROK.[60] When it did so, it changed the way North Korea was perceived by China and others in the region, and it changed other nations' policies toward the DPRK. It also changed DPRK policies toward China. Until 2009, Pyongyang had rebuffed most Chinese efforts to invest in extractive and other facilities in the DPRK and to build infrastructure that would facilitate cross-border trade. After the second nuclear test (and the failure of DPRK efforts to improve relations with the United States), however, Kim Jong Il adopted measures that opened the way for Chinese investment in every province.

Changes in the Soviet Union/Russia rival in magnitude the ones that have occurred in China but are different in both form and implications. But as the chapter by Lukin demonstrates, changes in Russia's relationships with the West in general and the United States in particular have had greater impact on its perceptions of and policies toward China than have the internal changes. This chapter also suggests that Vladimir Putin's reversion to a more authoritarian form of government and Xi Jinping's style of governance may have done more to influence relations with China than any of the economic, demographic, or societal changes in Russia.

Overview and Objectives of the Book

This is a book about China's interactions with Japan, the two Koreas, and the Soviet Union/Russia in the decades since 1978. The United States is sometimes a central player and always a backstage presence because of its centrality to the security and economic calculations of all the other countries. There is much that the book does not address, including relations between and among the players other than China, and precisely how China and the other players pursued the broad objectives that are the focus of the book. In other words, this is a book about what China has attempted to achieve with respect to other players in the region and, in broad terms, what each of the partners has sought from China or to address concerns about China, its actions, and/or its intentions. It is also a book about why each country has pursued the goals that it has and how outcomes have been shaped by the compatibility or contradictions of the goals pursued by individual countries and the skill with which they have pursued them.

This is not the book for anyone seeking a comprehensive overview of interactions in Northeast Asia during the past four decades or a detailed diplomatic history of interactions between and among the major players. Nor does it look in detail at investment, trade, and other economic interactions; changes in the regional military balance; or the influence and impact of particular political leaders. These are important subjects, but they are not central to the focus of chapters in this volume. What the book and the individual chapters do address are the declared, deduced, or imputed highest priorities of the People's Republic of China and its regional partners, and the broad strategies and policies adopted to achieve their priority objectives. Our goal is to provide an empirically based macro-level analysis of China-centered interactions in Northeast Asia since 1979.

China's highest priorities are security and development. The two goals are interconnected; security (including internal stability) is required for development, and development (modernization and economic growth) is necessary for military and comprehensive security. These declared priorities are the starting point for Beijing's assessment of what other countries can do to threaten or bolster China's security, and what they can contribute to China's quest for wealth and power. What is necessary to achieve security and sustained development changes over time, as do the intentions and capabilities of other countries. Such changes expand or shrink the range of possibilities and require modifications to the policies adopted to achieve overarching objectives and derivative goals. Exactly what Beijing (and, mutatis mutandis, Tokyo, Seoul, Pyongyang, or Moscow) does to achieve its objectives is a function of leadership preferences, what domestic conditions allow or require, and judgments about what is possible and the most effective way to achieve bundles of interconnected objectives.

Although the book explores China's relationships with only four Northeast Asian countries, its purpose is to provide a framework that can be used to examine, explain, and anticipate the character of Beijing's engagement with all regions of the world. As the chapters demonstrate, Beijing has adopted different methods to pursue similar security and developmental objectives in its relationship with other states in the region. Chapter 10 extends the analysis of patterns and dissimilarities by comparing the findings of this volume to those presented in the companion volume on China's relations with states in South and Central Asia.[61]

Individual chapters are structured to illuminate Chinese perceptions, priorities, and policies toward each of the countries examined here in a way that both identifies common or persistent elements and illustrates how and why they are modified to address particular aspects of each partner country. The chapters that address how Japan, the ROK, the DPRK, and Russia perceive China's rise and objectives help explain why they have responded as they have to perceived opportunities and dangers inherent in China's rise, and why China's policies have had only mixed success. Over time, changes in the international situation, respective levels of development, and the way publics and political leaders perceive others in the region have produced changes in emphasis and policy instruments, but all of the relationships examined here remain fraught and fragile. The chapters that follow help to clarify why that is so.

Notes

1. The introductory section of this chapter is a slightly modified version of the introductory pages of the first book in a projected series of volumes examining China's engagement with different regions since 1978. The first volume, edited by Thomas Fingar, is entitled *The New Great Game: China and South and Central Asia in the Era of Reform* (Stanford, CA: Stanford University Press, 2016). I decided to undertake this series because during the decades that I have studied China's interaction with other countries, especially the fifteen years during which I supervised and edited assessments of developments in and interactions among all countries on all issues while a senior official in the US government, I thought that I observed patterns of behavior in China's relations with other countries that varied by region and over time. The patterns appeared to result from changing Chinese assessments of the country's security situation and changing requirements of its quest for economic growth and rapid modernization. In addition to its other objectives, this book represents an attempt to refine and test preliminary judgments and hypotheses about China's priorities and calculus of decision.

2. See, for example, Robert Sutter, *Chinese Foreign Relations: Power and Policy Since the Cold War*, 4th ed. (Lanham, MD: Rowman and Littlefield, 2016), chap. 1; Avery Goldstein, *Rising to the Challenge: China's Grand Strategy and International Security* (Stanford, CA: Stanford University Press, 2005); Thomas Christensen, "China," in *Strategic Asia, 2001–2002*, ed. Richard Ellings and Aaron Friedberg (Seattle: National Bureau of Asian Research, 2001), 27–70; and Wang Jisi, "China's Search for a Grand Strategy," *Foreign Affairs* 90, no. 2 (2011): 68–79.

3. See the analysis and citations in Alastair Iain Johnston, "Is China a Status Quo Power?" *International Security* 27, no. 4 (2003): 5–56; and Feng Huiyun, "Is China a Revisionist Power?" *Chinese Journal of International Politics* 2 (2009): 313–334.

4. See, for example, Marc Lanteigne, *Chinese Foreign Policy: An Introduction* (New York: Routledge, 2009); and Linda Jakobson and Dean Knox, *New Foreign*

Policy Actors in China (Stockholm: Stockholm International Peace Research Institute, 2010).

5. See, for example, Su Hao, "Harmonious World: The Conceived International Order in Framework of China's Foreign Affairs," in *China's Shift: Global Strategy of the Rising Power*, ed. Masafumi Iida (Tokyo: National Institute for Defense Studies, 2009), 29–55; David Haroz, "China in Africa: Symbiosis or Exploitation?" *Fletcher Forum of World Affairs* 35, no. 2 (2011): 65–88, http://www .fletcherforum.org/wp-content/uploads/2013/12/Haroz_FA.pdf; and "Relations with Myanmar: Less Thunder out of China," *The Economist*, October 6, 2011, http://www.economist.com/node/21564279.

6. See, for example, David Shambaugh, *China Goes Global: The Partial Power* (Oxford: Oxford University Press, 2013); and Roderick MacFarquhar, "How Serious Is Xi Jinping About Tackling Corruption in China?" *The Atlantic*, June 28, 2013, http://www.theatlantic.com/china/archive/2013/06/how-serious-is-xi-jinping -about-tackling-corruption-in-china/277345/.

7. See, for example, Aaron L. Friedberg, "Hegemony with Chinese Characteristics," *National Interest*, July–August 2011, 18–27, http://web.clas.ufl.edu/users/ zselden/coursereading2011/Friedberg.pdf.

8. Ibid.; and Stephen M. Walt, "How Long Will China Tolerate America's Role in Asia?" *Foreign Policy*, December 2, 2013, http://www.foreignpolicy.com/ posts/2013/12/02/whats_the_big_question_answer_the_us_and_china.

9. See, for example, John J. Mearsheimer, "The Gathering Storm: China's Challenge to US Power in Asia," *Chinese Journal of International Politics* 3, no. 4 (2010): 381–396; and Aaron L. Friedberg, *A Contest for Supremacy: China, America, and the Struggle for Mastery in Asia* (New York: W. W. Norton, 2011).

10. See, for example, G. John Ikenberry, *Liberal Leviathan: The Origins, Crisis, and Transformation of the American World Order* (Princeton, NJ: Princeton University Press, 2011); and Bruce Jones, *Still Ours to Lead: America, Rising Powers, and the Tension Between Rivalry and Restraint* (Washington, DC: Brookings Institution, 2014).

11. An exception by a scholar who is both an IR specialist and an excellent China specialist is Thomas J. Christensen, *The China Challenge: Shaping the Choices of a Rising Power* (New York: W. W. Norton, 2015).

12. Examples include David Shambaugh, ed., *Tangled Titans: The United States and China* (Lanham, MD: Rowman and Littlefield, 2013); Robert Ross and Zhu Feng, eds., *China's Ascent: Power, Security, and the Future of International Politics* (Ithaca, NY: Cornell University Press, 2008); and Susan L. Shirk, *China: Fragile Superpower* (Oxford: Oxford University Press, 2008).

13. See, for example, Suisheng Zhao, ed., *Chinese Foreign Policy: Pragmatic and Strategic Behavior* (Armonk, NY: M. E. Sharpe, 2004).

14. Examples include Riordan Roett and Guadalupe Paz, eds., *China's Expansion into the Western Hemisphere* (Washington, DC: Brookings Institution, 2008);

Robert I. Rotberg, ed., *China into Africa: Trade, Aid, and Influence* (Washington, DC: Brookings Institution, 2008); Ian Storey, *Southeast Asia and the Rise of China: The Search for Security* (New York: Routledge, 2013); and Srikanth Kondapalli and Emi Mifune, eds., *China and Its Neighbors* (New Delhi: Pentagon Press, 2010).

15. This chapter does not intend or pretend to provide a comprehensive summary of this vast literature. An overview of what has been written and the approaches adopted can be found in Sutter, *Chinese Foreign Relations.*

16. See, for example, "Xi Jinping Expounds Security Commission Role," *Xinhuanet,* November 15, 2013, http://news.xinhuanet.com/english/china/2013 -11/15/c_132892155.htm.

17. The choice of countries and dyadic relationships explored in this book reflects a conscious decision to eschew coverage of China's interactions with "all" regional players in favor of examples that illustrate how Beijing's perceptions, priorities, and policies are shaped by geography, history, economic and security considerations, third-country relationships, developments in the global system, and the objectives and actions of other countries. Including Taiwan and Mongolia would have increased the number of cases and provided additional detail about China's relationships in the region but would not have changed bottom-line judgments about what shapes the goals and consequences of Beijing's initiatives toward other countries and reactions to other country actions affecting China. Insightful books on relations between Mainland China and Taiwan include Richard C. Bush, *Uncharted Strait: The Future of China-Taiwan Relations* (Washington, DC: Brookings Institution, 2013); Steven M. Goldstein, *China and Taiwan* (Cambridge, UK: Polity Press, 2015); and Baogang Guo and Chung-Chian Teng, eds., *Taiwan and the Rise of China: Cross-Strait Relations in the Twenty-First Century* (Plymouth, UK: Lexington Books, 2012). Mongolia's relevance to China's security was a function of its relationship with the Soviet Union until 1992, and it has not been a major contributor to China's quest for economic development and comprehensive modernization. For information on Sino-Mongolian relations, see Morris Rossabi, *Modern Mongolia: From Khans to Commissars to Capitalists* (Berkeley: University of California Press, 2005), chap. 9.

18. See, for example, Gi-Wook Shin and Daniel C. Sneider, eds., *History Textbooks and the Wars in Asia: Divided Memories* (New York: Routledge, 2011).

19. See the chapters in this book by Suisheng Zhao and Seiichiro Takagi.

20. See Andrew G. Walder, *China Under Mao: A Revolution Derailed* (Cambridge, MA: Harvard University Press, 2015).

21. See Ezra F. Vogel, *Deng Xiaoping and the Transformation of China* (Cambridge, MA: Belknap Press of Harvard University Press, 2011).

22. Chinese communist political writers eschew or disparage the utility of checks and balances as that concept is used in American political writings, but

many of the goals and mechanisms enshrined in writing on collective leadership aspire to limit the power of individuals. See John Wilson Lewis, *Leadership in Communist China* (Ithaca, NY: Cornell University Press, 1963); and John Wilson Lewis, *Major Doctrines of Communist China* (New York: W. W. Norton, 1964), chap. 6.

23. The new strategy is described at greater length in Chapter 2. See also Ezra F. Vogel, *The Four Little Dragons: The Spread of Industrialization in East Asia* (Cambridge, MA: Harvard University Press, 1991).

24. See Shiping Hua and Ruihua Hu, *East Asian Development Model: Twenty-First Century Perspectives* (New York: Routledge, 2015).

25. See Zheng Wang, *Never Forget National Humiliation: Historical Memory in Chinese Politics and Foreign Relations* (New York: Columbia University Press, 2012).

26. See John Wilson Lewis and Xue Litai, *Imagined Enemies: China Prepares for Uncertain War* (Stanford, CA: Stanford University Press, 2008).

27. This characterization is based primarily on analytic judgments but it is fully consistent with the announced responsibilities of the National Security Commission established in November 2013. See Yiqin Fu, "What Will China's National Security Commission Actually Do?" *Foreign Policy*, May 8, 2014, http://foreign policy.com/2014/05/08/what-will-chinas-national-security-commission-actually-do/.

28. See, for example, Timothy R. Heath, "China and the US Alliance System," *The Diplomat*, June 11, 2014, http://thediplomat.com/2014/06/china-and-the-u-s -alliance-system/.

29. See, for example, Joel Wuthnow, *Chinese Diplomacy and the UN Security Council: Beyond the Veto* (New York: Routledge, 2013).

30. For a more extended discussion of the reasons that what happens in Northeast Asia and other regions are the result of interaction among multiple ac-tors pursuing objectives vis-à-vis one another and third parties, rather than simply the result of Chinese policies to achieve Chinese goals, see Thomas Fingar, "China and South/Central Asia in the Era of Reform and Opening," in *The New Great Game: China and South and Central Asia in the Era of Reform*, ed. Thomas Fingar (Stanford, CA: Stanford University Press, 2016), chap. 1.

31. See Vogel, *Deng Xiaoping*, chap. 11.

32. See, for example, Harry Harding, *A Fragile Relationship: The United States and China Since 1972* (Washington, DC: Brookings Institution, 1992).

33. See Zbigniew Brzezinski, *Power and Principal* (New York: Farrar, Straus & Giroux, 1985), 218; and Chae-Jin Lee, "The Making of the Sino-Japanese Peace and Friendship Treaty," *Pacific Affairs* 52, no. 3 (Autumn 1979): 420–445.

34. Disagreement over Beijing's demand to include an antihegemony clause was the stated obstacle to conclusion of the treaty, and it no doubt was an im-

portant reason for the delay, but it ceased to be an insuperable obstacle after the United States urged Japan to finalize the agreement.

35. See Don Oberdorfer and Robert Carlin, *The Two Koreas: A Contemporary History*, 3rd ed. (New York: Basic Books, 2014).

36. See Elizabeth Wishnick, *Mending Fences: The Evolution of Moscow's China Policy from Brezhnev to Yeltsin* (Seattle: University of Washington Press, 2014); and Oberdorfer and Carlin, *Two Koreas*.

37. See Thomas Fingar and Fan Jishe, "Ties That Bind: Strategic Stability in the US-China Relationship," *Washington Quarterly* 36, no. 4 (Fall 2013): 125–138; and Thomas Fingar, "China's Goals in South Asia," in *The New Great Game: China and South and Central Asia in the Era of Reform*, ed. Thomas Fingar (Stanford, CA: Stanford University Press, 2016), chap. 2.

38. See Ezra F. Vogel, "Japanese-American Relations after the Cold War," *Daedalus* 121, no. 4 (Fall 1992): 35–60.

39. See the chapter in this volume by Takagi; and Michael Yahuda, *Sino-Japanese Relations After the Cold War* (New York: Routledge, 2014).

40. Oberdorfer and Carlin, *Two Koreas*.

41. See Richard C. Bush, *Untying the Knot: Making Peace in the Taiwan Strait* (Washington, DC: Brookings Institution, 2005).

42. See the chapters in this volume by Yu, Zhao, and Takagi.

43. See, for example, Pieter Bottelier, "China and the International Financial Crisis," in *Strategic Asia 2009–10: Economic Meltdown and Geopolitical Stability*, ed. Ashley J. Tellis, Andrew Marble, and Travis Tanner (Seattle: National Bureau of Asian Research, 2009), 71–102.

44. See the chapter in this volume by Liru Cui.

45. See the chapter in this volume by Takagi; and Linda Sieg, "Analysis: Japan Dilemma as Economic Dependence on China Grows," *Reuters*, September 2, 2010, http://www.reuters.com/article/2010/09/02/us-japan-china-idUSTRE 6810LQ20100902.

46. See, for example, Richard Katz, "Mutual Assured Production: Why Trade Will Limit Conflict Between China and Japan," *Foreign Affairs* 92, no. 4 (July–August 2013): 18–24.

47. See the chapter by Myung-Hwan Yu; and Jae Ho Chung, *Between Ally and Partner: Korea-China Relations and the United States* (New York: Columbia University Press, 2007), chap. 8.

48. See, for example, Choe Sang-Hun, "South Korea Tells China Not to Meddle in Decision over Missile Defense," *New York Times*, March 17, 2015, http://www.nytimes.com/2015/03/18/world/asia/south-korea-tells-china-not-to-meddle-in-decision-over-missile-system.html.

49. See, for example, Chung, *Between Ally and Partner.*

50. See, for example, Aaron L. Friedberg, *A Contest for Supremacy: China, America, and the Struggle for Mastery in Asia* (New York: W. W. Norton, 2011).

51. Figures, which are for 2014, are from the World Bank's World DataBank: http://data.worldbank.org/indicator/NY.GDP.MKTP.CD and http://data.world bank.org/indicator/NY.GDP.PCAP.CD.

52. See Homi Kharas and Harinder Kohli, "What Is the Middle Income Trap, Why Do Countries Fall into It, and How Can It Be Avoided?" *Global Journal of Emerging Market Economies* 3, no. 3 (2011): 281–289.

53. See Ashley J. Tellis and Travis Tanner, eds., *Strategic Asia 2012–13: China's Military* Challenge (Seattle: National Bureau of Asian Research, 2012); Richard D. Fisher Jr., *China's Military Modernization: Building for Regional and Global* Reach (Stanford, CA: Stanford University Press, 2010); and Anthony H. Cordesman, Ashley Hess, and Nicholas S. Yarosh, *Chinese Military Modernization and Force Development* (Washington, DC: Center for Strategic and International Studies, 2013).

54. For analysis of China's relations with other neighboring countries, see Fingar, *New Great Game.*

55. See, for example, Richard Katz, *Japan: The System That Soured* (New York: Routledge, 1998); and Sarah Hyde, *The Transformation of the Japanese Left* (New York: Routledge, 2009).

56. See, for example, A. David Adesnik and Sunhyun Kim, "South Korea: The Puzzle of Two Transitions," in *Transitions to Democracy: A Comparative Perspective,* ed. Kathryn Stoner and Michael McFaul (Baltimore, MD: Johns Hopkins University Press, 2013), chap. 11.

57. Oberdorfer and Carlin, *Two Koreas;* and Samuel S. Kim, "The Two Koreas: Making Grand Strategy amid Changing Domestic Politics," in *Strategic Asia 2007–2008: Domestic Political Change and Grand Strategy,* ed. Ashley J. Tellis and Michael Wills (Seattle, WA: National Bureau of Asian Research, 2007), 113–136.

58. See Young-Chan Kim, Doo-jin Kim, and Young Jun Kim, eds., *South Korea: Challenging Globalization and the Post-Crisis Reforms* (Oxford, UK: Chandos, 2008).

59. See Jonathan D. Pollack, *No Exit: North Korea, Nuclear Weapons and International Security* (New York: Routledge, 2011).

60. See Fingar and Straub in this volume; and Oberdorfer and Carlin, *Two Koreas.*

61. Fingar, *New Great Game.*

TWO

Sources and Shapers of China's Global Engagement

Thomas Fingar

China's rapid emergence as a major player on the world stage has evoked amazement, admiration, and anxiety. People everywhere instinctively know that this is an important development, but officials and ordinary citizens in China often seem as puzzled by what has happened and what it portends as do counterparts elsewhere. Puzzlement and uncertainty about China's accomplishments and objectives affect perceptions and policy decisions across a wide spectrum of issues and endeavors in all regions and most countries. China's rise, size, and activism magnify concern about Beijing's objectives and methods, but they also are seen as creating significant new opportunities. However, understanding of Beijing's objectives, strategies, and feedback mechanisms has not kept pace with its growing importance as a global actor, and efforts to explain and predict China's conduct have relied more on analogy, theory, and extrapolation than on empirical and comparative research.

The starting point for many explanations of China's behavior is to assume or assert that China is and behaves like the type of rising power posited by adherents of the realist school of international relations. According

---

This chapter presents a framework for understanding the priorities and requirements of China's strategy of development, and how that strategy shapes and is shaped by developments in the international system. The many areas of overlap between this chapter and that by Liru Cui (Chapter 3) underscore the significance of the points on which this American view differs from Cui's Chinese assessment.

to this school, the primary objectives of rising state behavior are to acquire and assert power, with the ultimate goal of becoming a dominant or hegemonic power.[1] China, realists argue, does what it does in particular relationships because it can, and because success will move it closer to the imputed goal of displacing the United States.[2] A second starting point eschews the "all major powers behave the same" model in favor of a "China is different" approach. One variant of this approach, which I call the Middle Kingdom school, sees contemporary China as the latest manifestation of "traditional" or "imperial" China determined to reclaim its rightful place as the preeminent power in the region and, by extension, the world.[3] A second variant, often espoused by Chinese scholars and officials, emphasizes that China is unlike other states because it will not seek hegemony and will not interfere in the internal affairs of other nations.[4] Liru Cui's chapter in this volume adopts this perspective.

Each of these interpretations has both strong and weak points, but here I am more interested in their shared propensity to ascribe primary importance to the power, goals, and methods that China brings to bear in its relationships with other actors. This has the perhaps unintended consequence of underestimating the importance of external—systemic—constraints and imperatives shaping Chinese behavior, and overestimating the importance and impact of Chinese actions. The former shortcoming assumes that China has greater freedom of action and wider latitude to determine what it will do and how it will do it than I believe to be the case. The latter makes partner or target actors far more passive than I assess them to be. In my experience, what China decides to do in particular cases is shaped by many factors, including the nature of the global order, China's goals and judgments about what is necessary to achieve those goals, and the anticipated and actual responses of other international actors. This chapter suggests a framework for assessing and integrating these and other shaping variables.

What Drives, Shapes, and Explains China's International Behavior?

Each of the approaches noted manifests a more or less existential interpretation of China's conduct on the world stage. Different scholars adopt different starting points, but the dynamic they posit is essentially the same: China does what it does because of what it is. Realists begin from the proposition that all powers behave in essentially the same way and that observed differences can be explained by differences in the amount and types of power they possess.[5] Rising powers are a subset of the more inclusive group, a distinguishing characteristic of which is that their power is increasing relative to other actors. Rising powers, of which China is an example, are assumed or asserted to behave in accord with their capabilities and relative place in the power-based hierarchy of nations.[6]

Rising powers defer to and act defensively toward countries above them in the hierarchy until they feel capable of displacing a more powerful state. Their behavior toward states with less power is more assertive than it is toward more powerful states, while at the same time guarding against expected attempts to displace them from their own positions on the power ladder. Applying this framework, the most important variable for understanding, explaining, and predicting behavior is the relative power of the states involved. Pushed to the extreme, this approach considers goals as determined by judgments about relative power and strategy as reflecting judgments about the best way to achieve successive objectives.

"China is special" explanations constitute a second existential approach. Adherents of the Middle Kingdom school regard history and culture as the most important shapers of China's foreign policy behavior. According to this approach, the best way to understand recent actions and to predict future behavior is to study the past for insight into how China has interacted with neighboring and more distant states. The approach acknowledges that China behaved differently when it was strong than when it was weak, and therefore implicitly incorporates insights from the realist school.[7] Another variant is the "China is different from in the past and different from other rising or major powers" school. Many Chinese descriptions of Chinese foreign policy behavior employ this approach and argue both that the best way to understand Chinese behavior is to pay attention to official statements and that actual conduct is the same as declaratory policy.[8]

Other variants of the existential approach focus on the authoritarian character of the regime, the fact that it is a Communist Party–led state, or the extent to which it has adopted a state capitalist economic model.[9] For example, many commentators have asserted that China prefers to work with other authoritarian regimes and prefers mercantilist arrangements to markets for ensuring access to resources. The reasons for these alleged preferences are said to derive from the nature of the regime.

Grand Strategy or Master Plan?

China's declaratory foreign policy may not be as determinative as suggested by Chinese commentators, but what it proclaims is not irrelevant or intended only to deceive. There are differences between what is proclaimed and what is actually done by all states and other international actors, but that is not a reason to disregard what officials claim to be doing. Indeed, analyzing why they proclaim what they do and examining deviation from declared policy should be integral to any attempt to understand a country's international behavior. Sometimes the tasks of assessment and evaluation are made easier by the existence of formal grand strategies articulating goals and priorities and means to achieve them. Opinions differ on whether China has a grand strategy.[10]

In theory, China (or any other country) could develop a detailed grand strategy that it treats as a state secret, but such a situation seems unlikely, because the primary reason for having a grand strategy is to facilitate understanding, at home and abroad, and to build support for specific policies and budget requests by linking them to a well-understood and presumably acceptable set of goals.[11] Applying this criterion, China has proclaimed lofty guiding principles but has not articulated a grand strategy. The absence of such an overarching strategy is consistent with the approach to reform and opening articulated by Deng Xiaoping in 1978 and reiterated numerous times since. That approach is well captured by the aphorism "to cross the stream by feeling the stones."[12] This is a "strategy" of careful, step-by-step experimentation that exploits opportunities and avoids costly mistakes. In American baseball parlance, it is a strategy of "take what they give you." Lacking an explicit declaration of grand strategy, analysts must infer and integrate elements of a coherent strategy from specific actions across a wide spectrum of issues and situations.[13]

Although priority objectives remain the same, the strategy and means used by Beijing to achieve them may be changing. Success has transformed China and a new generation of leaders, whose approach to politics was forged in the Cultural Revolution and whose experience as leaders was acquired during the period of steady growth and increasing capabilities.[14] For both objective and subjective reasons, they may want to modify or replace the legacy system they inherited. But what the replacement should look like is far from clear, and the perils, including political risks, of tampering too much with a system that is still producing results critical to regime legitimacy may be perceived as too great to risk a fundamental overhaul of the system put in place in the late 1970s. The short-term solution to this dilemma may be to vest greater power in the principal leader than has been enjoyed by any leader since Deng Xiaoping. Xi Jinping certainly appears to have more power than his three predecessors as president and head of the Communist Party, and many Chinese officials assert that China need no longer act as it did when it was poorer and weaker, but whether what we have seen since approximately 2012 constitutes a fundamentally different strategy remains to be seen.[15]

The preceding paragraphs are not intended to disparage the models, theories, and approaches others have employed to explain and predict China's conduct in particular places and/or on specific issues. Each of them provides insight helpful for understanding interstate relations and anticipating future behavior. But individually and collectively, they raise as many questions as they answer. For example, the implicit criticism of the realist and existentialist approaches assumption that foreign policy behavior is driven by immutable forces (e.g., relative power, culture, regime type) begs the question of what does drive (and shape) Chinese conduct on the world stage. If those aren't the key drivers, what are? If conduct is not the product of immutable forces, which factors are most important in shaping priorities and strategies to achieve them? Why does China do what it does in particular circumstances? How do others respond to or attempt to anticipate and shape Chinese behavior? These and similar questions must be addressed if we are to move beyond analogies and general theory-based explanations and predictions. More to the point, we—Chinese and citizens of other nations—must better understand goals, priorities, methods, and responses if we are to capture opportunities, avoid conflicts, and meet common challenges.

Framework for Analysis

The purpose of this chapter is to provide a framework for anticipating and analyzing China's behavior on the world stage. The framework identifies four compound variables: China's goals, priorities, and strategy; opportunities and constraints in the international system; the perceptions, goals, and actions of other states; and learning and feedback within dyads, among nations, and across regions. Other factors also influence China's conduct, notably—and increasingly—domestic interests and political maneuver, but I consider them less determinative than the factors examined here.[16] Which composite factor is most important almost certainly varies by place, time, and issue.

The framework undergirding this book treats China as a unitary actor and the key factors as composite variables representing the net outcomes of constantly changing objective circumstances and competition among players with variable skills and other resources. All contributors recognize that China is a multifaceted country with many actors, interests, and political agendas. Indeed, the proliferation of interests and the challenges of integrating them are inevitable consequences of modernization, and the difficulty of managing them within the confines of the highly centralized governmental structures and single-party rule are certain to increase. Competition and cooperation across sectors, issue areas, and other boundaries are continuous and critical to the establishment of priorities and the formulation of policies to achieve them. But the focus in this book is on the outcomes of those ongoing processes, not the processes themselves. As such, the outcomes present snapshots of a particular stage of China's interaction with its most important neighbors in the region. The result is, of course, an oversimplification of reality, but it is also a much more empirically based depiction of China and its interactions than are studies focused on testing or proving particular theories of international relations. Our goal is an empirically based, macro-level analysis of China-centered interactions in Northeast Asia during the past four decades.

CHINA'S GOALS AND PRIORITIES

Despite dramatic political changes, the priority objectives of China's domestic and foreign policies have been the same for almost two centuries. Those goals are to increase China's security, wealth, and power while preserving the "essence" of Chinese culture.[17] The Qing dynasty first attempted to achieve these goals through restoration and revitalization of imperial norms and institutions.[18] When that failed to yield desired results, it was supplemented by efforts to achieve self-strengthening through selective borrowing and partial reform.[19] After the Qing dynasty was overthrown in 1911, successive Republican governments adopted a variety of measures to achieve the same objectives.[20] Whether because of defects in the policies adopted or the fact that the country was almost continuously at war, or both, China was still a poor and relatively powerless country when the People's Republic was proclaimed in 1949.

The communist era began with a new strategy to achieve the goals of wealth and power. That strategy differed from earlier approaches in several important ways. One was the explicit decision to reduce China's vulnerability to aggression and interference from noncommunist powers by aligning the People's Republic of China (PRC) with the Soviet Union.[21] Mao Zedong's decision to "lean to one side" in the Cold War seems to have reflected a judgment that the best, and perhaps only, way to buy time for efforts at self-strengthening to achieve results that would reduce China's vulnerability was to "outsource" the nation's security to the Soviet Union. This could not have been an easy decision, because it made China dependent on and susceptible to instructions and interference from Moscow. However, given China's experience over the previous century and the failure of Nationalist governments to achieve wealth and power while simultaneously attempting to deal with Japanese aggression, and concern that Japan, the United States, or a combination of "imperialist" powers would attack the PRC while it was still weak, it was reasonable to rely on the Soviet Union for protection and assistance.

The decision to "lean" to the Soviet Union was expected to, and did, bring more than protection. It also brought substantial assistance and a blueprint for rapid modernization. Joseph Stalin was willing to assist China's efforts to modernize its economy and strengthen its military, but only if Beijing agreed to accept all components and requirements of the Soviet model.[22] Mao, and doubtless other Chinese leaders, chafed at subordination to Moscow, but any discomfort caused by the effective abandonment of long-standing efforts to preserve as much as possible of what was uniquely Chinese was probably ameliorated by the determination to supplant China's "feudal" culture with scientific socialism. Stated another way, Beijing's new rulers were prepared, even eager, to extirpate much of what earlier modernizers had regarded as integral components of the Chinese "essence" in order to accelerate the acquisition of wealth and power.

In conjunction with the restoration of peace after decades of war and destruction, alignment with and reliance on the Soviet Union produced significant advances in agricultural production, industrial capacity, education, living conditions, and military capabilities.[23] Whether sticking with the strategy would have brought similar rates of progress over an extended period or would have encountered the same kinds of structural problems as did the Soviet Union is a question that cannot be answered, because Beijing, or more accurately, Mao Zedong, decided to abandon the Soviet model in order to achieve even faster growth and cultivation of a uniquely Chinese model.[24] In many ways, this was but the latest in a succession of strategies to acquire wealth and power while preserving a Chinese essence.

The decision to abandon the Soviet model in favor of a uniquely Chinese path to modernity that would preserve distinctive aspects of Chinese culture, or more specifically, Mao's vision of what Chinese culture should be, ushered in a two-decade-long period of campaigns, movements, and failed experiments.[25] The failed experiments, compounded by splits in the leadership, deliberate destruction of party and state organizations and instruments of governance, and pursuit of foreign policies that made enemies of both the Soviet Union and the United States (and their allies), jeopardized China's security at the same time that they slowed—or reversed—progress toward greater wealth and power. China was becoming weaker, in both relative and absolute terms, at a time when it perceived and defined the international situation as increasingly dangerous. Mao determined that the threat to China's security objectives required a change in strategy. This determination, together with Richard Nixon's recognition of a possible opportunity to improve the US geopolitical position vis-à-vis the Soviet Union and in Vietnam, led to Nixon's 1972 visit to China and the start of US-China rapprochement.[26]

This background of failed experimentation, repeatedly disrupted attempts to become prosperous and powerful through modernization, uncomfortable vulnerability caused by China's growing weakness relative to the major powers, and incoherence with respect to a Chinese essence that had to be preserved or promoted provided the context and incentive for China's leaders to review the bidding after Mao died in September 1976. Their assessment of the situation produced important decisions with respect to goals, priorities, and strategy.[27] One decision accorded highest priority to rapid modernization—the acquisition of wealth and power. In certain respects, this was a return to the approach adopted in 1949, when Beijing decided to abandon its quest for a uniquely Chinese road to modernity in favor of adopting the "proven" path to success pioneered by the Soviet Union.[28] The late 1970s iteration of this strategy called for adoption of the path to rapid and sustained economic growth pioneered by Japan (with assistance from the United States).[29] The guiding premise seemed to be "stop experimenting in favor of following a proven path to wealth and power." Some in Beijing may have been reluctant to adopt a "Japanese model" because of historical enmity and discomfort about learning from a former vassal. But reluctance and discomfort were assuaged or explained away by shifting the focus from Japan to the United States. The operative slogan was "learn from the teacher, not the student." Washington was the "teacher" that had taught Japan how to take advantage of the "free world" system to speed development through the acquisition of technology, capital, and access to key markets.

By the time Deng and other leaders made the decision to follow the path of Japan, they seem to have become convinced that the United States was prepared to provide the necessary assistance. The Carter administration had signaled that it was ready to do so, and Beijing seized the opportunity.[30] Seizing the proffered opportunity was a necessary but not sufficient condition for successful adoption of the Japanese or Asian tiger model of development. Other requisites included sticking with the strategy long enough to achieve desired results. One of the lessons from the first thirty years of the PRC was that frequent shifts in policy, notably adoption of disruptive "revolutionary" methods as soon as the economy had begun to recover from previous failed experiments, was not a path to success. Lessons from their own experience and a calculated judgment that the "reform and opening" strategy would yield results if left in place for an extended period, and that the United States and other key countries would continue to assist (or at least not impede) China's drive for rapid modernization, made it prudent for the Chinese to "lock in" the strategy so that it could not easily be changed by political decisions in Beijing. Toward that end, and to overcome other manifestations of the "bad emperor" problem resulting from Mao's ability to make unilateral decisions, "reformers" in the leadership changed the structure and decision rules of the system in ways that were designed to prevent any one leader from acting unilaterally.[31] This double lock on the policy of reform and opening still makes it difficult to change policy quickly. It had the desired effect but may be nearing a point at which it deprives the system of the flexibility and agility needed to cope with the consequences of success. Indeed, that may be the reason Xi Jinping was selected to lead the country and given the mandate he appears to have.

History and the logic of previous Chinese strategies of development made it necessary to address security concerns. Deng and his cohorts did so by declaring that China needed a peaceful international environment for a protracted period in order to concentrate on speedy and sustained economic growth.[32] Sustained development, sloganized as the "four modernizations (agriculture, industry, science and technology, and defense), was the key to self-strengthening, and this, in turn, was the key to long-term security.[33] To skeptics who questioned abandoning Mao's longtime position that war was inevitable, Deng asserted that war was still inevitable, but immediate conflict was not. Indeed, he asserted that war could be avoided for at least two decades.[34] This appears to have become a rolling time frame; forty years after it was proclaimed, war can still be avoided for two or more decades.

To buttress Deng's analytical judgment about the likelihood of war, and to lock in the US commitment to assist China's modernization, Deng dropped the long-standing Chinese insistence that the "Taiwan issue" be resolved before the establishment of "normal" relationships.[35] This had the double benefit for the strategy of reducing the direct threat from the United States and its allies, and buttressing the value of the relationship with the United States as a deterrent to aggression from the Soviet Union.

China's reform and opening strategy was much more complex than has been summarized, but the goal here is to clarify priorities, not to provide a complete description. The highest priorities of China's foreign policy and strategy of development are achieving rapid and sustained economic growth in order to become prosperous, powerful, and influential on the world stage, as well as deterring threats to China's security and maintaining the peaceful international environment deemed necessary for attainment of rapid economic growth. Preserving the "essence" of Chinese culture, including "socialism with Chinese characteristics," has been relegated to a lower priority.[36] In the hierarchy of values shaping Chinese behavior, these generally have trumped all others for more than three decades. Together these objectives and priorities, locked in by structural and procedural changes made to prevent counterproductive excesses like those in the Maoist era, exercise a strong influence on China's policy and behavior on the world stage.

OPPORTUNITIES AND CONSTRAINTS IN THE INTERNATIONAL SYSTEM

Beijing's 1978 decision to pursue wealth and power by taking advantage of opportunities afforded by its unique access to the free-world system led by the United States has been vindicated by extraordinary economic achievements and substantial increases in China's role and influence on the world stage.[37] Evaluated in terms of progress toward China's priority objectives—prosperity, power, and security—the strategy has been remarkably successful. It has achieved much of what Deng and others hoped it would. Foreign investment and transfers of technology and access to foreign markets have contributed substantially to China's transformation from a poor agrarian nation to the world's second-largest economy, with more than 50 percent of its people now living in cities and hundreds of millions lifted out of abject poverty. No nation has attacked or seriously threatened China, relations with Taiwan are more extensive and cooperative than ever, and China has interests and a presence on every continent and in most countries.

China's achievements attest to the wisdom of the strategy and the way in which it has been executed by three political generations of Chinese leaders. Success has brought many benefits to the Chinese people and has increased the scope and impact of China's participation in the global system. But the strategy and its success have made China increasingly dependent on the international system that made success possible.[38] This development appears to have been either unanticipated or more consequential than envisioned by Deng and the colleagues who launched the policy of reform and opening. They appear to have assumed, and argued, that participation in the free-world system that was opened to them by the Carter administration would make China more capable and more prosperous, and that this, in turn, would make China increasingly less dependent on the global system.[39]

Greater wealth, power, and independence presumably would enable China to have greater freedom to abide by, reinterpret, or ignore the rules and norms of the international system, and to develop an increasingly independent foreign policy.[40] That may yet happen, but the pattern thus far suggests that China's success is inextricably tied to its integration into the global order that superseded the free-world system after the collapse of the Soviet Union, and that China's ability to act independently of the global order is decreasing. Stated another way, the character of the international system is a significant and increasingly important factor shaping China's international behavior.[41] It also means that China has an increasing stake in the viability and efficacy of the global order.

Constraints on and opportunities for China are a function of both its integration into and dependence on the global order, and the character of that order. For example, the current world order is not just an analytic construct; it is also an extensive, rule-based system constructed, led, and maintained by the United States. US leadership made it possible for China to take advantage of the free-world system more than a decade before the end of the Cold War. Washington could have continued to block access but decided that, if China was to be a partner in the struggle to contain and combat Soviet expansionism, it was better for that partner to be strong than weak. Enabling and actively assisting China to follow the path pioneered by Japan and the Asian tigers were critical to the success of the reform and opening strategy. Whether China would have had equal success if it had joined the US-led global system at the same time as former Warsaw Pact and non-aligned countries seems unlikely. With dozens of other emerging economies now in the game, China's head start is likely to have diminishing benefits unless it can make the transition from imitator to innovator.[42] Beijing seems aware of this and to be attempting to preserve its lead over other developing countries by stealing massive amounts of intellectual property.[43]

From Beijing's perspective, US leadership of the global order is both a positive and a worrisome attribute of the system. Positive attributes include US willingness and ability, at least to this point, to bear a disproportionate percentage of system maintenance costs.[44] This allows China, and others, to take advantage of US-provided public goods—as a classic free rider—and to concentrate on its domestic challenges. Prolonging US leadership is made even more attractive to China because, at least much of the time and on most issues, the United States acts as a liberal rather than as an imperial hegemon.[45] The US-led system is rule based, providing Chinese and others with know-how to take advantage of institutional arrangements, and the security arrangements integrated into the order have helped to preserve the peaceful international environment necessary for sustained growth and modernization of China's economy.

Aspects of the existing order that China finds worrisome include US preeminence and alliances. The reason these are troubling is that many Chinese suspect, or are convinced, that the United States is determined to contain and constrain China's power and influence, both in the region and on a global level. Those holding this view see it as only a matter of time until the US attempts to pull the rug from under China's development in order to prevent China from acquiring sufficient power and influence to challenge US hegemony. Beijing regularly denies that it desires or intends to displace the US at the top of the international order, but many people in many countries, including the United States, question the sincerity of that denial and take measures to hedge against the possibility that China will act contrary to its professed policy.[46] Maintenance of existing US alliances, and efforts by other nations to enlist the United States as a counterweight to China, are part of this hedging behavior, but Chinese tend to interpret them as part of a broader effort to contain China.[47]

The preeminent role of the United States in the global system and assumed, albeit perhaps exaggerated, ability of Washington to persuade or coerce other nations to resist Chinese initiatives or thwart Chinese ambitions constitutes another reason (in addition to direct dependence on US markets, technology, training, and the like) for Beijing to be reluctant to offend or anger the United States. The resultant actual and assumed leverage enjoyed by the United States is both worrisome and offensive to many in China because it threatens China's rise and ability to regain its assumed rightful place at the center of the global system. Moreover, US exploitation of the leverage it enjoys is considered a recurring phenomenon, not merely a theoretical possibility. Examples include pressure on Beijing to support sanctions on Syria and Iran that could jeopardize Chinese oil imports from the Persian Gulf, pressures to join and abide by international control regimes, and congressional threats to impose sanctions in response to China's monetary policies.

Although US influence in the global order is great, China may overestimate the extent to which the decisions and actions of other nations are a response to US pressure. Particularly in cases involving rules and norms of the international system, other nations want adherence as much as or more than the United States does.[48] Overstating the situation, Chinese sometimes think other nations are responding to pressure from Washington when they demand conformity to rules and norms that they subscribe to and often helped to develop. The important point here is not the accuracy or inaccuracy of Chinese assessments of US power but, rather, the fact that the international order has shared interests, including in the preservation of the system and adherence to its rules, and often acts as a quasi-independent influence on state behavior. What the international system is, how it operates, and its shared interests in preserving and perpetuating arrangements from which all members have benefited, often at low costs, are important facts of life that create incentives, opportunities, and constraints for China and all other participants.

PERCEPTIONS, GOALS, AND ACTIONS OF OTHER PLAYERS

International affairs are two-way streets, and what happens is a function of the goals and actions of both players in every dyad and multiple players in many regional or issue-focused groupings. The situation is made even more complex by the tendency—or necessity—of many states to factor in the desires, demands, or anticipated reactions of third parties (e.g., allies, key markets, firms with global production chains). China's deep and deepening integration into the global system increases the complexity and potential for unanticipated or unwanted consequences in a growing number of relationships.

China's relationships with other nations are, to a degree, shaped by history and proximity, primarily because these factors influence perceptions and interpretive frameworks. Nations on China's periphery, particularly those in Northeast and Southeast Asia, view many Chinese statements and actions through the lens of historical memory. Often the frame of reference is the way Chinese dynasties treated them when China was strong and they were regarded as culturally inferior subjects of Chinese suzerainty. When China was weak, they had more independence; when it was strong, they were often treated as vassal states.[49] Those who "remember" the behavior of earlier Chinese regimes often view China's rise with concern, despite assurances from Beijing that it will never (i.e., not again) seek hegemony or in other ways threaten its neighbors.[50]

History, like international relations, works both ways. China seems not to remember, or not to consider relevant, the actions of its own predecessor regimes. However, it assiduously keeps alive memories of affronts to China by predecessors of the current regime in Japan (e.g., Japan's aggression and occupation of China in the twentieth century).[51] Similarly, both the Republic of Korea (ROK) and the Democratic People's Republic of Korea (DPRK) view Chinese actions through lenses colored by their perceptions of Beijing's relationship with the "other" Korea as well as by relations between Korean and Chinese dynasties.[52]

In addition to historical and cultural legacies, proximity—how near or far other countries are from China—also shapes perceptions of security threats. Japan is regarded as posing a threat to China's security because it is close, because it has a strong economy and strong military, and because it is allied with the United States.[53] History, hedging, and the magnitude of US power make the United States a threat to China even though it is far away. European nations are not regarded as threatening China's security because they are distant, weaker, and judged to have no territorial or other designs on China, despite their history of aggression in the nineteenth and twentieth centuries.[54]

Geographic proximity influences historical legacies and perceptions of security dangers but does not determine how China and other nations perceive one another. It does appear to be the case, however, that China has had more strained relationships with nations close to its borders than it has with more distant lands. Conversely, states closer to China appear to be more worried than more distant states about China's intentions and capabilities, and more eager to enlist the United States as a counterbalance.

Another factor shaping the perceptions, and ultimately the goals and strategies of other nations, is the nature of the Chinese system. One element in this compound factor is the nature of China's economic system. Whether it is seen primarily as a market for raw materials, agricultural products, or manufactured goods, or as a competitor for one or more of these categories, colors perceptions of the relationship. Dependence and perceived vulnerabilities to pressure, unfair competition, or other actions influence judgments about how likely and how damaging such actions might be. This, in turn, shapes hedging behaviors to minimize risks. That said, China is also perceived as an important locomotive for regional and global economies, and many other nations want to hitch their economic wagon to the Chinese train.

Another element is the character and perceived stability of the system. China is an authoritarian, one-party state with few checks on the ability of political leaders to make decisions, change policies, and adopt more threatening behaviors. Despite its considerable economic success, China has little soft power; few citizens of other nations want their countries to be more like China, because becoming more like China is perceived as jeopardizing individual freedom and the scope of entrepreneurial success. Many see corruption, cronyism, monopolistic behavior, and other undesirable attributes as inherent to the Chinese system. This makes the system unappealing and, for some, potentially unstable.[55]

What is the net effect of the various elements of other state perceptions (e.g., the extent to which China is perceived to be aggressive, stable, or economically fragile)? The answer is, "It depends." Each "other" country assesses the implications of what it perceives to be China's intentions and ability to achieve them, as well as the options it has for minimizing deleterious consequences for itself while taking maximum advantage of opportunities afforded by China's rise and ambitions. Each also considers possibilities and potential consequences of various hedging behaviors, including relationships with third countries. They prepare policy options geared to what they think China might do and adjust them in response to actual Chinese behavior. China tries to anticipate the objectives, tactics, and moves of other nations when determining its own course of action. On all sides, there is continuous learning and feedback.

LEARNING AND FEEDBACK

Globalization, democratization, and instant communications have dramatically reduced the number, scope, and duration of "confidential" arrangements in the international arena. Governments almost everywhere feel increasingly compelled to explain decisions to legislatures and ordinary citizens, and to respond to criticism and requests for even more information about specific actions, goals, and strategies to achieve them. This is partly the result of the spread of democracy in recent decades, but even authoritarian regimes are finding it necessary to provide more information to their citizens. This trend is reinforced by the growth of markets and multinational supply and production chains. As more actors in all countries require more information to accomplish their objectives, governments have responded by making more information available. Nonstate actors (e.g., firms, international financial institutions) have added to both the demand for and the supply of information. It is not too much of an exaggeration to say that information about any international transaction quickly becomes available to governments and other actors everywhere.

Greater transparency has many consequences, including exposing governments to closer scrutiny and more pressure from interested—and increasingly well-informed—constituencies. Chinese officials frequently report that public sentiment—expressed by netizens using the Internet—is an increasingly important constraint on government action. For example, netizen pressure may have influenced Beijing to take a tougher stand on territorial disputes with Japan and Southeast Asian states.[56] The Republic of Korea's government postponed the signing of an intelligence sharing agreement with Japan in June 2012 because of the popular outcry after the existence of the agreement was revealed.[57]

Arguably to a greater extent than ever before, governments must consider the reactions of their own publics and publics in the country or countries directly affected by a prospective action. But, also to a growing extent, they must consider how governments, firms, and actors elsewhere in the region and beyond will view prospective actions. Whether this leads to better decisions or to patterned behavior cannot be answered without empirical research. What we can say is that it makes decision making more complicated and more cumbersome (because it requires input from more constituencies), and it facilitates learning among nations and across regions. One of the objectives of this project is to determine whether and how transactions in one dyad or region inform and influence goals and strategies with respect to other issues or in other regions.[58] I hypothesize that transnational learning plays a role in shaping both China's approaches and the objectives and approaches of partner states in each successive transaction. How much of an influence and how impacts vary over time, from region to region, and according to the type of issue involved, and how significant that influence is in comparison to the other shaping factors noted earlier are questions that cannot be answered without detailed comparative analysis.

Applying the Framework

The framework outlined in this chapter can be used to generate initial predictions and hypotheses about China's relationships with countries in particular regions, in this case, Northeast Asia. For example, the posited hierarchy of goals suggests that China's approach to dealing with Japan, the ROK, and the DPRK will include elements designed to address its security concerns (i.e., to reduce the danger of military conflict and/or attempts to interfere in China's internal affairs) but will accord highest priority to achieving Beijing's economic and developmental objectives (e.g., via direct investment, transfers of technology, markets for Chinese products), and that Beijing will attempt to limit the deleterious impact of historical memory and military relationships with the United States.

The framework suggests that there may be conflict, or useful complementarities, between the universalistic, or global, characteristics, norms, and rules of the international system, and the particularistic, or cultural, attributes shaped by shared cultural roots and relationships between China and its neighbors. It suggests that China might be more interested in seeking "special" arrangements based on culture and history (e.g., special affinity among Asian or Confucian cultures). However, it also suggests the possibility that, as longtime members of the US-led liberal order, Japan and the ROK might prefer arrangements consistent with rules and norms of the global order and the way they interact with other partners. The framework also suggests that Japan and both Koreas might view issues and opportunities through a different historical lens than does China, seeing more of the downside or negative consequences for themselves of special arrangements with the country that regarded them as inferior vassals during the period of greatest cultural affinity. Finally, the framework suggests that each of the countries involved will factor in what it has observed and learned about the prospective partner's interactions with other states and the way it expects the United States to view specific agreements and overall relationships.

In addition to providing a starting point by suggesting what to look for and what to expect, the framework enjoins analysts to be wary of single-factor explanations for the conduct of China and its partner states. Analysis may lead to the conclusion that one or two factors or sets of factors are far more important than others in shaping behavior, but the framework enjoins them to at least consider the impact of other factors and to attempt to order their relative importance on the basis of empirical research rather than theories of international relations or existential assertions about the behavior of particular types of regimes. The resultant analysis is almost certain to be more multifaceted than conventional wisdom. It is also likely to be more accurate.

Notes

1. See, for example, John J. Mearsheimer, *The Tragedy of Great Power Politics* (New York: W. W. Norton, 2001).

2. See, for example, Aaron L. Friedberg, *A Contest for Supremacy: China, America, and the Struggle for Mastery in Asia* (New York: W. W. Norton, 2011).

3. See, for example, Liu Mingfu, *Zhongguo Meng: Hou Meiguo Shidai de Daguo Siwei yu Zhanlue Dingwei* [China's Dream: Major Power Thinking and Strategic Posture in a Post-American Era] (Beijing: Zhongguo Youyi Chuban Gongsi, 2010); and Robert Ross, *Chinese Security Policy: Structure, Power, and Politics* (New York: Routledge, 2009), chap. 3.

4. See, for example, Hu Jintao, "Build Towards a Harmonious World of Lasting Peace and Common Prosperity," speech at the High-Level Plenary Meeting of

the United Nations' 60th Session, September 17, 2005, http://sy.china-embassy
.org/eng/xwfb/t213754.htm. This chapter provides neither a literature review nor a
detailed critique of the different schools of thought regarding China's past and future behavior on the world stage. To do so would be useful but difficult because of
the very uneven quantity and quality of work on specific countries and regions, as
well as the fact that most efforts at synthesis have been by international relations
specialists who have done little work specifically on China, and by China specialists who focused overwhelmingly on US-China relations or a "strategic triangle"
with the United States and China as two of the corners. One of the exceptions to
this generalization is Robert G. Sutter, *Chinese Foreign Relations*, 4th ed. (Lanham,
MD: Rowman and Littlefield, 2012).

5. This chapter conflates the many variants of realism in writings on international relations. See, for example, Liu Feng and Zhang Ruizhuang, "The Typolo-
gies of Realism," *Chinese Journal of International Politics* 1, no. 1 (2006): 109–134.

6. See the discussion and sources cited in Thomas J. Christensen, "Fostering
Stability or Creating a Monster?," *International Security* 31, no. 1 (Summer 2006):
81–126.

7. See, for example, John King Fairbank, ed., *The Chinese World Order: Traditional China's Foreign Relations* (Cambridge, MA: Harvard University Press, 1968);
and Mohan Malik, "China and Strategic Imbalance," *The Diplomat*, July 14, 2014,
http://thediplomat.com/2014/07/china-and-strategic-imbalance/.

8. See, for example, Huang Deming, Kong Yuan, and Zhang Hua, "Sympo-
sium on China's Peaceful Development and International Law," *Chinese Journal of
International Law* 5, no. 1 (2006): 261–268.

9. See, for example, Minxin Pei, *China's Trapped Transition: The Limits of De-
velopmental Autocracy* (Cambridge, MA: Harvard University Press, 2006); and Ian
Bremmer, *The J Curve: A New Way to Understand Why Nations Rise and Fall* (New
York: Simon and Shuster, 2006).

10. See, for example, Wang Jisi, "China's Search for a Grand Strategy: A Ris-
ing Great Power Finds Its Way," *Foreign Affairs* 90, no. 2 (2011): 68–79; and Avery
Goldstein, *Rising to the Challenge: China's Grand Strategy and International Security*
(Stanford, CA: Stanford University Press, 2005).

11. On reasons for having a grand strategy, see Thomas Fingar, "Intelligence
and Grand Strategy," *Orbis* 56, no. 1 (2006): 118–134.

12. The aphorism may have been used for the first time in the context of reform and opening when Chen Yun cited it in his speech in December 1980. See
"Jingji Xingshi yu Jingyan Jiaoxun" [The Economic Situation and Our Experience and Lessons], in *Chen Yun Wenxuan 1956-1985* [Selected Works of Chen Yun,
1956–1985] (Beijing: Renmin Chubanshe, 1995), 251.

13. An excellent example of such an attempt can be found in Goldstein, *Rising to the Challenge*.

14. See Cheng Li, ed., *China's Changing Political Landscape: Prospects for Democracy* (Washington, DC: Brookings Institution, 2008).

15. See Xi Jinping, *The Governance of China* (Beijing: Foreign Languages Press, 2014).

16. See, for example, Linda Jakobson and Dean Knox, *New Foreign Policy Actors in China* (Solna, Sweden: Stockholm International Peace Research Institute, 2010), http://books.sipri.org/files/PP/SIPRIPP26.pdf.

17. See, for example, Benjamin Schwartz, *In Search of Wealth and Power: Yen Fu and the West* (Cambridge, MA: Harvard University Press, 1964).

18. Mary Clabaugh Wright, *The Last Stand of Chinese Conservatism: The T'ung Chih Restoration, 1862–1874* (Stanford, CA: Stanford University Press, 1962).

19. See, for example, Ssu-yu Teng and John K. Fairbank, *China's Response to the West: A Documentary Survey, 1839–1923* (Cambridge, MA: Harvard University Press, 1954).

20. See John K. Fairbank, ed., *The Cambridge History of China*, vol. 12, *Republican China, 1912–1949*, pt. 1 (Cambridge: Cambridge University Press, 1983).

21. See Sergei N. Goncharov, John W. Lewis, and Xue Litai, *Uncertain Partners: Stalin, Mao, and the Korean War* (Stanford, CA: Stanford University Press, 1993), chap. 3.

22. See Jan S. Prybyla, *The Political Economy of Communist China* (Scranton, PA: International Textbook, 1970).

23. See, for example, A. Doak Barnett, *Communist China: The Early Years, 1949–1955* (New York: Praeger, 1964).

24. Andrew G. Walder, *China Under Mao: A Revolution Derailed* (Cambridge, MA: Harvard University Press, 2015).

25. Roderick MacFarquhar and John K. Fairbank, eds., *The Cambridge History of China*, vol. 14, *The People's Republic*, pt. 1 (Cambridge: Cambridge University Press, 1987), chaps. 7–11; and Roderick MacFarquhar and John K. Fairbank, eds., *The Cambridge History of China*, vol. 15, *The People's Republic*, pt. 2 (Cambridge: Cambridge University Press, 1991), chaps. 1–4.

26. Henry Kissinger, *On China* (New York: Penguin, 2011), chaps. 7–10.

27. My effort to reconstruct and interpret the decision-making process and its outcomes is based, in part, on Ezra F. Vogel, *Deng Xiaoping and the Transformation of China* (Cambridge, MA: Belknap Press of Harvard University Press, 2011), chaps. 7–12; and Li Lanqing, *Breaking Through: The Birth of China's Opening-Up Policy* (New York: Oxford University Press, 2009).

28. On early Soviet achievements, see, for example, R. Davies, Mark Harrison, and S. G. Wheatcroft, eds., *The Economic Transformation of the Soviet Union, 1913–1945* (Cambridge: Cambridge University Press, 1994).

29. See Takatoshi Ito, "Japan and the Asian Economies: A 'Miracle' in Transition," *Brookings Papers on Economic Activity* 2 (1996): 205–272, http://www.brookings.edu/~/media/Files/Programs/ES/BPEA/1996_2_bpea_papers/1996b_bpea_ito_weinstein.pdf.

30. See, for example, Thomas Fingar and Victor H. Li, "United States-China Relations in 1979: Agreements, Protocols, Accords, and Understandings," *Chinese Law and Government* 14, no. 1 (Spring 1981): 3–32; Vogel, *Deng Xiaoping*, chap. 11; and Harry Harding, *A Fragile Relationship: The United States and China Since 1972* (Washington, DC: Brookings Institution, 1992), chap. 3.

31. See Carol Lee Hamrin and Suisheng Zhao, eds., *Decision-Making in Deng's China: Perspectives from Insiders* (Armonk, NY: M. E. Sharpe, 1995).

32. Deng Xiaoping, "The Present Situation and the Tasks Before Us" (speech, January 16, 1980), in *Selected Works of Deng Xiaoping (1975–1982)*, by Editorial Committee for Partly Literature, Central Committee of the Communist Party of China (Beijing: Foreign Languages Press, 1984), 224–258.

33. See Richard Baum, ed., *China's Four Modernizations: The New Technological Revolution* (Boulder, CO: Westview Press, 1980).

34. See, for example, Ren Xiao, "The International Relations Theoretical Discourse in China: A Preliminary Analysis" (Sigur Center Asian Papers No. 9, Sigur Center for Asian Studies, George Washington University, Washington, DC), April 2000, http://www.gwu.edu/~sigur/assets/docs/scap/SCAP9-Xiao.pdf.

35. Vogel, *Deng Xiaoping*, 323–333.

36. On subordinating socialism to other objectives, see Edward S. Steinfeld, *Playing Our Game: Why China's Rise Doesn't Threaten the West* (New York: Oxford University Press, 2010), chap. 3.

37. See, for example, Loren Brandt and Thomas G. Rawski, "China's Great Economic Transformation," in *China's Great Economic Transformation*, ed. Loren Brandt and Thomas G. Rawski (New York: Cambridge University Press, 2008), 1–26.

38. Phillip C. Saunders, "Supping with a Long Spoon: Dependence and Interdependence in Sino-American Relations," *China Journal* 43 (January 2000): 55–81.

39. See Thomas Fingar, "Introduction: The Quest for Independence," in *China's Quest for Independence: Policy Evolution in the 1970s*, ed. Thomas Fingar (Boulder, CO: Westview Press, 1980), 1–23.

40. See Ministry of Foreign Affairs of the People's Republic of China, "China's Independent Foreign Policy of Peace," August 18, 2003, http://www.fmprc.gov.cn/eng/wjdt/wjzc/t24881.htm.

41. This point is developed further in Thomas Fingar, "China's Vision of World Order," in *Strategic Asia 2012–13: China's Military Challenge*, ed. Ashley J. Tellis and Travis Tanner (Seattle: National Bureau of Asian Research, 2012), 343–373.

42. Most developing countries have experienced difficulties making the transition and fall into what is called the middle-income trap. Whether China will be more successful than all others remains to be seen. See, for example, Barry Eichengreen, Donghyun Park, and Kwanho Shin, "When Fast-Growing Economies Slow Down: International Evidence and Implications for China," *Asian Economic Papers* 11, no. 1 (2012): http://www.mitpressjournals.org/doi/pdf/10.1162/ASEP_a_00118.

43. See *The IP Commission Report: The Report of the Commission on the Theft of American Intellectual Property* (Seattle: National Bureau of Asian Research, 2013).

44. Fingar, "China's Vision of World Order."

45. Chinese do not use these terms, which come from John Ikenberry, but they certainly understand the distinction. See G. John Ikenberry, *Liberal Leviathan: The Origins, Crisis, and Transformation of the American World Order* (Princeton, NJ: Princeton University Press, 2011).

46. See, for example, Evan S. Medeiros, "Strategic Hedging and the Future of Asia-Pacific Stability," *Washington Quarterly* 29, no. 1 (2005–2006): 145–167.

47. See Fingar, "China's Vision of World Order"; and Friedberg, *Contest for Supremacy*.

48. See the discussion in Ikenberry, *Liberal Leviathan*, especially "Power and Strategies of Rule," chap. 3.

49. See, for example, Benjamin I. Schwartz, "The Chinese Perception of World Order, Past and Present," in Fairbank, *Chinese World Order*, 276–288.

50. See Zheng Bijian, "China's 'Peaceful Rise' to Great-Power Status," *Foreign Affairs* 84, no. 5 (September–October 2005): 18–24; and Bonnie S. Glaser and Evan S. Medeiros, "The Changing Ecology of Foreign Policy-Making in China: The Ascension and Demise of the Theory of 'Peaceful Rise,'" *China Quarterly* 190 (2007): 291–310.

51. See, for example, Kent Calder, "China and Japan's Simmering Rivalry," *Foreign Affairs* 85, no. 2 (March–April 2006): 129–139.

52. See Samuel S. Kim, *The Two Koreas and the Great Powers* (New York: Cambridge University Press, 2006).

53. See Wu Xinbo, "The End of the Silver Lining: A Chinese View of the US-Japanese Alliance," *Washington Quarterly* 29, no. 1 (Winter 2005–2006): 119–130.

54. See Frans-Paul van der Putten and Chu Shulong, *China, Europe and International Security: Interests, Roles, and Prospects* (Oxford, UK: Routledge, 2011), especially chaps. 2 and 6.

55. See, for example, Joseph S. Nye Jr., "American and Chinese Power After the Financial Crisis," *Washington Quarterly* 33, no. 4 (October 2010): 143–153.

56. See, for example, Elizabeth C. Economy, "China: The New Virtual Political System," Council on Foreign Relations, April 2011, http://www.cfr.org/china/china-new-virtual-political-system/p24805. See also Thomas Christensen, "The Advantages of an Assertive China: Responding to Beijing's Abrasive Diplomacy," *Foreign Affairs* 90, no. 2 (2011): 54–67.

57. Choe Sang-Hun, "South Korea Postpones Military Pact with Japan," *New York Times*, June 29, 2012, http://www.nytimes.com/2012/06/30/world/asia/south-korea-postpones-military-data-pact-with-japan.html?_r=1&ref=world.

58. Other books in the series are Thomas Fingar, ed., *New Great Game: China and South/Central Asia in the Era of Reform* (Stanford, CA: Stanford University Press, 2016); and Donald Emmerson, ed., *The Deer and the Dragon: China and Southeast Asia in the Era of Reform* (forthcoming).

THREE

China's Global Engagement
A Chinese Perspective

Liru Cui

China's extensive and still increasing engagement on the world stage is a dynamic process shaped by continuities and changes in the international system, adherence to the principles and priorities undergirding the modernization strategy adopted in the late 1970s, and the evolution of needs and possibilities made possible by more than three decades of sustained economic growth.[1] The "reform and opening" strategy adopted in 1978 to make China more modern, more prosperous, and more secure through participation in the international system was a sharp break from policies that had led to self-imposed seclusion for more than six hundred years.[2]

The decision to break from highly autarkic policies intended to preserve China's autonomy and protect its economy and society from the perils of dependence on external actors and sources of supply was both difficult and unavoidable. Recurring attempts to insulate China from external influences and to achieve security through self-reliance had failed to achieve either goal and left the country weaker and less influential than it had been for centuries. The new strategy eschewed experimentation and autarky in favor of following a proven path to sustained development. But it also made China more vulnerable to decisions and developments beyond its borders

This chapter presents a Chinese view of China's strategy, how it is perceived by other nations, and how pursuit of that strategy shapes China's diplomatic priorities and policies. It examines many of the same developments and issues as does the chapter by Thomas Fingar (Chapter 2) but interprets many of them in a different way.

and beyond the control of its political leaders. The pages that follow present a Chinese interpretation of what Beijing was and is attempting to accomplish, the response of other nations to China's success, and China's vision of how the international system is likely to evolve.

Goals and Priorities of the Reform and Opening Strategy

The reform and opening strategy evolved over time, but from the beginning it was conceived to have several mutually reinforcing components. Thus, for example, the economic component was designed to enhance efficiency, encourage entrepreneurial behavior, and improve living conditions. Other parts of the economic component sought to attract and utilize foreign capital, technology, and market opportunities.[3] The primary objective of the diplomatic component of the strategy was to ensure that the international environment was favorable for achieving rapid modernization.[4] The primary goal has remained constant through more than three decades, but the policies employed to achieve that goal have evolved over time and in response to changing conditions in different regions and nations.[5]

No one predicted or could have imagined that China's new strategy of development would transform the world's most populous poor country into an economic and trade powerhouse in the short span of thirty years. But that is exactly what happened, and long before China surpassed Japan as the world's second-largest economy in 2010, people everywhere were beginning to pay attention to China's actions and accomplishments.[6] Some viewed developments with a mixture of admiration and envy; others did so with concern about what China's success might mean for them, or with calculation of the ways in which they might be able to benefit from China's achievements. Such perceptions and calculations created new challenges and opportunities for Beijing and shaped the evolution of Chinese foreign policy.

Among the most demanding challenges facing Chinese decision makers are those inherent in managing relationships with countries (and companies) that are both partners and competitors. China's continued success and sustained rise depend increasingly on its ability to collaborate with partners who worry about the consequences of China's rise for their own future success and may become less willing to jeopardize their own prosperity and security by cooperating with a China that seeks and seems destined to overtake them in the competition for market share and political influence.

Successful management of these challenges requires assuaging concerns that China's accomplishments endanger the prosperity or security of other nations and persuading others that China's "rise" contributes to global peace and prosperity.[7]

Domestic Factors Shaping China's Diplomacy

China's diplomacy, like that of other countries, is designed to protect and pursue national interests and prioritized objectives. Since the late 1970s, China's highest priority has been to modernize the country as rapidly as possible; its diplomatic strategies and negotiating positions have been formulated to achieve that objective. Stated another way, modernization is China's highest priority, reform and opening are the principal means to achieve that objective, and China's foreign policies are designed to ensure the success of policies to modernize the country through participation in the global economy. The goal has remained constant, but the methods used to pursue it have changed in concert with changes in China's capabilities and responsibilities on the world stage.

Modernization is a shorthand way of describing China's century-long quest for prosperity, power, and recovery of its "rightful" position in world affairs.[8] In other words, it is both a goal and the means to achieve other, more important objectives. The strategy devised to achieve modernization and the accomplishments it has achieved have been described as China's "Second Revolution."[9] Describing reform and opening in this way conveys to the Chinese people both an understanding of the strategy's significance and why it is necessary to do whatever is required to ensure success. That is also the meaning of the oft-repeated injunction to "take development as the central task" in the drive to achieve "socialist modernization" and a "socialist market economy."[10] To achieve these goals, the country must open itself to, and integrate with, the outside world.[11]

Opening to the outside world is not the only requirement for successful modernization. Other, and even more important, requisites are the preservation of party leadership and the maintenance of domestic stability.[12] The importance of these factors is illustrated by the disintegration of the Soviet Union when Mikhail Gorbachev attempted to modernize the country through glasnost and perestroika.[13] What happened in the Soviet Union attests to the wisdom of the very different approach adopted by China's leaders.[14]

Another important feature of China's post-Mao approach to modernization is its pragmatism. Deng Xiaoping enjoined his colleagues in the party to put aside futile arguments about ideology and political rectitude in order to concentrate on the priority objective of national self-strengthening through modernization. His pithy admonition of "less empty talk, more hard work" and his insistence that pragmatism should trump principle if acting pragmatically would advance the cause of modernization guided all aspects of reform and opening, including China's diplomacy.[15]

Pragmatism, and the logic of the reform and opening strategy, caused Beijing to pursue modernization through greater engagement with the Western-dominated economic and political order led by the United States. What China needed (e.g., training, technology, capital, access to markets) was more abundant in the "free world," and as importantly, the United States and its partners were willing to engage with China and assist its drive for modernization. When the Cold War ended, what had been the "free world system" became a truly global system. As a result, global engagement has been the central theme of China's diplomacy for more than three decades.

China's modernization goal—sometimes called the modernization "dream"—will be achieved in three stages. In the first stage, the country will escape from the constraints of poverty that for so long limited the well-being of the people and the security and influence of the nation. The second stage will be characterized by the moderate prosperity and capabilities of a middle-income country, and in the third stage China will join the ranks of the world's most developed countries.[16] China is now in transition from the first to the second stage.

During the first stage, China approached the outside world from a position of weakness and passivity in order to learn from and selectively adopt norms and practices of more developed countries. At the beginning, China's modernization posed no threat to the developed nations of the West, but rivalry and inherent contradictions became more apparent as developed countries realized the implications of the progress being made by a country of 1.3 billion people moving rapidly toward moderate prosperity.

Modernization is so important to China that it will do everything possible to achieve that goal and will pursue every opportunity to achieve win-win outcomes through cooperation with other nations. Chinese leaders have asserted repeatedly their determination to modernize without detriment to the interests of others. That said, they are equally determined to be treated as equals and to ensure that China's rights and interests are fully respected.

Opportunities and Anxieties in the International System

Leaders of other nations regularly assert that they welcome and support China's rise, but with serious reservations.[17] Western history and culture, and the policies of the West-dominated world make clear that those who have long enjoyed primacy are ambivalent about the arrival of a strong China able to challenge their entrenched interests and global dominance. Indeed, contradictions between their statements and behavior in recent years attest to the implicit qualification of public claims to welcome China's success.

As China continued to modernize and build capacity, the Western world recognized that it had the potential to become a world power. This was unsettling to the West and sparked growing concern about a number of developments:

- Sustained economic growth has increased China's economic clout and political influence and is considered by some to pose a growing "threat" to the West.
- Some in the West see China's increasing engagement in all parts of the world as fraught with dangers to Western interests and security.
- China's modernization of its military capabilities to safeguard its interests and deter threats has caused groundless concern in other countries.
- The fact that China's goals, approaches, and priorities in managing regional and global issues do not always align with those of the West fuels suspicion and concern.
- Many have also taken note of the fact that China and the West often hold different views on what is needed to make the international system better suited to contemporary political and economic realities.

China's rise has been enormously beneficial to the world economy as a whole and to Western nations in particular, but from the perspective of Western history and culture, it is also the source of new problems and challenges. Some of the problems are a normal, and therefore acceptable, part of increased interactions among multiple players with both competing and congruent interests. Established or traditional powers would rather not have to deal with these problems, but they accept the need to do so. Other challenges are more difficult to accept because they threaten the existing structure and distribution of power in the global system.

Problems and challenges created by China's increasing involvement on the world stage have sparked consternation and heated debate in the West and among some of China's neighbors. One reason for concern and debate is that countries have never before had to contend with a rising country like China. Lacking clear precedents, other countries walk a fine line between efforts to constrain China and efforts to benefit from its growing strength and stature. Occasionally they veer too far to one side or the other, but most of the time, they choose to cooperate with China, albeit with safeguards to hedge against unwanted possibilities. Such hedging is understandable, but it has the inherent danger of going too far and degenerating into blatant efforts to contain China's rise even though countries generally are careful to deny that such is their intent.[18]

China's diplomacy and global engagement adapt to the ever-changing international situation and to its own changing status in the global system. Doing so requires finding ways to advance China's modernization goals by doing what is necessary or possible in the international arena without exaggerating or underestimating increases in its own power and influence. The world is changing in many ways, and so is China's national strength. This requires continuous recalibration of diplomatic goals and strategies to achieve the overarching goal of sustained modernization.

Relations between countries always evince elements of cooperation and conflict. This is normal. Specific disputes and clashes of interest can and must be addressed, but they can be resolved only at the micro level. At the macro level, it simply is not possible to eliminate all tensions and conflict. China and its partners continuously work to resolve specific problems and disagreements, but new problems arise and it is necessary to go through the process over and over. What is changing, however, is that China's actual and relative strength and interests are increasing over time.

Fine-Tuning China's Diplomacy

As noted earlier, China's diplomacy is shaped by the priority accorded to the quest for modernization. As a result, the central task of diplomacy is to foster an external environment conducive to reform and openness. After the end of the Cold War, economic growth replaced concerns about security as the top priority of most countries. This development was fully consistent with China's own focus on development. Indeed, for the foreseeable future maintenance of comparatively high growth rates and sustainable progress will continue to be the linchpin of Beijing's domestic and foreign policies. This focus will further enhance China's role as a significant engine of global growth and deepen its integration into the world economy. Integration into the global system provides an additional guarantee that China will not abandon its commitment to peaceful development, because doing so would endanger the system on which China depends for its own success.[19]

China is now in transition from poverty to middle-income status, and the focus of reform has shifted from growth to enhancement of the social safety net and popular well-being. Achieving greater fairness, justice, and prosperity for all will command greater attention during the coming ten years because that is the only way for China to build a harmonious society.[20] Doing so will also solidify the foundation of party legitimacy and long-term governance. The leadership team elected in 2012–2013 will guide this transformation and oversee China's ascent to greater influence in the international system. Creation of a more just and equitable society at home will further burnish China's credentials as a role model and major player on the world stage.

Changes at home and in the international system require adjustments to China's diplomacy. That adjustment has already begun and is characterized by a shift of focus from building a socialist market economy and integrating China into the global system toward acting in accordance with China's new global status. In other words, China needs to be more active with its growing strength and influence, and to take a more constructive role, together with others, in transforming the US-led and West-dominated system one step at a time. This being the case, China's diplomacy has also changed in ways that seek and assert a larger role for Chinese views and priorities. But seeking greater attentiveness to China's concerns and objectives does not mean that Beijing aspires to disrupt the international system or to become a regional or global hegemon.

China's diplomacy accords highest priority to neighboring countries and to the broader Asia-Pacific region, where a new geopolitical and geoeconomic order is emerging. The historic transition now under way involves most of the countries in the region, but China is singled out for special attention because it has the largest economy in Asia and its rapid rise is somewhat disconcerting to many. It will be a formidable challenge for Beijing to manage its escalating clashes of interests with some of its neighbors, but it will seek to do so by working for shared prosperity and using its traditional approach of seeking common ground while reserving differences.[21]

Peaceful Rise: Viability of China's Aspirations

The term *rise* has often been used to describe sustained rapid growth of a large country leading to substantial increases in national strength and international stature.[22] As used here, the phrase "China's rise" refers to the modernization process begun in 1978 with the adoption of the reform and opening strategy of development that has enabled the country to become stronger and allowed many Chinese people to become rich in an amazingly short time. Its vast territory and huge population make it inevitable that China will become a world power.

The phrase and concept of "peaceful rise" originated as a response to increasing assertions of the "China threat" theory.[23] The idea that China's increasing wealth, power, and influence are inherently or inevitably inimical to the interests of other nations emerged in the 1990s and seems to have been spawned by the combination of increasingly visible Chinese achievements and speculative concern that China would challenge the West-dominated international system in ways analogous to the Soviet Union. With the collapse of the Soviet Union and the end of the Cold War, China became the most viable candidate to inherit the title of "chief opponent." It is, after all, a huge developing nation with steadily increasing capabilities and a political system very different from that of the West.

The concerns of some in the West are understandable, but Chinese believe their fears are unjustified or exaggerated. To address their concerns and refute the "China threat" fallacy, Chinese Communist Party theorist Zheng Bijian put forward a counterthesis describing China's "peaceful rise."[24] Zheng buttressed his argument by describing China's political and diplomatic conduct since the policy of reform and opening was launched in 1978. Although his argument should have been convincing, the depth of concern was such that many seized on his use of the word *rise* to summarize China's accomplishments as proof that a stronger China is inherently threatening to the interests of other nations. To avoid the negative connotation and interpretation of the word *rise*, the Chinese government substituted the term *peaceful development* to describe the same phenomenon.[25]

Recognizing the intensity and implications of concern and fear about China's growing global role, Beijing explained in detail the guiding principles of its foreign policy in white papers published in 2005 and 2011.[26] Despite these authoritative explanations, the phrase "China's rise" continues to be used most often by Western mainstream media as the bumper-sticker description of China's changing role in world affairs. The way the phrase is used emphasizes the negative implications of China's actions and accomplishments and reluctance to use the more neutral formulation of the Chinese government.[27] In the end, it is the concept, not the wording, that is most important.

Describing China's rise as "peaceful" means that the process and manner of the country's ascendancy have not entailed confrontation, use of force, or violent conflict. Nor have they increased international tensions or evoked fear-based collective resistance to what China is doing. China's behavior, in other words, has been rational and intended to produce outcomes that, most of the time, can be characterized as win-win by all involved parties.

Moreover, because the process has been and should remain peaceful, it avoids major confrontations and is viewed positively by most people and places. Such a pattern of modernization is unusual for a large country. Indeed, the pattern emerges more from practice than from the application of theories of international relations. The best indicator of how China will act in the future is the way that it has acted during the three decades of rapid development. What China is doing and the way it is doing it are without precedent.[28] That, doubtless, is one of the reasons outsiders find China's rise difficult to understand and more troubling than it should be. Chinese leaders emphasize the peaceful character of the country's rise not simply to ally the worries of their neighbors but also because they genuinely believe that other nations will benefit from the general accomplishments of a stronger China.

Challenges Facing China's Peaceful Rise

The viability of China's peaceful rise will not be determined by China alone. China's rapid rise has triggered doubts and concerns about Beijing's intentions that are exacerbated by the crisis of confidence resulting from Western decline and changes in the balance of power. Dwindling self-confidence in the West has intensified worry about China's capabilities and intentions.

nationalism

This situation is in stark contrast to, and reinforced by, rising national pride and pent-up resentment about China's humiliation at the hands of foreign powers during the period of semicolonial rule.[29] Nationalism and resentment make many Chinese more eager for assertive competition than for cooperative teamwork. This, in turn, makes it increasingly difficult for the Chinese side to yield as easily as before on matters affecting the national interests of both sides.

Heated debate in the West on the existence, character, and implications of a "Chinese model" reflects underlying worries about the emergence of a potentially disruptive rival with interests incompatible with those of the currently dominant powers. At the same time, ordinary people in the West are increasingly puzzled and pessimistic about the future of capitalism as they struggle with unprecedented economic and political woes. Under these conditions, the "threat" of an ascendant China is highly salient and often exaggerated. The global financial tsunami that began in 2007 and China's steady economic and political gains have prompted Western countries to react more negatively to China's policies and to adopt more visible "hedging" strategies to deter or defeat anticipated assertive behavior by China. This has underscored the contradictions in the China policies of Western nations that claim to welcome China's rise but act in ways designed to thwart or contain Chinese influence.

Chinese have always doubted the sincerity of Western rhetoric professing to welcome China's arrival, in part because Western sanctions and efforts to contain China have been unceasing. Examples include US weapons sales to Taiwan, Western sanctions and embargoes against China, and frequent US naval exercises close to China's coast.[30] It is no wonder that many Chinese regard China's emphasis on peaceful rise as wishful thinking and unilateral capitulation. They assume that the United States will do everything possible to retain hegemony and Western dominance, and that this will lead to irreconcilable clashes. Unilateral concessions to relax tensions would be regarded as likely to fuel Western intransigence. Many Chinese also think that China is already strong enough to strike back in self-defense.[31] Such views mirror, in certain respects, attitudes in Washington. The result is a situation in which hawks and hotheads on both sides of the Pacific corroborate and reinforce one another in an ever more antagonistic vicious circle.

Nationalism

Looking ahead, China will face even more formidable challenges in its effort to sustain its peaceful rise for another five to ten years. One such challenge is the need to transform its model of internal development and to adopt a more responsive and responsible form of governance. Reducing economic inequality, improving social services and the social safety net, and reducing corruption are essential to improve the lives of the Chinese people and to increase China's soft power even as it continues to increase its hard power.[32]

China's foreign policy and diplomatic strategy will remain fundamentally the same for several more years because they are deeply rooted in the country's domestic situation and continuing drive for sustained growth and rapid modernization. That means, among other consequences, that China will continue to follow a course of peaceful development. China's approach to international relations derives from and reflects the country's unique combination of vast territory, a huge, industrious population, a centuries old inclusive culture, growing strength and pride in the nation, and a regime with strong decision-making and executive powers. These—and other—steadily strengthening internal dynamics provide a firm foundation for sustained peaceful development. Continuation of China's peaceful path of development will gradually alleviate external concerns, increase the country's ability to exercise both hard and soft power, and make it possible for Beijing to assume heavier international responsibilities and provide more public goods for the global system.

A second challenge is to emphasize what is positive in the complex mix of cooperative and conflictual dimensions of China's relationships with other nations, both to take full advantage of the opportunities they present and to avoid preoccupation with inevitable negative aspects. An aphorism used by Deng Xiaoping is apt here: "when you open the windows to let in fresh air, it is inevitable that you will also allow a few flies to enter." His point was that China must not forgo benefits because they sometimes come with unwanted side effects.

The challenge of staying focused on what is positive and most important also entails giving priority to the management of relations with other major powers and groups such as the United States, Europe, Japan, and India. The key to sustaining China's peaceful rise through the coming decade is to strive for mutual accommodation. Mutual accommodation, mutual respect, and mutual benefit must be essential attributes of China's new type of cooperative partnership with the United States.[33] China must give second priority to improving relations with its neighbors. This will require managing disagreements and disputes in ways that create a positive environment for cooperation. To do this, China should play a more active role in building the framework and institutions for regional cooperation.

Regional security institutions are still much less developed than are those for economic relationships. This is an important matter because preserving security and regional stability are crucial for sustained peaceful ascendancy. China needs to improve greatly its ability to manage crises and to defuse tensions before they get out of control. For example, we live in a time when economic frictions are commonplace and rivalry for energy and other resources is intensifying. This creates a critical need for mechanisms to reduce tension and expand cooperation. The need for such mechanisms is even greater in the much less regulated spheres of sea, sky, space, and the cyber world.

China also must find ways to cope with looming global challenges, such as those associated with imbalances in economic growth; climate change; natural disasters; insecurity related to energy, food, and water; and exploitation of the oceans, outer space, and cyberspace. Collaboration among the great powers on these issues is crucial but woefully inadequate. As the world's second-largest economy (in terms of gross domestic product), China has a huge stake in the management of these issues and must assume greater international responsibilities and play a larger role in fostering international cooperation to address them. China should also find ways to provide more public goods to the international community.

Perhaps the biggest challenges of all derive from the need to rebuild and reform the international order. China needs to play a larger role than it has heretofore, but to do so, it must first have a clear understanding of the relationship between attainment of its national goals and the requirements for a new global system. In other words, before it begins pressing for changes to the current system, from which China benefits greatly, it must be confident that the proposed changes will alleviate significant problems without putting at risk China's own development or that of other emerging economies.

China's approach to reforming the international order should avoid the temptations and pitfalls of excessive nationalism and power politics. It should not seek to become a superpower like the United States. Instead, it should work hard to build a harmonious society at home and a harmonious international system.[34]

To sustain the momentum of its peaceful rise, China must continue to have the support and cooperation of other nations. Such support and cooperation are indispensable. To ensure that China obtains the support it needs, Beijing should make clear that it would respond to any attempt to contain China by curtailing the benefits of cooperation with China. Fortunately, at a time when structural clashes are inevitable, structural inertia resulting from years of collaboration may act as a powerful break that can check impulsive moves toward confrontation and conflict.

The West must genuinely accept China's ascendancy. Western rhetoric claims that it does, but the rhetoric is not sincere, and Western countries have always been at best ambiguous about whether they welcome or fear China's rise. Their strategic thinking and policy designs seem to bestow conditional acceptance on China's rise, but the real proof of attitude and intentions is what they do to protect their own national interests when coping with China's rise and internal dynamics.

At the end of the day, it must be acknowledged that China's development has been integrally linked to Western nations' pursuit of their own national interests. Beijing deliberately changed its own approach to development in order to achieve sustained growth by joining the prevailing international system. Sustained high growth has been achieved, and it has paved the way for eventual rejuvenation of China's society and political system. During the past thirty years, China has acted pragmatically and with consideration for the concerns of others by not challenging the rules and norms of the existing international system. It has done so, in part, because China's traditional culture is inclusive, and inclusiveness is urgently needed for world development in the era of globalization. The importance of this need is recognized in the economic theory of inclusive growth.[35] The only way to achieve sustainable growth is through inclusive development.

China's diplomacy has entered a new era fraught with challenges and opportunities. The greatest challenge is to preserve a generally robust and harmonious relationship with the outside world as China itself becomes stronger and more influential. Whether China can successfully meet these challenges depends, to a considerable degree, on its own actions and decisions. This is particularly the case with respect to its future path of development. Decisions and policies over the past three decades have been described as constituting the Chinese model of development. The nature, future, and transferability of this "model" have been much debated by scholars and officials around the globe, including in China.[36] Chinese are justifiably proud of what has been achieved, but we must avoid excessive exuberance and acknowledge that the so-called Chinese model is in fact a development path with Chinese characteristics that is still under construction. Before China can claim that it has found a new way to achieve sustainable development that reflects the core values of an advanced civilization, it must implement thoroughgoing reforms in its political and economic institutions, and make extensive improvements in cultural, social, and other fields. Until it does, China's soft-power appeal will be limited.

China's Vision of the Future International System

China's pursuit of modernization is being realized through participation in and integration into the prevailing international system. China has accepted the rules and norms of the system it is joining, but it has also changed the system by infusing new interests and ideas. Indeed, China's trajectory of development over the past thirty years has been marked by growing participation in global institutions and acceptance as an integral component of the international system. This is infusing globalization and the international system with China's win-win methods and peaceful approach to development. This, in my view, makes China's peaceful rise a model and logical starting point for the next phase of globalization.

In important respects, China's peaceful rise is a product of globalization. Economic development is a dynamic force that drives human society forward, and economic globalization is the dynamic that drives the transformation of international economics and politics. Changes in the balance of economic power pave the way for changes to the strategic configuration of the international system. This is a fundamental aspect of change in the global system, but the ways changes occur are just as important. Globalization drives and shapes the transformation of the international system, but the approach used by key participants determines the character of emerging economies and their impact on the system as a whole.

One of the most important impacts is the return to a more multipolar world. The rise of emerging economies was facilitated by West-led globalization through their integration into the prevailing international system.

They did this by cooperating with Western developed nations in ways that created extensive interdependencies. In this respect, it is more appropriate to characterize China's peaceful rise as the logical outcome of a broader process than as the result of wise choices by Chinese leaders. That being the case, China's insistence that its rise is peaceful is not mere propaganda; it is an accurate description and logical outcome of the way it modernized through participation in the processes of globalization. It also explains how and why China has become a crucial stakeholder in the global economy. The processes that brought that about are among the most salient features of the globalization era.

The contention that China should act as a responsible stakeholder was first proposed by former deputy secretary of state Robert Zoellick in a speech to the National Committee on US-China Relations on September 21, 2005.[37] The idea is important because it marks a shift in US strategy from one predicated on the idea that China is a threat to one that accepts China's rise and assumes that it is ready to shoulder significant international responsibilities. Zoellick's assessment is perceptive in recognizing that great power relations in the era of globalization are different from in earlier eras. Economic integration and interdependence bind great powers and other major economic entities more tightly than before, and it is becoming increasingly costly to break such bonds. One consequence of this increased interdependence is that boundaries between politics and economics have become blurred, and international relations increasingly manifest both rivalry and cooperation. The rise of emerging economies contributes to greater multipolarity. But in the context of globalization, the result is myriad partnerships rather than a larger number of zero-sum competitive relationships.

Another characteristic of the globalization era is the emergence of multiple patterns of development. Previously there were only a few successful paths to development. But in the current era, diverse patterns and pathways have proved successful, and multiple models are available to countries that are just beginning to take advantage of new opportunities for rapid modernization. This is a marked change from the three Cold War models of Western neoliberal market economies, socialist planned economies, and nonaligned improvisation, and from the neoliberal model of markets plus democracy that was temporarily ascendant immediately after the disintegration of the Soviet empire. Western developed states called for universal adoption of the neoliberal model, but China insisted on going its own way and developing its own path to modernity.

Beijing's insistence on going its own way has both theoretical and practical value, because China's rise has demonstrated that following a peaceful approach and pursuing a strategy of development keyed to its own national conditions can lead to rapid and sustained economic growth. China's experience—or model—shows that unprecedented achievements can be achieved by eschewing conflict and slavish imitation of what worked in other, and very different, political, social, and economic situations. It also shows that, in the globalization era, diversity is as important as multipolarity. This lesson has far-reaching significance for refashioning the global economic and political order.

The world has again become multipolar, with many different types of state-to-state relations and multiple patterns of development. The post–World War II international system is in the midst of a historic transformation from a West-dominated world under US leadership to a system in which leadership is shared with developing nations and emerging economies. Responding to and shaping this transformation pose major challenges for China's global engagement and for the international system as a whole. It will be difficult but imperative to forge a new, stable, and effective international system better suited to new realities than the old system that helped create a world very different from the one that existed seventy years ago.[38]

Notes

1. See Li Lanqing, *Breaking Through: The Birth of China's Opening-Up Policy* (Oxford: Oxford University Press, 2009).

2. See, for example, Jakub J. Grygiel, *Great Powers and Geopolitical Change* (Baltimore, MD: Johns Hopkins University Press, 2006), chap. 6.

3. Li, *Breaking Through*; and Barry Naughton, *Growing Out of the Plan: Chinese Economic Reform, 1978–1993* (Cambridge: Cambridge University Press, 1996).

4. See, for example, Harry Harding, *China's Second Revolution: Reform After Mao* (Washington, DC: Brookings Institution, 1987).

5. See, for example, the essays in Thomas W. Robinson and David Shambaugh, eds., *Chinese Foreign Policy: Theory and Practice* (Oxford, UK: Clarendon Press, 1994); and Robert G. Sutter, *Chinese Foreign Relations*, 4th ed. (Lanham, MD: Rowman and Littlefield, 2012).

6. See, for example, Jeffrey Sachs, "China's Lessons for the World Bank," *The Guardian*, May 24, 2007, http://www.theguardian.com/commentisfree/2007/may/24/chinaslessonsfortheworldb.

7. An early attempt to provide such reassurance is Zheng Bijian, "China's 'Peaceful Rise' to Great-Power Status," *Foreign Affairs* 84, no. 5 (September–October 2005): 18–24.

8. See, for example, Orville Schell and John Delury, *Wealth and Power: China's Long March to the Twenty-First Century* (New York: Random House, 2013).

9. See, for example, Harding, *China's Second Revolution.*

10. See, for example, Hu Jintao, "China to Follow the Path of Socialism with Chinese Characteristics," keynote report at the 18th Communist Party of China (CPC) National Congress, November 8, 2012, http://english.gov.cn/2012-11/08/content_2260243.htm.

11. See Li Lanqing, *Breaking Through*; and Hu Shuli, "China Must Keep Opening Up to Boost Reform," *South China Morning Post*, August 21, 2014, http://www.scmp.com/comment/insight-opinion/article/1211620/china-must-keep-opening-boost-reform.

12. See, for example, "Communist Party of China Will Always Strive Forward," June 20, 2011, http://www.china.org.cn/opinion/2011-06/30/content_22892821.htm.

13. See arguments and sources in Christopher Marsh, *Unparalleled Reforms: China's Rise, Russia's Fall, and the Independence of Transition* (Oxford, UK: Lexington Books, 2005).

14. Ibid.

15. On Deng Xiaoping's famous quotation about white cats and black cats, see Qin Hanxiong, "Deng Xiaoping Zhumingde Maolun Yuanzi Nali?" [Where did Deng Xiaoping's Famous Cat Theory Come From?], *Xinhua*, April 24, 2011, http://news.xinhuanet.com/2011-04/24/c_121341795.htm. See also "Constitution of the Communist Party of China" (2002), http://www.china.org.cn/english/features/45461.htm.

16. Zheng, "China's 'Peaceful Rise.'"

17. See Ian Storey, *Southeast Asia and the Rise of China: The Search for Security* (London: Routledge, 2011).

18. See, for example, Andrew J. Nathan and Andrew Scobell, "How China Sees America: The Sum of Beijing's Fears," *Foreign Affairs* 91, no. 5 (September–October 2012): 32–47.

19. See, for example, Thomas Fingar, "China's Vision of World Order," in *Strategic Asia 2012–13: China's Military Challenge*, ed. Ashley J. Tellis and Travis Tanner (Seattle: National Bureau of Asian Research, 2012), 343–373.

20. See, for example, "Communiqué of the Sixth Plenum of the 16th CPC Central Committee," NEWSGD.com, October 12, 2006, http://www.newsgd .com/news/china1/200610120003.htm; and Alice Miller, "Hu Jintao and the Sixth Plenum," *China Leadership Monitor*, no. 20, http://media.hoover.org/sites/default/ files/documents/clm20am.pdf.

21. Other chapters in this volume illustrate some of the historical and contemporary sources of tension in China's relationships with other countries in Northeast Asia.

22. See, for example, John Mearsheimer, *The Tragedy of Great Power Politics* (New York: W. W. Norton, 2001); and Andrew F. Hart and Bruce D. Jones, "How Do Rising Powers Rise?" *Survival* 52, no. 6 (2011): 63–88.

23. See, for example, Emma V. Broomfield, "Perceptions of Danger: The China Threat Theory," *Journal of Contemporary China* 12, no. 35 (2003): 265–284; and Shannon Tiezzi, "Beijing's 'China Threat' Theory," *The Diplomat*, June 3, 2014, http://thediplomat.com/2014/06/beijings-china-threat-theory/.

24. Zheng, "China's 'Peaceful Rise.'"

25. Bonnie S. Glaser and Evan S. Medeiros, "The Changing Ecology of Foreign Policy-Making in China: The Ascension and Demise of the Theory of 'Peaceful Rise,'" *China Quarterly* 190 (June 2007): 291–310.

26. See State Council of the People's Republic of China, "China's Peaceful Development Road," *Chinadaily.com*, December 22, 2005, http://www.chinadaily .com.cn/english/doc/2005-12/22/content_505678.htm; and Information Office of the State Council, "Full Text: China's Peaceful Development," September 2011, http://english.gov.cn/official/2011-09/06/content_1941354.htm.

27. See, for example, "The Dragon's New Teeth," *The Economist*, April 7, 2012, http://www.economist.com/node/21552193; and Shannon Tiezzi, "China's 'Peaceful Rise' and the South China Sea," *The Diplomat*, May 17, 2014, http://thediplomat .com/2014/05/chinas-peaceful-rise-and-the-south-china-sea/.

28. Other chapters in this volume, notably those by Fingar, argue that the strategy and path of development that China is pursuing are essentially the same as those followed earlier by Japan, Taiwan, and the ROK.

29. See Zheng Wang, *Never Forget National Humiliation: Historical Memory in Chinese Politics and Foreign Relations* (New York: Columbia University Press, 2012).

30. Jiawen Yang, Hossein Askari, John Forrer, and Hildy Teegan, "US Economic Sanctions Against China: Who Gets Hurt?" *World Economy* 27, no. 7 (2004): 1047–1080; and Shaun Waterman, "China's Top General Calls US Naval Exercises Inappropriate," *Washington Times*, July 11, 2011, http://www.washingtontimes.com/ news/2011/jul/11/chinas-top-general-calls-us-naval-exercises-inappr/?page=all.

31. See, for example, the views cited in Jason Miks, "'Time for China to Strike Back,'" *The Diplomat*, September 30, 2011, http://thediplomat.com/2011/09/time -for-china-to-strike-back/.

32. See Information Office of the State Council, "Full Text: China's Peaceful Development," September 2011, section II, http://news.xinhuanet.com/english 2010/china/2011-09/06/c_131102329_3.htm.

33. Xi Jinping declared these attributes of a new type of relationship when responding to questions from the *Washington Post* during his 2012 visit to the United States. See "Views from China's Vice President," *Washington Post*, February 12, 2012, https://www.washingtonpost.com/world/asia_pacific/views-from-chinas -vice-president/2012/02/08/gIQATMyj9Q_story.html.

34. See Yongnian Zheng and Sow Keat Tok, "'Harmonious Society' and 'Harmonious World': China's Policy Discourse Under Hu Jintao" (Briefing Series Issue 6, China Policy Institute, University of Nottingham), October 2007, https:// nottingham.ac.uk/cpi/documents/briefings/briefing-26-harmonious-society-and -harmonious-world.pdf.

35. Inclusive growth benefits many and is at no one's expense. See Jesus Felipe, "Inclusive Growth: Why Is It Important for Developing Asia?" *Cadmus* 1, no. 4 (April 2012): 36–58, http://www.cadmusjournal.org/files/pdfreprints/vol1issue4/ Inclusive_Growth_Jesus_Felipe.pdf.

36. See, for example, Joshua Kurlanzick, "China's Model of Development and the 'Beijing Consensus,'" *China-US Focus*, April 29, 2013, http://www.chinaus focus.com/finance-economy/chinas-model-of-development-and-the-beijing-con sensus/; and Andre Boltho and Maria Weber, "Did China Follow the East Asian Development Model?" *European Journal of Comparative Economics* 6, no. 2 (2009): 267–286.

37. Robert B. Zoellick, "Whither China: From Membership to Responsibility," September 21, 2005, http://2001-2009.state.gov/s/d/former/zoellick/rem/ 53682.htm.

38. On the waning efficacy of legacy institutions established after World War II, see, for example, National Intelligence Council, *Global Trends 2025: A Transformed World*, http://www.dni.gov/files/documents/Newsroom/Reports%20 and%20Pubs/2025_Global_Trends_Final_Report.pdf.

FOUR

Beijing's Japan Dilemma
Balancing Nationalism, Legitimacy, and Economic Opportunity

Suisheng Zhao

China's relationship with Japan is complex and sensitive. Geographic proximity, cultural similarities, historical interactions involving dramatic reversal of their relative positions in the twentieth century, genuine and exaggerated security concerns, and economic opportunities push and pull the relationship in different directions and complicate the challenges facing policy makers in both countries. This chapter examines the Chinese side of the equation with the goal of explaining why Chinese leaders have adopted postures and policies toward Japan that risk accelerating the slowdown of China's economy and undermining the performance-based pillar of party legitimacy.

Geographic proximity, cultural similarity, and economic complementarities create numerous incentives and opportunities for China to pursue its modernization goals through cooperation with Japan. Chinese leaders have recognized and acted to capitalize on these opportunities since the earliest days of reform and opening, but doing so has been complicated and constrained by the need to balance security, political, and economic priorities. The task of devising acceptable trade-offs is never easy, but in the case of China's relations with Japan, it is compounded by dilemmas created or exacerbated by the decision of Mao Zedong and other founding leaders to make nationalism—especially anti-Japanese nationalism—a major pillar of Communist Party legitimacy.

nationalism

This chapter examines the Sino-Japanese partnership from a Chinese perspective. It notes the importance of Japan to China's security and developmental strategies while demonstrating how Beijing's concerns about public opinion and legitimacy cause it to act in ways that jeopardize economic growth and exacerbate its security concerns.

The reform and opening strategy adopted in the late 1970s has made economic performance an important—if not the most important—source of legitimacy in the post-Mao era. Japan has contributed greatly to China's post-Mao quest for modernity, wealth, and power by opening its markets and providing enormous amounts of aid, capital, technology, and training. China's leaders understand the importance of maintaining basically good relations with Japan to avoid jeopardizing the high rates of growth that undergird party legitimacy, but as growth has slowed, they have leaned more heavily on nationalism to justify the party's monopoly of power in an increasingly pluralistic society. Standing up to Japan is a central element in the party's legitimization mythology. This produces a dilemma because compensating for weakening economic performance by adopting harsher rhetoric and actions toward Japan risks accelerating the slowdown, but ignoring public ire at alleged Japanese actions inimical to China's interests—ire fueled by the official media—might be even more dangerous to party legitimacy.

The anti-Japanese component of Chinese nationalism, the importance of the anti-Japanese struggle in the narrative used by the Communist Party to legitimate its political monopoly, and Japan's relationship with the United States are both constraints on what China can do and instruments that can be used to achieve Beijing's security, economic, and political objectives. Other studies have focused on ways in which China has attempted to utilize Japan's relationship with the United States to address security concerns, as well as the importance of Japan to the success of China's economic policies.[1] This chapter focuses more narrowly on the challenges and constraints that result from the interconnection of history, nationalism, concerns about political legitimacy, and the imperatives of sustained economic growth. The framework outlined in Chapter 1 predicts that preserving security, stability, and sustained development will trump other goals and considerations most of the time. I agree with that assessment but focus here on considerations and examples that require amending the framework to accommodate the particular effects of the nationalism-party-legitimacy-Japan nexus.

History, Memory, and Mythology

Imperial Japan was China's most cruel and destructive enemy during the half century that began in 1895 and lasted until the end of World War II. This was also the period in which Chinese nationalism became more intense and the Communist Party attempted to distinguish itself from Chiang Kai-shek's Nationalist Party by claiming to have played a larger role in Japan's defeat. Seizing the banner of anti-Japanese nationalism helped the communists achieve victory during the civil war, and the communist government has kept alive the memories and mythology of its role in the anti-Japanese struggle to bolster its legitimacy.[2]

China and Japan established formal diplomatic relations in 1972 and signed a treaty of peace and friendship in 1978, but the normalization communiqué and superficial friendship accord did not resolve or bring closure to the historical issues.[3] On the basis of what they are taught in school, and what they watch on television and read in official media, many Chinese people believe that Japan has refused to acknowledge or accept responsibility for its wartime atrocities and do not know about or discount the fact that Japan has been strongly pacifist for seventy years. Chinese leaders have assiduously cultivated negative beliefs about Japan when it was in their interest to do so, but they find it increasingly difficult to manage the complex—and critically important—relationship with Japan because of the intensity of public sentiment regarding anything that has to do with Japan and the increasing importance of public opinion to their own legitimacy.

Geopolitically, China and Japan belonged to opposing camps during most of the Cold War. China regarded Japan as a security threat because of geographic proximity and its position in the US-led containment strategy aimed at the Soviet Union and, from 1950 until the early 1970s, the People's Republic of China. The perceived security threat posed by Japan, alone or in alliance with the United States, causes Beijing to be extremely alert for any sign that Japan is rebuilding its military strength. Genuine, if exaggerated, security concerns demand vigilance; the strength of anti-Japanese nationalism requires an immediate response to even the possibility of resurgent militarism. Vigilance and political sensitivity help explain the way in which Chinese scholars debated the implications of government efforts under Shinzo Abe to modify policies governing collective self-defense and to amend or reinterpret the Japanese constitution. Reflecting one school of thought, a Chinese scholar drew parallels between these developments and the rise of Japanese militarism before the Sino-Japanese War in 1894–1895. He argued, "This expansion of Japan's conception of its self-defense marks a return to the 'line of interest' referred to by Yamagata in 1890," when imperial Japan was preparing to launch wars against Korea and China.[4]

The steady buildup of Chinese military power over the past two decades has given Beijing new capabilities to buttress media and diplomatic protests by reminding Japan that China is now a more formidable power and assuring the Chinese public that it will not be complacent in the face of alleged or imputed threats from Japan. Territorial disputes are often the putative source of friction, but the underlying cause is the determination of Chinese leaders to do everything they can to discourage Japan from seeking to play a larger role in regional or global affairs.

Security concerns, unresolved historical issues, and the political uses and imperatives of Chinese nationalism push China's Japan policy in a negative direction, but they are not the only factors at work. Others include the importance of sustained economic growth to the success of Beijing's quest for wealth and power, and the performance pillar of regime legitimacy. Anti-Japanese nationalism is one pillar of legitimacy, but during the era of reform that pillar has been secondary to the ability of the regime to create jobs, raise incomes, improve living conditions, and in other ways improve the life of the Chinese people. Hostility to Japan does not help achieve those objectives and, if not managed successfully, can become a dangerous threat to the success of Deng Xiaoping's strategy of economic development.[5] Chinese leaders understand this, and a second focus of this chapter examines how Chinese pragmatism has helped to maintain a degree of stability and superficial friendship sufficient to capitalize on economic opportunities.

Unresolved Historical Issues and Anti-Japanese Nationalism

The late premier Zhou Enlai famously characterized the relationship between China and Japan as "two thousand years of friendship and fifty years of misfortune" (两千年的友好，五十年的不幸). The influential Peking University professor Wang Jisi has elaborated on the judgment expressed by Zhou by arguing that it is especially unfortunate that the fifty years of misfortune have overwhelmed (压倒了) two thousands of years of friendship and overshadowed what has happened in the decades since diplomatic relations were established.[6]

The fifty years of unfortunate history began with China's humiliating defeat by Japan in the war of 1894–1895. The impact of this defeat is well summarized by the observation that, at the time, "China was already accustomed to rapacious Western powers squabbling over its riches, but had remained self-confident in the knowledge of these powers' irrelevance. However, the assault from Japan, a speck of dust in its own backyard, shattered this self-assurance and was experienced as a shocking and intolerable humiliation."[7] The defeat led to efforts by the first generation of Chinese nationalists to rejuvenate China and avenge the humiliation. Japanese expansion into China after the Versailles Peace Treaty triggered the anti-imperialist May Fourth Movement in 1919 and Japan's invasion of China in the 1930s and 1940s further intensified anti-Japanese nationalism. It is important to understand that the intensity of anti-Japanese nationalism in China was and is a function of more than just the oft-cited brutality of the Japanese aggressors. As important, or perhaps more important, is the humiliation that China experienced as a result of repeated defeats by a former "student" that the Chinese dismissively called dwarfs (倭人) or little Japan (小日本).

The Sino-Japanese War ended in 1945, but historical wounds have not healed. Eager to seize the opportunity to normalize relations that was created by Nixon's surprise opening to China, leaders in China and Japan intentionally deferred sensitive history issues. Tokyo scrambled to contain the political consequences of the "Nixon shock," and to lock in perceived opportunities it had been unable to pursue in the face of earlier American opposition. Kakuei Tanaka, who became prime minister on July 5, 1972, immediately put normalization of relations with China at the top of his agenda. Beijing was equally eager to move because of uncertainty about the extent and durability of the new relationship with Washington and hope that the Japanese would prove more responsive to China's wishes than the United States and quickly invited Tanaka to visit.

China also had another reason to move quickly. Its economy was in shambles after six years of the Cultural Revolution, and Beijing hoped—expected—to be able to obtain substantial Japanese economic assistance. Beijing appears to have calculated that it could better capitalize on Japanese guilt if it did not push Tokyo into a defensive position by highlighting wartime atrocities or demanding reparations. China's approach was signaled by Zhou Enlai, who told Tanaka that Beijing drew a distinction between the small number of "militarists" and the vast majority of Japanese people, and that the Chinese and Japanese nations had both been traumatized by the war. Sidestepping political disputes over historical memory cleared the way for immediate Sino-Japanese strategic collaboration.[8] On September 29, 1972, only seven months after Nixon's trip to China, Tanaka and Zhou signed the joint communiqué announcing the normalization of diplomatic relations.

The normalization accord deliberately did not address war reparations, whether or how Japan should apologize for its actions in China, or bilateral territorial disputes. Kicking the issues down the road did not solve them. Indeed, it created conditions that led to sharply different public perceptions of what had been agreed and created opportunities for both the Chinese government and the Chinese people to manipulate historical memory for political effect. For example, influenced by what they learned in school and from official media, many Chinese believe that Japan has not compensated and apologized sufficiently for its wartime crimes, and suspect that Japan is ambivalent about, if not hostile to, China's modernization. They hold these views despite the extraordinary amounts of aid and investment funds that Japan has provided to China. Chinese leaders episodically replay the "guilt card" by issuing statements reviving memories of Japanese atrocities and warning about the dangers of remilitarization. Far fewer official statements report the magnitude and importance of Japan's contributions to China's rise.[9]

Mao Zedong and Deng Xiaoping sought to improve relations with Japan by burying historical memories, but the past repeatedly came back to haunt their successors. Communist Party general secretary Hu Yaobang made high-profile efforts to promote better relations with Japan in 1984–1986, including inviting seven thousand Japanese young people to visit China. But his efforts to achieve reconciliation were contentious within the party and did not gain support or produce results. President Jiang Zemin tried again a few years later. Japan was the first "Western" country to lift the sanctions it had imposed on China after the 1989 Tiananmen Incident. In acknowledgment of this development, Jiang received the Japanese emperor in Beijing in 1992 and made a high-profile visit to Japan later that year. After these visits, the Japanese government issued two important statements addressing World War II issues, the 1993 statement on "comfort women" by Chief Cabinet Secretary Yohei Kono, and Prime Minister Tomiichi Murayama's 1995 apology for aggression and colonial rule.[10]

If these statements were intended to put sensitive history issues behind in order to focus on the future, they failed to achieve their goal. The Chinese people—and many Chinese leaders—were not willing to declare the statements adequate to redress past wrongs or to surrender the political leverage they were perceived to provide. Whether pushed by other leaders and prodded by public opinion or reflecting his own view of the matter, Jiang downplayed efforts for reconciliation in favor of using almost every public occasion during his 1998 visit to Japan to remind Japanese leaders that the past was far from forgiven or forgotten.[11] Party propagandists depicted Jiang's message as intended to pave the way for closer relations in the future by resolving issues from the past, but other evidence indicates an additional motivation.[12] For example, at a seminar on security in Northeast Asia held in Shanghai shortly before Jiang's visit, Chinese strategists reminded him, "One of China's strategic goals should be to delay Japan's advancement toward becoming a major military power."[13]

Anti-Japanese nationalism was fueled by the patriotic education campaign conducted by the Chinese government in the 1990s to buttress regime legitimacy after the collapse of communist ideology. The legitimacy of Communist Party rule derived, in part, from its proclaimed role in opposing the Japanese invasion. When other sources of legitimacy—in this case, ideology—weakened, officials manipulated historical memories to rebuild support by rekindling animosity toward Japan. During this campaign, state-run museums mounted exhibitions depicting Japanese atrocities. Museums, such as the Memorial Hall of the Victims in Nanjing Massacre by Japanese Invaders and the museum memorializing the victims of Japan's infamous Unit 731 that conducted germ warfare and chemical experiments on live humans, vividly reminded the Chinese public about the country's "century of humiliation" at the hands of Japan and other imperialist powers. Anti-Japanese content was—and is—a regular feature in Chinese media, which often portrays a stereotype of Japanese "devils" as cruel and stupid warriors. Japanese soldiers regularly run amok on Chinese television and movie screens. The violence and anti-Japanese tone in many Chinese television dramas send a somewhat mixed message that killing "Japanese devils" was both glorious and easy. The seventieth anniversary of the end of World War II provided an opportunity to ratchet up efforts to remind ordinary Chinese of the party's role in ending Japan's occupation and humiliation of China and Beijing seized that opportunity by staging a massive military parade and flooding broadcast and print media with anti-Japanese diatribes.[14]

Anti-Japanese nationalism in China is also sustained by Chinese media coverage of the claims of right-wing Japanese politicians who deny that

Japan committed wartime atrocities, and by Chinese government and media criticism of visits to the Yasukuni Shrine by Prime Minister Junichiro Koizumi (in 2001–2006) and by Prime Minister Shinzo Abe (in 2014). The Chinese people need little prodding to interpret these developments in the worst possible way, but official media ensure and intensify public outrage by depicting the visits and statements by right-wing politicians as deliberate and dangerous evocation of Japan's militarist past and as a repudiation of the pacifist policies the country has followed since 1945. Distorting the past by both sides complicates the bilateral relationship and causes Japan's numerous apologies and billions of dollars in development assistance to be overshadowed by emotional Chinese nationalist reactions to Japanese denial of historical atrocities.[15]

Anti-Japan virulence is also a staple of online sites. Websites popular among young Chinese nationalists were riddled with slogans such as "destroy Japanese dogs" or "annihilate the Japanese people." *Resistance War Online*, launched in 2007, was ranked one of the top-ten 2D online games of 2008, and one of the top-ten original online games of 2008 and 2009.[16]

The result of Japan's difficulty in accurately remembering the past and China's difficulty in forgetting it was predictable. Hatred of Japan is deeply embedded in the minds of Chinese people who are not told that Japan today is a relatively open society with a robust national conversation about history between atrocity-denying right wingers and pacifists committed to telling historical truth and fighting efforts to whitewash wartime atrocities. What they are told is quite different. For example, the 1990s Chinese best seller *The China That Can Say No* criticized the country's leaders for not demanding war reparations because they were overly eager to normalize relations with Japan in the 1970s and claimed, "Japan has always turned its back on China. . . . Japan has never made any effort to narrow the historical gap with Asian countries."[17] The popularity of the book attests to how effectively it played to widespread public sentiment. The fact that it was widely read doubtless reinforced negative sentiment toward Japan. The strength and prevalence of nationalist animosity toward Japan is illustrated by the words of a woman in Xi'an whose son had smashed the skull of the owner of a Japanese car with a bicycle lock during the anti-Japanese riots in 2012. Asked to give the source of her son's "patriotic" rage, she said, "When we turn on the TV, most of the dramas are about the anti-Japanese war. How would it be possible not to hate Japanese?"[18]

Chinese Pragmatism and Superficial Friendship

Despite the poisonous effect of historical memories, China maintained a superficial friendship with Japan after relations were normalized in 1972 in order to enhance its strategic position vis-à-vis the United States and the Soviet Union. The friendship continued in the 1980s, when Deng Xiaoping insisted that China implement a good-neighbor policy (睦邻政策) to create conditions favorable for China's economic modernization. After the Cold War ended in the 1990s, the good-neighbor policy toward Japan and other Asian countries acquired greater importance because, in addition to promoting development, it was to provide China with the strategic advantage it needed to increase its influence in regional affairs and leverage that could be used to manage relations with the United States and other Western powers.

To maintain the superficial friendship, Beijing adopted a pragmatic approach in the sensitive territorial dispute involving the Diaoyu/Senkaku Islands. That approach, which was followed for several decades, was to assert China's claim to the islands, which it insisted had been seized unlawfully by imperial Japan in the late nineteenth century, while agreeing to defer resolution of the dispute to a later time. This approach was employed to sidestep the issues during the negotiations to exchange diplomatic recognition in 1972. Chinese leaders adopted this approach because they did not want the dispute over the uninhabited islets to interfere with their grand geostrategic objectives. According to Zhang Xiangshan, an adviser to then premier Zhou Enlai, Prime Minister Tanaka raised the islands issue in the negotiation with Zhou. Zhou responded to the question about China's position by saying that he "did not want to discuss the issue, as it would not be good to talk about it at this time" (现在谈没好处). After a few brief exchanges, both sides agreed to postpone the issue in order to settle more urgent normalization issues first.[19]

The Diaoyu/Senkaku Islands reemerged as a controversial issue in March 1978, after the right-wing Japan Youth Federation erected a lighthouse on the largest of the islets to symbolize Japan's sovereignty claims. The East China Sea People's Liberation Army (PLA) naval commander reportedly planned a major naval exercise and to send a flotilla of more than eighty armed fishing vessels to circle the isles as a show of force. Deng Xiaoping overruled the plan because he attached greater importance to Japanese acceptance of an anti-Soviet hegemony clause in the Peace and Friendship Treaty to be concluded in a few months than he did to the islets.[20] At the ceremony to mark the signing of the treaty, Deng enjoined Japanese prime minister Takeo Fukuda to "follow our established policy and postpone the solution for another twenty or thirty years" (一如既往, 搁置它20年, 30年嘛). Deng further added, "The [islands] issue is too complicated to discuss at this time. We may not be wise enough to resolve this issue, but our next generation may be smarter and find a solution."[21]

Beijing passed a maritime territory law in 1992 that described the islands as part of China's territory, but Deng's successors continued the commitment to shelve the dispute for more than a decade. There were many incidents related to the territorial dispute during that decade, but the two countries handled them in a relatively cool-headed way to ensure that they did not escalate into major crises. One example was the incident in July 1996 in which ethnic Chinese people in Taiwan and Hong Kong responded angrily when members of a right-wing Japanese group renovated the lighthouse they had constructed on the disputed islands some time previously. Beijing's response was carefully calculated to avoid enflaming relations during the already-tense period of the sixty-fifth anniversary of the Japanese invasion of Manchuria, known as the September 18 Incident. Leaders in Beijing feared the island dispute would fan popular anti-Japanese sentiment that, in turn, would force the government to take actions that would damage relations with Japan at a time when China still badly needed Japanese economic assistance and investment. Chinese media did not report the incident until tensions had subsided.

China's policy began to change in the new century. In contrast to its earlier practice, the Chinese government did nothing to stop seven Chinese activists from leaving a Chinese port with the declared intention to land on one of the disputed islands in March 2004. China's foreign ministry lodged an official protest when the Japanese police and coast guard detained the Chinese activists. After the activists were released and returned to Shanghai, they were hailed as national heroes.[22] The change in approach coincided with reports that the disputed waters held substantial quantities of oil, gas, and other valuable mineral resources. China overtook Japan as the second-largest oil consumer in 2003 and become the third-largest oil importer in 2004. In 2003, the China National Offshore Oil Corporation began drilling in the gas field called Chunxiao by China and Shirakaba by

Japan. The field is located near the median line that Japan regards as the border of its exclusive economic zone. China does not recognize the median line and claims jurisdiction over the entire continental shelf. Although the gas field lies largely on the Chinese side of the median line, Japan claimed that Chinese drilling near the line would tap into geological structures on the Japanese side.

Beijing used its growing economic and military power to support its more assertive policy approach. Ignoring Japanese complaints, China deployed five warships in September 2005 to support its claim of sovereignty by accompanying the Chinese research vessel surveying for oil and gas under the seabed near the Chunxiao field. This was the first time that China had deployed warships in this way. Members of the public welcomed the shift to a more assertive policy vis-à-vis Japan. Large-scale anti-Japanese demonstrations took place in major Chinese cities in early 2005 to protest Japanese prime minister Koizumi's visit to the Yasukuni Shrine and the publication of Japanese history textbooks that minimized the country's war crimes. Shortly before the demonstrations began, more than twenty million Chinese signed an Internet petition opposing Japan's bid for a permanent seat on the UN Security Council. The Chinese government initially tolerated and even encouraged the demonstrations, but soon after they began, Beijing took steps to limit and then end them. The reasons probably had more to do with fear that they would morph into antigovernment protests than desire to protect relations with Japan.[23] However, the government canceled high-level bilateral meetings with Japanese officials, including the scheduled meeting between Prime Minister Koizumi and visiting Chinese vice minister Wu Yi.[24]

Despite adopting a less compromising position toward Japan in the first decade of the new century, China's leaders still tried to maintain the superficial friendship and were careful to prevent the nationalist sentiment of Chinese people from seriously damaging the relationship with Japan. Describing nationalism as a force that must be "channeled," Beijing acted to restrain or even ban anti-Japanese demonstrations, as it did shortly before the anniversary of the May Fourth Movement, which was triggered by anger over the Versailles Treaty's giving Japan control of parts of China's Shandong Province in 1919. To preclude demonstrations, the government sent a blizzard of text messages to mobile phone users warning against "joining illegal demonstrations." Several organizers of online petition drives were detained. Tiananmen Square was closed to the public for a government-organized coming-of-age ceremony for eighteen-year-olds on May 4. In the meantime, Chinese leaders looked for opportunities to improve relations with Japan. When newly elected prime minister Shinzo Abe expressed his desire to visit China, Beijing grasped the opportunity and extended an invitation. Abe's visit to China in October 2006 helped mend Japan-China relations after a prolonged chill brought on by Koizumi's visits to the Yasukuni Shrine. Lauding the visit as a breakthrough in strained China-Japan relations, Chinese premier Wen Jiabao make an official visit to Japan in the spring of 2007, the first visit to Japan by a top Chinese leader since 1998.[25]

Economic Confidence and Assertive Nationalism

Beijing's policy toward Japan became more strident in 2009. The change occurred in the context of a general shift toward greater assertiveness, if not aggressiveness, in China's foreign policy that roughly coincided with the global economic slowdown. The shift was striking because from the onset of the reform era, the explicit goal of China's foreign policy was to facilitate modernization of China's domestic economy by creating and maintaining a peaceful international environment (外交服务于国内经济建设). Beginning in approximately 2009, however, China seemed to reverse the order and to use its growing economic power to pursue more ambitious foreign policy objectives. The shift may have been undertaken, in part, in response to goading from hypernationalists in the party and the public who saw the global economic downturn as an opportunity for China to reclaim its great power status. Whether because they shared this assessment of the global situation or to forestall criticism from inside and outside of the regime, or both, Chinese leaders become more assertive in their defense and pursuit of the so-called core national interests of state sovereignty and territorial integrity.[26]

An incident involving the Japanese coast guard and Chinese fishing vessels in waters near the disputed Diaoyu/Senkaku Islands provided an opportunity to demonstrate and test the utility of the new policy. On September 7, 2010, a Chinese fishing boat collided with—or rammed—two Japanese coast guard vessels. The incident confronted the new Democratic Party of Japan (DPJ) government with the need to manage the sensitive and important relationship with China while at the same time demonstrating that it would defend Japan's sovereignty as vigorously as had Liberal Democratic Party (LDP) governments. Japanese officials detained the captain of the fishing boat and announced that they would pursue the matter through the domestic legal system. Doing so violated the Sino-Japanese Fisheries Agreement, which specified that the areas around the Diaoyu/Senkaku Islands was to be treated as part of the high seas in which vessels are subject to flag-state jurisdiction. In the past, Japanese authorities had quickly deported intruders from China and Hong Kong. The break with past practice was interpreted in China as a sign that the new Japanese government would be more aggressive in its dealings with China if Beijing did not respond vigorously to the Japanese challenge.

The arrest of the Chinese captain sparked a wave of anti-Japanese agitation on the Internet in China, because recognizing Tokyo's judicial right would be de facto recognition of Japan's sovereignty over the islands. Perceiving both a political imperative to stand up to the Japanese challenge and that the power balance with Japan was tilting in China's favor, Beijing adopted an unusually hawkish position. The Chinese government quickly demanded the "immediate and unconditional" release of the captain. China's top-ranking foreign policy officials from State Councilor Dai Bingguo on down called in the Japanese ambassador a total of six times to protest, including an unceremonious summons at midnight. Although calling in the ambassador in this way was unprecedented and could be a breach of diplomatic etiquette and protocol, Beijing wanted there to be no uncertainty about how China would respond to anyone—especially Japanese—that failed to respect Chinese sovereignty or treated China as an inferior. Beijing rapidly escalated both its rhetoric and the level at which the issue was handled. Premier Wen Jiabao, whose visit in 2007 was credited with improving the tone and substance of the relationship, personally called on Japan to release of the captain while refusing to meet with Japanese prime minister Naoto Kan during the UN development conference in New York City.[27]

Rather than defusing the diplomatic row, the Chinese government raised the stakes. Specific measures included suspending high-level exchanges with Japan, calling off the scheduled round of talks on joint exploitation of the Chunxiao gas fields in the East China Sea, and discouraging Chinese citizens from traveling to Japan. Beijing's most dramatic move was to block shipments to Japan of rare earth elements crucial for the production of electronic components, hybrid cars, wind turbines, and guided missiles.[28] These minerals are not actually rare, but mining and processing them is damaging to the environment. In 2010, China accounted for 93 percent of world production and more than 99 percent of total exports. As a further retaliatory measure, the Chinese arrested four Japanese nationals in Hebei Province, accusing them of illegally entering a defense zone and videotaping military targets. Taken together, these unprecedentedly hard-line positions were clearly intended to demonstrate to Japan and to others that China was not to be trifled with and that Beijing was prepared to use its economic might to achieve political objectives.

The combination of diplomatic paroxysm and economic blackmail worked. After the arrest of the four Japanese nationals in China, the Naha District Public Prosecutor's Office released the detained captain, noting that the decision was made "taking into account the impact on our citizens and Japan-China relations."[29] The Chinese government sent a chartered plane to retrieve him and gave him a hero's welcome upon his arrival. After the Japanese government acceded to Chinese pressure, Beijing added new demands by calling for both an apology and compensation for the boat captain's "unlawful" detention.[30]

The fishing boat incident marked a turning point in China's position toward Japan. Thereafter, Beijing increased its naval activities around the disputed islands with the goal of challenging Japan's territorial claim. The Chinese government actively looked for a pretext to challenge Japan's de facto control of the disputed islands. The pretext came in April 2012, when the vocal nationalistic governor of metropolitan Tokyo, Shintaro Ishihara, offered to purchase some of the islands from a private Japanese owner who wanted to sell. Uichiro Niwa, Japan's ambassador to China, warned that purchasing the islands "will result in an extremely grave crisis in relations between Japan and China," but Ishihara pressed ahead with his efforts to raise funds for the purchase.[31] A group of Japanese right-wing nationalists swam ashore from nearby boats and raised the Japanese flag on August 19 as a tit-for-tat response to Chinese nationalists who had landed and planted flags on the islands earlier. A second group of activists from the Tokyo metropolitan government went to the waters near the islands, calling themselves a survey team to prepare to buy the islands. These actions inflamed Chinese passions and triggered anti-Japanese protests across a number of Chinese cities.

To defuse the crisis by preempting Ishihara's provocative plan, Prime Minister Yoshihiko Noda's government began secret negotiations with the private landowner in late May and announced the purchase ("nationalization") of three of the five islands on September 10, 2012. According to Japanese accounts, the government would not construct any port facilities or improve the lighthouse, as Ishihara planned, but instead would preserve the islands as they were for the time being.[32] Japanese officials were caught between the rock of Ishihara's initiative, which polls indicated was backed by a majority of Japanese voters, and the hard place of outraging China by having the national government buy the islands. Mistakenly hoping that Beijing would regard purchase by the national government as the lesser of two evils, they chose that option.[33] Japanese officials sought to convey the message through both public comments and back channels that the nationalization was forced upon the government by domestic politics and did not enhance Japan's claims under international law. Although the Japanese proposal for a formal meeting between Noda and President Hu Jintao at the Asia-Pacific Economic Cooperation summit in early September was rejected by China, the head of the foreign ministry's Asian and Ocean Affairs Bureau was dispatched to Beijing on the day the purchase deal was signed.[34]

The Noda government grossly miscalculated the willingness of Beijing to understand the perceived need of DPJ politicians to respond as they did to Japanese domestic politics and failed to foresee the intensity of Chinese anger fueled by characterization of the purchase as an intolerable effort to humiliate China. China and Japan have diametrically opposite interpretations of what happened and why it happened. Japan viewed its purchase of the islands as necessary to prevent a crisis about sovereignty; China interpreted the nationalization as a direct violation of the already-fragile status quo. From the Chinese perspective, it was a game changer intended to strengthen Japan's claim by exercising direct government control. Japan could now claim that it had applied domestic law when purchasing the islands. The Chinese linked the nationalization of the islands to the attempt to apply domestic law after detention of the fishing boat captain two years earlier and interpreted the actions as indicative of a Japanese strategy to reinforce its claim to the islands that could not go unchallenged.

This interpretation made it politically impossible for Chinese leaders to accept the change of status even if they had wanted to do so in order to protect the relationship with Japan that was still so important to China's quest for modernization and sustained economic growth. One Chinese analyst interpreted the situation as one in which Chinese felt that Japan had taken advantage of China's restraint to systematically strengthen its control over the islands. Japan's change in position, from agreeing that a dispute existed to denying one entirely, was a fundamental shift that had to be rebuffed.[35] Nationalization of the islands was perceived as more than just a response to domestic politics, and more important, it was seen as a calculated attempt to take advantage of and humiliate China by breaching the tacit understanding to maintain the status quo.

Chinese observers, some with a predisposition toward conspiracy theory explanations, often depicted seemingly small incidents as indicative of much broader and more significant Japanese intentions. Thus, for example, some Chinese argued, and presumably believed, that the Japanese government had planned to nationalize the islands for years but was waiting for the right moment or conditions. According to this interpretation, Ishihara's ploy was coordinated in advance with the Noda government because the politicians thought that circumstances favored moving before China became stronger, and that Ishihara's extreme position was deliberately crafted to allow Noda to appear less radical and therefore more acceptable to Beijing. This scenario would allow both Noda and Ishihara to reap political benefits and, if the ploy succeeded, would allow Japan to strengthen its claim to the islands. It was not only academics and ill-informed members of the public that subscribed to such interpretations. A senior Foreign Affairs Ministry official asserted, "Japan's explanation is just an excuse and the Tokyo governor and the Japanese government have cooperated to play a duet."[36] Similarly, an article in the *People's Daily* claimed, "The intensifying tension between China and Japan over the Diaoyu Islands is not a farce being played out by Japanese right-wing politicians but a well-orchestrated plan of the Japanese government."[37]

This assessment of the situation made it imperative for Beijing to demonstrate both resolve and military capability. A *People's Daily* commentary stated, "With respect to the Diaoyu Islands, the will of the Chinese government and people to defend territorial sovereignty is firm. Long gone are the days when the Chinese nation was subject to bullying and humiliation from others. China has the complete ability and will continue to do whatever it takes to firmly defend territorial sovereignty" (中华民族任人欺凌的时代早已一去不复返).[38] To demonstrate its resolve, the Chinese government deployed a seemingly well-coordinated response that included lodging angry protests, ratcheting up state media coverage of the nationalization, publicizing bellicose commentary, threatening economic sanctions, and dispatching patrol ships to the disputed waters.

On the day the Japanese government announced the purchase of the islands, China's Ministry of Foreign Affairs issued a statement claiming that the purchase "constitutes a gross violation of China's sovereignty over its own territory and is highly offensive to the 1.3 billion Chinese people."[39] Foreign Minister Yang Jiechi summoned Japanese ambassador Uichiro Niwa to lodge a strong protest. Premier Wen Jiabao, during a speech at the China Foreign Affairs University the previous day, vowed that China would "never yield an inch" of the Diaoyus.[40] China's leader-in-waiting, Xi Jinping, struck a similar note in his meeting with US defense secretary Leon Panetta. He denounced Japan's purchase as a "farce" and urged Tokyo to "rein in its behavior and stop any words and acts that undermine China's sovereignty and territorial integrity."[41]

Editorials and headlines in Chinese media urged people to rally around the flag, and the Chinese government rolled out a series of economic retaliatory responses. Almost all Chinese tours to Japan were canceled after Jiang Zengwei, Chinese vice minister of commerce, hinted that the government saw nothing wrong with peaceful boycotts of Japanese goods.[42] Japanese companies were experiencing delays in obtaining work visas for their employees. China's customs authorities tightened clearance procedures for goods imported from Japan, including key components for electronic and other labor-intensive products used by Japanese companies to assemble products at Chinese plants.[43] China was Japan's largest trading partner and a major market for Japanese cars and electronics. The retaliations were quickly felt by Japanese businesses, as they devastated Japanese auto sales and overall Japanese investment in China.[44] Data from the Japan External Trade Organization showed that the pace of year-over-year declines in Japanese exports to China accelerated to 16.7 percent for January–June, from 14.8 percent for July–December. Japan's imports of Chinese goods fell 6.1 percent.[45]

In addition to the official responses, the Chinese government tolerated the large anti-Japan demonstrations in more than one hundred Chinese cities, leading to violence and destruction of Japanese property and interests. Protests in Beijing and Shanghai turned violent at times, but those in other cities involved significantly more violent acts, such as the looting of Japanese shops and restaurants, smashing Japanese-made cars, burning buildings of some Japanese companies, and ransacking some Japanese supermarkets.

Protestors broke into a dozen Japanese-run factories in Qingdao, setting fire to a Panasonic factory and a Toyota dealership.[46]

Years of propaganda demonizing the Japanese primed Chinese youth for the demonstrations. The majority of the demonstrators did not quite know why they wanted the islands, but they knew they disliked the Japanese because of wartime crimes against China. An office worker said, "It's more than about the Diaoyu Islands. It's about wanting to avenge all the millions of Chinese the Japanese killed in the war."[47] A young computer worker said Chinese should stand up to Japan, remembering its brutal occupation of much of China before and during World War II: "We cannot lose the Diaoyu Islands. We cannot forget our national shame."[48]

Manipulated Memories Fuel Public Pressure

Chinese perceptions and interpretations of the territorial dispute are shaped by historical memories as those memories have been construed and kept alive by propaganda outlets and social media. One strand of the constructed memory nurtures a strong sense of grievance and resentment for real and imputed Japanese offenses. Another strand emphasizes Japan's cultural debt to China. Together, these strands support the idea that Japan should and will accede to Chinese demands because of gratitude for all that Japan has received from China and remorse for all the bad that Japan has done to China. This dynamic and its consequences are captured in the assessment of a Chinese scholar: "Whenever there was a conflict of interest with Japan, the Chinese people always expected Japan to make concessions because it owed China so much in history. If the Chinese government wants to compromise, the public rage will quickly turn against the 'traitorous' government."[49]

Decades-long efforts by the regime to inculcate a particular view of Japan and the growing importance of public opinion that is a consequence of modernization, urbanization, and the erosion of ideological, charismatic, and other sources of legitimacy increasingly drive and constrain Beijing's policy options vis-à-vis Japan. This dynamic is especially clear—and important—in the post-2009 resurgence of the territorial dispute. A Chinese scholar has described the dynamic in the following way: "Every time Japan and the Diaoyu/Senkaku dispute come up in the news, people in China become emotional and angry. Chinese leaders and officials cannot afford to be seen as soft towards Japan."[50] The resultant burst of anti-Japanese nationalism both forced the government to act and constrained its ability to manage the dispute, because if it did nothing, or if it were perceived as too accommodating to Japan, it would lose even more of its already-dwindling legitimacy. Many Chinese, and many in the leadership, believe that China's rising power gives their country the ability to settle historical and territorial disputes on China's terms. The notion that because China is no longer weak it should no longer tolerate Japanese (or any other country's) affronts to China's sovereignty is reinforced by the belief that it is no longer necessary to treat Japan with kid gloves in order to obtain the investment, technology, and markets required to achieve rapid modernization. Those who believe (probably incorrectly) that Japan now needs China more than China needs Japan press the government to adopt hard-line positions. Their short-term objective is to force Japan to acknowledge that ownership of the islands is contested. The longer-term goal is to make China the unchallenged and indispensable power in the region.

Beijing started to challenge Japan's de facto control by conducting regular maritime patrols around the islands to create a "new normal" soon after the fishing boat incident in 2010. At a press conference on July 11, 2012, China's Foreign Ministry spokesman acknowledged that three Chinese fishery administration patrol ships on a routine patrol had entered into the twelve-nautical-mile waters of the Diaoyu Islands. Previously, Chinese spokespeople answering such questions acknowledged that Chinese vessels had entered "the vicinity" of the islands. A *People's Daily* commentary a few months later stated that the patrol missions had become routine (常规行动) and that the Japanese needed to accept that. China would continue to undertake such missions on a regular basis to defend its territorial sovereignty and legal rights: "China needs persistence and it has the will and strength to be persistent."[51]

Beijing pushed hard because it judged that Japan had limited bargaining power. A *China Daily* article stated, "Japan's repeated resorts to Article 5 of the US-Japan treaty show a lasting shortage of bargaining power to back Tokyo's claim."[52] A *Global Times* editorial on the first anniversary of Japan's nationalization of the disputed islands claimed Chinese victory in what it called the "Cold Confrontation" because "Japan has failed in its effort to consolidate its actual control of the Diaoyu Islands. . . . Taking this opportunity, Chinese marine law enforcement expanded its forefront into the surrounding waters of the Diaoyu Islands, and established a regular system of law enforcement. . . . China has not only shaken Japan's effective control over the islands, but more importantly, showed to the rest of the world its resolution to protect its sovereignty, both assertively and forcefully."[53] Two months later, another editorial celebrated that, "despite provocative rhetoric, Japan has generally accepted China's way of safeguarding its rights over the Diaoyu Islands and a complicated new situation has come into being."[54]

Chinese media kept up the pressure by referring repeatedly to the possibility of war. Calls for war did not represent Beijing's official policy, but many Chinese commentators argued that if war occurred, China would be capable of defeating Japan. A *Global Times* editorial stated, "China's comprehensive military power is stronger than Japan's. Once a war breaks out, China could also endure the economic consequences better than Japan." Such views are extreme and almost certainly not representative of the thinking of most senior Chinese leaders. When queried about them, officials and many academics are quick to point this out and often explain the appearance of such statements as a manifestation of China's greater freedom of expression and more open media. That may be true, but a more likely explanation is that top leaders find it useful to permit the publication of views they believe will resonate with important segments of the Chinese public and disconcert foreign audiences. The latter objective would be a Chinese variant of what Richard Nixon described as his madman theory.[55]

Although sometimes overshadowed by dramatic and prominent expressions of extreme views, more sober arguments were and are made by influential Chinese. For example, recognizing the strength of negative public attitudes and the inefficacy of existing mechanisms (and inability to develop additional ones), some Chinese scholars have urged both sides to act in a rational way. Peking University professor and frequent adviser to the Chinese government Wang Jisi wrote that it would be a mistake to believe that China could use its growing economic and military power to suppress rivals (压制对手) and force Japan to accept its terms because there were no historical examples of great powers suppressing other countries. China and Japan experienced not only wars and hostilities but also many periods of warmth, gratitude, and hopefulness. He wrote that it pained him to see the deteriorating relationship and called for strategic wisdom and efforts to restore a more normal state of affairs.[56] Shanghai-based Ren Xiao took a similar approach, warning that it would be a mistake to draw a parallel between Abe's attempts to reinterpret or amend the constitution and the rise of Japanese militarism in the previous century.[57]

Unfortunately, rational voices have often been overwhelmed by emotional anti-Japanese nationalist sentiments. The role of track II diplomacy involving influential opinion leaders of both countries is quite limited when it comes to the dialogue between China and Japan. The vast majority of track II programs between the two countries are government-led activities designed to create the superficial appearance of friendship, with very limited influence on government policies.

Riding the Anti-Japan Tiger

Many Chinese have vivid, albeit secondhand and sometimes distorted, memories of Japanese aggression and humiliation of their country, and perceive Japan to be insufficiently remorseful for past sins and atrocities. This predisposes them to assign most of the blame for current tensions to the Japanese people and their government. Many Japanese believe that their country has apologized enough for the actions of long-dead leaders, and that Chinese are insufficiently grateful for all that Japan has done to facilitate their country's modernization and willfully blind to how different the Japan of today is from the militarized nation that caused great harm in China and elsewhere in Asia. This predisposes them to resent Chinese actions and criticism, and to worry about China's rising power intentions. No country is responsible alone for the deterioration of the relationship. Self-righteousness and lack of empathy can only intensify their rivalry. Both Tokyo and Beijing would benefit from avoiding a cycle of action and reaction. China wants Japan to acknowledge and repent for past atrocities, but China also needs to be very wary of and move beyond the easy temptation of anti-Japanese nationalism.

The Communist Party deserves much of the blame for the high level of anti-Japanese hostility in China but appears to have lost the ability to control or utilize the sentiments it once found useful. Leaders recognize, more clearly than does the Chinese public, how important Japan is to the continued success of China's quest for wealth, power, security, and influence. They also recognize the enormous risks of making Japan an enemy and active opponent of China's rise. But Beijing appears increasingly pushed by the strength of public opinion to adopt uncompromising stands on Japan-related issues, especially the Diaoyu/Senkaku territorial dispute. In a very real sense, they created the tiger of anti-Japanese public opinion and now have no choice but to ride it—falling off or failing to appear resolute will further undermine the regime's already eroding legitimacy. However, if they appease public opinion by adopting even more hostile policies toward Japan, they run an equally great risk of undermining legitimacy, because alienating Japan would have significant negative consequences for sustained economic growth, the most important pillar of regime legitimacy. Beijing is on the back of a dilemma that is largely of its own making but is nonetheless a very real dilemma.

Notes

1. See, for example, Richard C. Bush, *The Perils of Proximity: China-Japan Security Relations* (Washington, DC: Brookings Institution, 2010); and Michael Yahuda, *Sino-Japanese Relations After the Cold War: Two Tigers Sharing a Mountain* (Abingdon, UK: Routledge, 2014).

2. The classic work on the Communist Party's exploitation of anti-Japanese nationalism is Chalmers Johnson, *Peasant Nationalism and Communist Power: The Emergence of Revolutionary China 1937–1945* (Stanford, CA: Stanford University Press, 1962).

3. See "Joint Communiqué of the Government of Japan and the Government of the People's Republic of China," 1972, http://www.mofa.go.jp/region/asia-paci/china/joint72.html; and "Treaty of Peace and Friendship Between Japan and the People's Republic of China," 1978, http://www.mofa.go.jp/region/asia-paci/china/treaty78.html.

4. In December 1890, Japanese prime minister and "father" of Japanese militarism Aritomo Yamagata claimed that there were two lines to be guarded for Japan's self-defense. The first was the sovereignty line, which traced the border of Japan's national territory. The second was the interest line, which referred to any area within which the safety of the sovereignty line was intimately related. Liu Jiangyong, "Then and Now: Sino-Japanese Relations 120 Years After the War," *East Asia Forum*, October 22, 2014, http://www.eastasiaforum.org/2014/10/29/then-and-now-sino-japanese-relations-120-years-after-the-war/.

5. See Ezra F. Vogel, *Deng Xiaoping and the Transformation of China* (Cambridge, MA: Belknap Press of Harvard University Press, 2011).

6. 王缉思, 刘洋 (Wang Jisi and Liu Yang), "中美与中日关系同时滑坡并非有利局面" 环球财经 [Stress in Sino-US and Sino-Japanese Relations at the Same Time

Is Not Good], *Global Finance*, September 1, 2014, http://www.21ccom.net/articles/world/zlwj/20140901112316.html.

7. Liah Greenfeld, "Roots of Japan-China Rivalry," *Japan Times*, September 27, 2012, http://www.japantimes.co.jp/opinion/2012/09/27/commentary/world-commentary/roots-of-japan-china-rivalry/#.VQLSWcYmU7o.

8. Yinan He, "History, Chinese Nationalism and the Emerging Sino-Japanese conflict," *Journal of Contemporary China* 16, no. 50 (2007): 1–24.

9. See, for example, Tsukasa Takamine, "The Political Economy of Japanese Foreign Aid: The Role of Yen Loans in China's Economic Growth and Openness," *Pacific Affairs* 79, no. 1 (Spring 2006): 29–48.

10. See "Statement by the Chief Cabinet Secretary Yohei Kono on the Result of the Study on the Issue of 'Comfort Women,'" August 4, 1993, http://www.mofa.go.jp/policy/women/fund/state9308.html; and "Statement by Prime Minister Tomiichi Murayama on the Occasion of the 50th Anniversary of the War's End," August 15, 1995, http://www.mofa.go.jp/announce/press/pm/murayama/9508.html.

11. See, for example, Nicholas D. Kristof, "Burying the Past: War Guilt Haunts Japan," *New York Times*, November 30, 1998, http://www.nytimes.com/1998/11/30/world/burying-the-past-war-guilt-haunts-japan.html.

12. "Facing the Future with a Farsighted View—Warmly Greeting President Jiang Zemin's Successful Visits to Russia and Japan," *Renmin Ribao*, December 1, 1998, as reported by *Xinhua* Domestic Service, November 30, 1998.

13. 任晓 (Ren Xiao), "东北亚安全形势的现状与未来" [The Current and Future Security Situation in Northeast Asia], 国际展望 [International Outlook] 7 (1996): 11.

14. See, for example, "China Celebrates 70th Anniversary of Victory of World Anti-Fascist War," *Global Times*, September 3, 2015, http://www.globaltimes.cn/special-coverage/Anniv-of-Victory/; "Even More Anti-Japan War Dramas Will Fill China's Airwaves in Run-up to Victory Day Celebrations," *Shanghaiist*, August 30, 2015, http://shanghaiist.com/2015/08/30/more_anti_japan_dramas.php; and Andrew Jacobs, "As China's Economy Falters, Military Parade Offers Chance to Burnish Image," *New York Times*, September 1, 2015, http://www.nytimes.com/2015/09/02/world/asia/as-economy-falters-military-parade-offers-chance-to-burnish-chinas-image.html?_r=0.

15. Robert A. Manning, "China and the US-Japan Alliance," *East Asia Forum*, October 28, 2013, http://www.eastasiaforum.org/2013/10/28/china-and-the-us-japan-alliance/.

16. Hongping Annie Nie, "Gaming, Nationalism, and Ideological Work in Contemporary China: Online Games Based on the War of Resistance Against Japan," *Journal of Contemporary China* 22, no. 81 (May 2013): 500.

17. 宋强 (Song Qiang) et al., 中国可以说不 [The China That Can Say No] (Beijing: Zhonghua Gongshang Lianhe Chuban She, 1996), 112–113.

18. Murong Xuecun, "China's Television War on Japan," *New York Times*, February 10, 2014, http://www.nytimes.com/2014/02/10/opinion/murong-chinas -television-war-on-japan.html.

19. 张香山 (Zhang Xiangshan), "中日复交谈判回顾" [Recollection of Sino-Japanese Normalization Negotiation], 日本研究 [Japan Studies] 1 (1998): http:// www.china.com.cn/chinese/HIAW/143113.htm.

20. Willen van Kemenade, *China and Japan: Partners or Permanent Rivals* (The Hague: Netherlands Institute of International Relations Clingendael, 2006), 68.

21. 侯杰 (Hou Jie), "邓小平谈钓鱼岛归属问题：先搁置它二三十年" [Deng Xiaoping on Sovereignty over the Diaoyu Islands: Shelve the Problem for Two-Three Decades], May 18, 2012, http://cul.china.com.cn/lishi/2012-05/18/ content_5018247.htm.

22. See, for example, Irene Wang and Alice Yan, "Capital Fetes Seven Diaoyu 'Heroes,'" *South China Morning Post*, March 29, 2004, http://www.scmp.com/ article/450162/capital-fetes-seven-diaoyu-heroes.

23. See, for example, Robert Marquand, "Beijing Keeps Lid on Anti-Japan Sentiment," *Christian Science Monitor*, May 4, 2005, http://www.csmonitor .com/2005/0504/p05s01-woap.html.

24. See "Vice Premier Wu Yi Cancels Meeting with Koizumi," *China Daily*, May 24, 2005, http://en.people.cn/200505/24/eng20050524_186438.html.

25. See coverage and assessment of the visit by Tao Wenzhao, "History Should Be a Lesson, Not an Obstacle," *China Daily*, April 19, 2007; and Takanori Kato, "China Walking Media Tightrope," *Daily Yomiuri*, April 30, 2007.

26. Suisheng Zhao, "Foreign Policy Implications of Chinese Nationalism Revisited: The Strident Turn," *Journal of Contemporary China* 22, no. 82 (July 2013): 535.

27. See, for example, Chisa Fujioka and Chris Buckley, "China Snubs Japan PM over Boat Row, Rules Out Meeting," *Reuters*, September 21, 2010, http:// www.reuters.com/article/2010/09/21/us-japan-china-idUSTRE68I06520100921.

28. Keith Bradsher, "Amid Tension, China Blocks Vital Exports to Japan," *New York Times*, September 22, 2010, http://www.nytimes.com/2010/09/23/ business/global/23rare.html?pagewanted=all&_r=0. This move, though dramatic, had the easily predictable effect of demonstrating to all countries and purchasers of all Chinese products that China had become an unreliable supplier.

29. Sachiko Sakamaki, "Japan Cites China Relations in Releasing Boat Captain," *Bloomberg*, September 24, 2010, http://www.businessweek.com/news/2010 -09-24/japan-cites-china-relations-in-releasing-boat-captain.html.

30. See "China Reiterates Demand for Japan's Apology, Compensation," *China Daily*, September 26, 2010, http://www.chinadaily.com.cn/china/2010-09/26/content_11348360.htm.

31. Editorial, "No Need to Pander to China over Senkaku Islands," *Yomiuri Shimbun*, June 12, 2012, http://www.yomiuri.co.jp/dy/editorial/T120612003987.htm.

32. Junya Hashimoto, "Government Drew Up Multiple Plans for Senkaku Use," *Yomiuri Shimbun*, September 13, 2012, http://www.yomiuri.co.jp/dy/national/T120912004075.htm.

33. Linda Sieg, "Analysis: Mistrust, Rivalry and Bad Timing Fan Japan-China Row," *Reuters*, September 19, 2012, http://www.reuters.com/article/2012/09/19/us-china-japan-row-idUSBRE88I0KL20120919.

34. Akihisa Nagashima, a member of the Democratic Party of Japan in the Lower House, who handled the Senkaku Islands issue as a special adviser to Noda, said in his book, "We exhausted all available diplomatic channels to reach Chinese Vice Foreign Minister Zhang Zhijun and State Councilor Dai Bingguo." After rounds of discussions, the Japanese officials became "positive about the prospects of being able to elicit a 'tacit acceptance' from China," "Japan, China Were Close to Preventing Current Turmoil over Senkakus, DPJ Lawmaker Says," *Asahi Shimbun*, October 22, 2013, http://ajw.asahi.com/article/behind_news/politics/AJ201310220059.

35. Ren Xiao, "Diaoyu/Senkaku Disputes—A View from China," *East Asia Forum*, November 4, 2013, http://www.eastasiaforum.org/2013/11/04/diaoyusenkaku-disputes-a-view-from-china/. Another Chinese scholar argued, "Japan broke the agreement to 'shelve disputes' to work for the future [that had been] reached by former Chinese Premier Zhou Enlai and former Japanese Prime Minister Tanaka Kakuei. . . . Japan went ahead with its plan to 'purchase' the islands, and tried to eliminate all obstacles to 'private ownership' and ultimately 'nationalization' of the islands to reinforce its control over them." See Zhou Yongsheng, "Sino-Japan Ties Not Easy to Improve," *China Daily*, February 5, 2013, 9.

36. Editorial, "Clash over Senkaku Islands Would Achieve Nothing," *Asahi Shimbun*, September 16, 2012, http://ajw.asahi.com/article/views/editorial/AJ201209170058.

37. Jin Baisong, "Consider Sanctions on Japan," *China Daily*, September 17, 2012, http://www.chinadaily.com.cn/opinion/2012-09/17/content_15761435.htm.

38. 钟声 (Commentary) "日本，不要自讨没趣" [Japan: No Need to Invite a Rebuff], 人民日报 (*People's Daily*), July 18, 2013, http://world.people.com.cn/n/2013/0718/c14549-22232913.html.

39. "Statement of the Ministry of Foreign Affairs of the People's Republic of China," September 10, 2012, http://www.fmprc.gov.cn/eng/zxxx/t968188.htm.

40. Li Xiaokun and Zhang Yunbi, "Wen Vows No Concession," *China Daily*, September 10, 2012, http://usa.chinadaily.com.cn/china/2012-09/11/content _15748555.htm.

41. "Xi Calls Japan's Island Purchase 'a Farce,'" *Xinhua*, September 19, 2012, http://www.chinadaily.com.cn/china/2012-09/19/content_15769128.htm.

42. "商务部: 中国消费者有权对日对购岛岛中国场"" [Ministry of Commerce: Chinese Consumers Have the Right to Express a Position on the Purchase of the Islands], 人民网 (People's Daily Online), September 14, 2012, http://finance .people.com.cn/n/2012/0914/c1004-19005817.html.

43. "China Delays Approval of Working Visas: Firms Made to Wait as Beijing Retaliates amid Senkakus Flare-up," *Japan Times*, September 23, 2012, https:// engineeringevil.com/2012/09/22/china-delays-approval-of-working-visas/.

44. In September 2012, Toyota's sales of new vehicles in China dropped 48.9 percent from a year earlier, Honda's sales plunged 40.5 percent, Nissan's slid 35 percent, Mitsubishi's dived 63 percent, and Mazda's sales sank 36 percent. See "Japanese Car Sales Plunge in China After Islands Dispute," *Associated Press*, October 9, 2012, http://www.guardian.co.uk/business/2012/oct/09/japanese-car -sales-china-islands-dispute.

45. Mitsuru Obe, "Japan Exports to China at 4-Year Low," *Wall Street Journal*, August 14, 2013, http://online.wsj.com/article/SB10001424127887324139404579012 481067770274.html.

46. "Anti-Japan Protests Escalate, Turn Violent," *South China Moring Post*, September 17, 2012, http://www.scmp.com/news/china/article/1038664/anti-japan -prot. See also Alan Taylor, "Anti-Japan Protests in China," *The Atlantic*, September-ber 17, 2012, http://www.theatlantic.com/photo/2012/09/anti-japan-protests -in-china/100370/.

47. "China Hints That It Sees Nothing Wrong with Boycott of Japanese Goods," *Reuters*, September 14, 2012, http://ajw.asahi.com/article/behind_news/ politics/AJ201209140018.

48. "Anti-Japan Protests in China Swell, Turn Violent," *New York Times*, September 15, 2012, http://www.nytimes.com/aponline/2012/09/15/world/asia/ap -as-asia-disputed-islands.html.

49. Yinan He, "History, Chinese Nationalism and the Emerging Sino-Japanese conflict," *Journal of Contemporary China* 16, no. 50 (2007): 11.

50. Ren, "Diaoyu/Senkaku Dispute."

51. 钟声 (Commentary), "中国需要这样的坚守"" [China Needs Such Persis-tence], *People's Daily*, October 8, 2012, 3.

52. Zhang Yunbi, "Analysts: Japan's Chaotic Voices to Harm Ties," *China Daily*, July 26, 2012, http://usa.chinadaily.com.cn/china/2012-07/26/content_15618083.htm.

53. Editorial, "Advantage China in Diaoyu Dispute," *Global Times*, September 12, 2013, http://www.globaltimes.cn/content/810627.shtml.

54. Editorial, "Tokyo's Complaints over ADIZ Hypocritical," *Global Times*, November 25, 2013, http://www.globaltimes.cn/content/827360.shtml.

55. See H. R. Haldeman, *The Ends of Power* (New York: Times Books, 1978), 122; and James Carroll, "Nixon's Madman Strategy, *Boston Globe*, June 14, 2005, http://www.boston.com/news/globe/editorial_opinion/oped/articles/2005/06/14/nixons_madman_strategy/.

56. Wang Jisi and Liu Yang, [Stress in Sino-US and Sino-Japanese Relations].

57. "任 晓 (Ren Xiao), 超越"耻辱" [Beyond "Humiliation"], 上海思想界 (ShanghaiThoughtCircle), no. 9, 2014, http://www.chinaelections.org/article/105/235423.html.

FIVE

Japan and the Rise of China
From Affinity to Alienation

Seiichiro Takagi

Japan and China view each other through lenses colored by proximity, history, economics, and their relationships with the United States. The salience and relative importance of each factor depends on what is happening in both the domestic and the external arenas. Generally speaking, when things were going well in Japan, particularly during the period of sustained growth and widespread admiration of the Japanese economic miracle, Tokyo and the Japanese public evinced confidence in their own country and support for China's modernization.[1] Perceptions and policies changed gradually, however, after Japan's "bubble economy" burst in 1991, effects of which were felt with some time lag, and as China's "rise" acquired momentum. Over time, Japanese perceptions of China became less positive and Tokyo's policies became more reactive and defensive.

The dynamic at work involved more than just the reversal of economic trajectories, however. Over time, the Japanese and Chinese economies became increasingly intertwined and interdependent; Chinese citizens became more vocal, and at times more violent, in their criticism of Japanese actions; and China's government became more assertive about its growing economic

This chapter examines Sino-Japanese relations from a Japanese perspective. It argues that Japan supported and benefited from China's reform and opening strategy and demonstrates how China's military buildup and assertive actions near the disputed Senkaku/Diaoyu Islands eroded Japanese public and political support for Chinese goals.

and military power. Economic interdependence constrained the willingness of both sides to take actions likely to be as costly to the one imposing penalties as to their target. In addition, changing perceptions of military capabilities and intentions transformed Japanese (and Chinese) thinking with respect to the US-Japan alliance.

The pages that follow present a brief analytical history of the evolution of Japanese attitudes and policies toward China during the era of reform and opening.[2] China's achievements and actions influenced Japanese assessments of dangers and opportunities resulting from China's rise. But Japanese perceptions and policy responses were also shaped by historical memory, public opinion, the availability and cost of possible courses of action, and for a brief period, domestic politics.

The rapid rise of China was profoundly shocking to Japanese because it challenged a key aspect of Japan's post–World War II national identity. Since the 1980s, being the world's number-two economic power had become a defining characteristic of Japan's identity and self-image. China's economic performance during the first decade of reform and opening (from December 1978 through the Tiananmen Incident in June 1989) was erratic and caused little concern in Japan. Japan's own rate of growth was high and a source of national self-confidence. But Japanese self-confidence eroded during the decade after the bubble economy burst in 1991 and China began to achieve sustained double-digit growth after coping successfully with the difficulties of post-Tiananmen alienation from Western-camp nations and the collapse of the Soviet Union, as well as the reinvigoration of the reform and opening policy in 1992. China's performance became increasingly worrisome, as Japan remained mired in the prolonged period of low growth now characterized as the "lost decade." The worries were initially focused on the relocation of Japanese manufacturing operations to China to take advantage of cheap labor, but the so-called hollowing out of Japan's economy was compounded by military developments, especially after the turn of the century. A symbolically important point was reached in 2010, when China's gross domestic product (GDP) surpassed that of Japan and China captured the title "world's second-largest economy." The initial impact of this development was limited, but it became more important over time. How it became more important, and how and why Japanese perceptions of China changed, are the focus of this chapter.

Factors Inclining Japan to Assist China's Quest for Modernity

Japan's initial response to China's reform and opening policy was both supportive and substantial. The timing of the announcement of the new policy in December 1978, just four months after Japan and China had signed the Treaty of Peace and Friendship that completed the process of diplomatic normalization begun in 1972, was quite conducive to Japan's positive response.[3] A critical element of the new policy was China's willingness to accept foreign economic assistance. Japan responded positively and quickly; Tokyo began to provide official developmental assistance (ODA) to China in 1979 and became the largest provider of bilateral ODA to China in 1980. Japan retained its number-one position through the 1990s.

A key factor in Tokyo's decision to respond positively to China's new willingness to engage with the outside world was its calculation that supporting reform and opening through economic exchanges was critical to inducing China to align with the Western camp rather than return to the socialist fold. But that was not the only reason. Japan's decision to assist China was made easier by two additional factors, war guilt and US policy. Memory—and recognition—of Japan's invasion and occupation of China before 1945 was still quite vivid among Japan's senior politicians and business leaders. This, in conjunction with China's renunciation of reparations, created a sense of obligation to help China's quest for development.[4] The second enabling factor was US approval of Tokyo's decision to assist China. Japan would have been reluctant to assist China if doing so might jeopardize its security alliance with the United States. The establishment of full diplomatic relations between the United States and China on January 1, 1979, assuaged that concern.

When the socioeconomic consequences of reform and opening led to the Tiananmen Incident in June 1989, Japan initially opposed attempts by other Western nations to impose political and economic sanctions because they would lead to the international isolation of China. Tokyo ultimately joined the Western sanctions, albeit reluctantly, to avoid its own isolation, but Japan was the first Western nation to lift them.[5] Japan's approach was vindicated in early 1992 when Deng Xiaoping made his famous sojourn to southern China to rekindle and accelerate the reform and opening policy.[6] The renewed commitment to reform was formalized at the Communist Party's Fourteenth Party Congress in mid-October.[7] Soon afterward, the

Japanese emperor visited China to celebrate the twentieth anniversary of the establishment of diplomatic relations. His visit significantly improved Japanese public perceptions of China and led to the acceleration of Japanese investment in China. The more positive mood persisted despite the bursting of Japan's bubble economy in 1991 and Chinese promulgation, in February 1992, of the Territorial Waters Law, which asserted that the Senkaku (called Diaoyu by China) Islands belonged to Taiwan, and thus to China.[8]

Throughout the 1990s, when the Japanese economy experienced sustained postbubble stagnation, Japan continued to be the number one provider of bilateral ODA to China. The Chinese nuclear weapons test in May 1995 triggered a domestic debate on the wisdom of providing ODA to China, but the debate resulted only in the suspension of the financially meager grant-in-aid program.[9] Suspending this program was intended to signal Japanese concern without causing serious damage to China's economy.[10] Bilateral trade and Japan's investment in China continued to grow. Less positive developments included President Clinton's visit to China in June 1998, which made Japanese somewhat uneasy because he did not stop in Japan, and Jiang Zemin's visit to Japan later in the same year.[11] Jiang's incessant lecturing on the "lessons of history" alienated many in Japan.[12] However, most Japanese were not very worried about China's continued economic growth and the increases in military expenditures it made possible because the alliance with the United States had been reaffirmed for the post–Cold War era in April 1996.[13] Indeed, the mid-1990s debate in the United States over whether to contain, engage, or "con-gage" China had little resonance in Japan.[14]

After the turn of the century, Prime Minister Junichiro Koizumi, who assumed the office in April 2001, angered the Chinese by repeatedly visiting the Yasukuni Shrine, which the Chinese regard as the symbol of Japanese militarism. Koizumi was not an anti-China politician. In fact, he was the first Western world leader to assert, at the Boao Forum for Asia in April 2002, that the rise of China is not a threat, but rather an opportunity and a challenge, to Japan.[15] During the Koizumi administration (2001–2006), Japan-China economic ties continued to develop despite recurring political frictions. This led the Chinese to characterize the relationship as *zheng leng, jing re* (politically cold and economically hot).

The political component of the relationship began to improve with the end of the Koizumi administration. Shinzo Abe, Koizumi's successor, visited

Beijing immediately after he formed his cabinet in October 2006. At his postsummit press conference, he said that both sides agreed to characterize the bilateral relationship as the *senryakuteki gokei kankei* (strategic relationship of mutual benefit), or *zhanlue huhui guanxi* in Chinese.[16] The trip was later described as "ice-breaking."[17] The imagery and positive trend in political relations were extended with subsequent trips to "melt the ice" (by Chinese premier Wen Jiabao in April 2007), to "warm the water" (by Prime Minister Yasuo Fukuda in December 2007), and to "welcome spring" (by President Hu Jintao in May 2008).[18]

The trend appeared likely to continue after the historic change of government from the Liberal Democratic Party (LDP), which had been in power almost continuously since 1955, to the newly formed Democratic Party of Japan (DPJ) in September 2009. The first DPJ prime minister, Yukio Hatoyama, was clearly inclined to reduce what he regarded as excessive emphasis on the relationship with the United States by enhancing Japan's relationship with China. How, and with what consequences, he might have done that remains a mystery, because he resigned in May of the following year after realizing that his mishandling of the Futenma marine air base relocation issue had complicated relations with the United States without achieving anything of value in the relationship with China.[19]

The near-term potential for positive developments in Japan's relationship with China was effectively derailed by the September 2010 incident near the Senkakus in which a Chinese fishing crew was detained after ramming two Japanese coast guard vessels. The aftermath of the collisions and detention alienated many Japanese and strengthened the anti-China forces in Japan.[20] Chinese expressions of friendship and support after the triple disaster of earthquake, tsunami, and nuclear power-plant failures in the northeastern prefectures of Japan's main island in 2011 created a short-lived opportunity to rebuild positive momentum in the relationship, but the positive effect was quickly dissipated by another and more intractable flare-up of the Senkaku issue in 2012.[21]

Though brief, this summary of developments in Japan's relationship with China during the era of reform and opening illustrates the complex interaction of geostrategic, political, economic, and historical factors shaping Japanese perceptions and policies toward its increasingly powerful neighbor. All are important, but not equally so, and the relative importance of each has varied over time.

Geography is always an extremely important factor in the history and character of Sino-Japanese relations. Proximity enabled the millennia-long infusion of culture from China, facilitated post-Meiji Japan's imperialistic expansion into China, and has made possible China's recent attempts to pressure Japan with paramilitary forces. The history of Japan's invasion of China continues to bedevil the bilateral relationship. China and/or the Chinese people construe defense of Japanese interests as evidence of Japan's refusal to accept responsibility for past actions, and Japanese increasingly resent efforts by China to exploit history and Japanese remorse to stigmatize and pressure Japan. Perceptions that increased wealth and power are enabling China to act more assertively remind Japanese of China's imperial past and fuel worries about its future ambitions.

Japan's relationship with the United States is a much more recent but no less important factor shaping Japanese responses to China's rise. Were it not for the alliance with the United States, Japanese would worry more about the security implications of China's growing strength and military capabilities. Japan might also be less willing to assist China's quest for development and to accept the consequences (as well as the benefits) of growing economic interdependence. Stated another way, Japan can accept greater risks in its relationship with China because of its alliance with the United States. As a result, Japan's bilateral relationships with China and the United States must be managed as part of an inescapable strategic triangle. Despite this imperative, Japan often appears to lack an overarching strategy to guide relations with the two giants.

With this overview of the way Japan-China relations have evolved since 1978 and brief discussion of factors shaping Japanese perceptions and responses to China's rise setting the stage, the remainder of this chapter focuses more narrowly on specific examples of how and why the relationship has changed.

Media Reaction to China's Rise

On January 20, 2011, China's National Statistical Office announced that the country's GDP grew by 10.3 percent in 2010. Although the comparable statistics for Japan had not yet been published, all major Japanese newspapers reported the Chinese announcement on the front page of their evening editions. The headline message of all of them was that China was certain to surpass Japan as the world's second-largest economy. However, this was not the most prominent news story on that day. Two of the five major papers treated the news as the second item on the front page; Hu Jintao's visit to the United States received more prominent treatment. The January 20 announcement was not the first time that Japan was made aware that it might soon lose its second-place standing to China. Five months earlier, on August 16, 2010, major newspapers reported that China's nominal GDP had surpassed that of Japan in the second quarter. Notably, however, previous reporting focused on Japan's lackluster economic performance, not on how well China had done.

Japan's response to having been surpassed by China in terms of GDP was less excited or dismayed than many in China or elsewhere thought it would be or had been. At the time, Japan's "defeat" in a GDP competition was not particularly salient. Indeed, Hisayoshi Ina, an editor at *Nihon Keizai Shimbun*, characterized Japan's response to the news as "dull."[22] Many commentaries acknowledged the historical significance of the reversal, but they also noted that China's rapid growth had created many serious problems. The problems they mentioned included aggravation of income imbalances between city and countryside and between coastal and inland regions, environmental degradation, and retarded development of social safety nets. They also pointed out the gap between the responsibilities that China would henceforth be expected to assume and China's will and ability to assume them.

Some commentaries also noted that China's pattern of growth, which depended heavily on the export of consumer products manufactured with cheap labor, could not be sustained because of rising wages and decline of the working-age population after the mid-2010s. Some commentaries downplayed the significance of the reversal of positions by noting that China's population was ten times that of Japan and that China's per capita GDP was only one-tenth as large. "True" wealth, they argued, should be measured in terms of well-being, not just the size of economy.

Perhaps the most important reason that Japan took China's GDP "victory" in stride is that reversal of the countries' aggregate economic positions had long seemed inevitable. Given Japan's postbubble economic stagnation and continued double-digit economic growth in China, Japanese who paid attention to economic performance considered it only a matter of time until China would surpass Japan in terms of GDP. Many in Japan knew about the Goldman Sachs report of 2001, which popularized the term *BRICs* and contained a scenario in which China overtook Japan as the world's second-largest economy.[23] In fact, a table in that report showed that China's GDP (measured in terms of purchasing power parity) had surpassed that of Japan in 2000.[24] A business magazine, *Nikkei Bijinesu*, had predicted in 2007 that China's GDP could surpass that of Japan as early as 2010.[25] The article quotes Qinghua University economics professor Hu Angang as saying that World Bank data indicated China's GDP (calculated in terms of purchasing power parity) surpassed Japan's in 1995.[26]

Shifts in Public Opinion

Changes in Japanese public opinion regarding China's rise are readily apparent in the annual Survey on Diplomacy conducted by the Cabinet Office from 1978, when the Treaty of Peace and Friendship was signed, to 2012.[27] Figure 5.1 shows the time series of responses to the question "Do you feel affinity with China?" The "feel affinity" line represents the combined percentage of respondents who answered "yes" and "more or less, yes"; the "don't feel affinity" line represents the combined percentage of answers "no" and "more or less, no."

As Figure 5.1 shows, the recent public perceptions of China are dramatically different from those in the decade following the signing of the Peace and Friendship Treaty in August 1978. In that decade, the "feel affinity" (FA) group far outnumbered the "don't feel affinity" (DFA) group. Although there were some fluctuations, FA constituted about 70 percent or more every year except 1978, and DFA never surpassed 30 percent. Examination of the reason for the dramatic reversal after 1988 is instructive.

The sharp drop in FA and corresponding increase in DFA in 1989 clearly reflects the impact of the Tiananmen Incident in June of that year. But the FA percentage was still significantly higher than the percentage of DFA. This pattern persisted until 1994, except for the 4.5 percent increase of FA and a similar decrease of DFA in 1992. The uptick in FA in 1992 clearly reflects the positive atmosphere created by the emperor's visit to China for the commemoration of the twentieth anniversary of the establishment of formal diplomatic relations. Three years later, in 1995, public opinion entered a new phase, which lasted until 2003. During this phase, FA and DFA were almost the same and evinced little fluctuation.

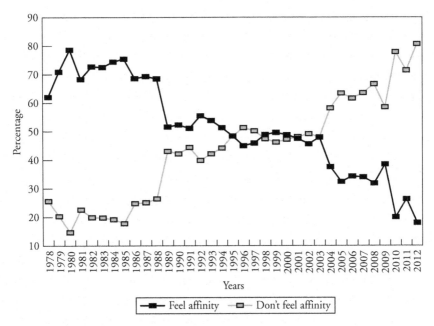

FIGURE 5.1 Feelings of affinity with China
SOURCE: Cabinet Office, "Public Opinion Poll on Diplomacy" (in Japanese), October 2012, http://www8.cao
.go.jp/survey/h24/h24-gaiko/zh/z10.html.

In 2004, the DFA percentage rose sharply, with a corresponding drop in FA. Further change in the same direction continued for three more years with the DFA percentage fluctuating between 60 percent and 70 percent, and FA moving between 30 and 40 percent. This pattern continued for three more years. The deterioration of public perceptions of China in 2004 reflects the impact of anti-Japanese sentiment expressed by spectators at the Asian Cup soccer games during the summer. The tournament was held in China, and members of the Japanese team had been subjected to malicious booing during preliminary matches in various Chinese cities. The situation became much worse when the Japanese team defeated the Chinese team in the final round. Disappointed spectators threw plastic bottles at the bus carrying Japanese players and the car of Japanese embassy staff. The further deterioration of positive feelings toward China in 2005 reflects the impact of anti-Japanese demonstrations that swept across major cities, including Beijing and Shanghai, during the spring. The figures for 2007 and 2008 are striking because they indicate no improvement in opinion toward China despite the exchange of visits by Prime Minister Abe in 2006, Prime Ministers Wen and Fukuda in 2007, and President Hu in 2008.

The improvement of the FA value in the 2009 poll might reflect the cumulative effect of the frequent exchange of visits in the preceding three years and the more positive atmosphere created by the inauguration of the new DPJ government. Even with this uptick, however, the FA percentage in 2009 reached only the level in 2006. In the following year, the percentage of DFA rose sharply to the all-time high of 77.8 percent, with a corresponding drop in the FA percentage. The probable cause was the fishing boat incident near the Senkaku Islands in early September, China's high-handed behavior during the ensuing row, and anti-Japanese demonstrations in major Chinese cities. The situation improved a little in the following year, probably in response to the suspension of China's anti-Japanese campaign after the triple disaster in March, and Premier Wen Jiabao's visit to the disaster site in May. However, the fact that DFA declined only to 71.4 percent, the third highest in the period under study, shows that the improved perception of China was fragile. In 2012, when the poll was taken in the month following the massive anti-Japanese demonstrations triggered by the Japanese government decision to purchase the privately held Senkaku Islands on September 11, the DFA percentage reached the all-time high of 80.6 percent.

The pattern of changes in Japanese feelings of affinity with China suggests that public opinion does not respond directly to reports about China's rise. Comparison of these findings with the results of other polls provides further clues to the state of Japanese public opinion. The BBC World Service poll on the influence of other countries conducted between December 6, 2011, and February 17, 2012, shows that 50 percent of Japanese respondents considered China's influence to be "mainly negative"; only 10 percent considered it "mainly positive."[28] In an *Asahi Shimbun* poll conducted in August and September 2012, only 3 percent said that they "like China." In the same poll, 38 percent said that they "dislike China," and 55 percent answered "neither."[29] This result suggests that many of those who did not feel much affinity with China did not necessarily dislike China. Rather than dislike, it appears that their primary inclination was one of emotional detachment.

Sources of Strategic Distrust

In a 2010 monograph on US-China strategic distrust, American coauthor Kenneth Lieberthal began the section expounding views in the United

States with the curious—but probably accurate—statement that "strategic distrust of China is not the current dominant view of national decision makers in the US government."[30] But he also pointed out that Americans worry about a variety of developments on the Chinese side because they consider the future of China to be very uncertain.[31] Although he focuses on US government officials, Lieberthal implies that these concerns and resultant distrust are shared by at least a portion of the American public.

In the case of Japan, we know more about public opinion than about the views of government decision makers. Among the Japanese public, strategic distrust of China is strong and takes many forms, some of which drive policy decisions and others of which constrain the options of decision makers. This section examines sources of strategic distrust of China within Japanese society. As used here, "strategic distrust" refers to belief that the distrusted nation pursues long-term goals that threaten one's core national interest.[32] Specific sources of strategic distrust in Japan's perception of China are summarized in the following sections.

CHINA'S RAPID EXPANSION OF MILITARY CAPABILITY

China's military buildup, which began in earnest in the 1990s, is the most important source of Japan's strategic distrust. It is widely known in Japan that China's military expenditures have grown by more than 10 percent in every year but one since 1989.[33] The increased expenditures have been used to raise the pay of soldiers and to purchase food and other items previously produced by military units themselves, but much of the money has been used to procure more and better equipment. In the 1990s, military modernization was achieved primarily through purchases of advanced weapons from Russia (e.g., Su-27 and Su-30 fighters, a Sovremennyy-class destroyer). China shifted from purchase to domestic production of advanced equipment in this century, deploying new systems such as the J-10 fighter. China's space program has successfully launched and recovered manned satellites. The program's military side was revealed in 2007 when China used a missile to shoot down a defunct Chinese weather satellite.[34]

China's rapid expansion of its military capability is increasingly apparent, and worrisome, in the seas surrounding Japan. Activities of Chinese naval vessels have been observed with increasing frequency, technical sophistication, and scale. From the late 1990s to the early 2000s, Japan was most concerned about increasing activities by nonmilitary Chinese research vessels operating in Japan's exclusive economic zone. Since approximately 2005, however, the activities of Chinese naval vessels have become a greater source of concern. In January 2004, a nuclear-powered submarine made a submerged transit through Japanese territorial waters near Okinawa. In September 2005, Chinese naval vessels were observed in the vicinity of the oil and gas fields near the median line dividing the exclusive economic zones of Japan and China in the East China Sea. The following year, a Chinese Song-class submarine reportedly surfaced near the US aircraft carrier *Kitty Hawk* in international waters near Okinawa.[35]

The frequency of Chinese naval activities near Japan has increased even more rapidly in the past eight years. In October 2008, four naval vessels, including Sovremennyy-class destroyers, passed through the Tsugaru Strait between Honshu and Hokkaido, sailed southward, and then passed between Okinawa's main island and Miyako Island.[36] In April 2010, a fleet of ten vessels, including two Sovremennyy-class destroyers and two kilo-class submarines, reportedly conducted an exercise in the East China Sea before passing between Okinawa's main island and Miyako Island on the way to and from the Pacific Ocean.[37] These military maneuvers are discomforting to Japanese because, among other reasons, a Chinese carrier-based helicopter flew dangerously close to a Maritime Self-Defense Force destroyer that had been observing the activities of the Chinese fleet.[38] These and other activities of Chinese naval vessels through 2015 are described with a graphic in a Ministry of Defense white paper from 2015.[39]

The impact of these developments on Japanese strategic distrust of China can be observed in surveys tracking the views of the Japanese public as a whole and those who are better informed about international affairs, and in analyses prepared by strategic affairs specialists. Comparison of public opinion polls in recent years shows predictable hardening of judgments. According to the *Yomiuri Shimbun* polls conducted in November 2006 and October 2010, respondents who considered China to be a "military threat to Japan" increased from 54.5 percent in 2006 to 79 percent in 2010.[40] The figure for 2010 seems consistent with the result of the *Asahi Shimbun* poll conducted from August to September 2012 that asked, "Do you feel China's military power is a threat to Japan, or not?" Seventy-four percent of the respondents answered that they did and only 22 percent said that they did not.[41]

Polls conducted annually since 2005 by Genron NPO show a similar trend in the responses of national samples and samples of "knowledgeable" Japanese.[42] Both groups were asked the same questions repeatedly, including, "Which countries and areas (on the list provided) do you think pose a military threat to your country?" The list included China, Republic of Korea, North Korea, Russia, India, the Middle East, the United States, the European Union, and others. Multiple answers were allowed. In the 2008 survey, which was conducted in June and July, China was mentioned by 54.8 percent of the general national sample and 66.3 percent of the "knowledgeable" sample. The result of the 2012 survey, conducted in April and May, when Tokyo governor Ishihara's intention to purchase the Senkaku Islands had been announced but the national government had not yet decide to preempt that purchase, was that China was mentioned by 58.7 percent of the general national sample and 81.3 percent of the "knowledgeable" sample.[43] These poll results confirm that a growing percentage of Japanese perceive China to be a military threat, indicate that the threat perception is higher among the "knowledgeable," and show that the increase in the perception of China as a military threat is significantly steeper for the "knowledgeable" than for the public as a whole.

"Knowledgeables" may be more inclined than ordinary Japanese to see China as a military threat because of their exposure to the ideas of experts on strategic issues. One of the most articulate and empirically minded among these experts is Professor Emeritus Shigeo Hiramatsu of Kyorin University.[44] His 1995 book *The Threat of China's Expanding Military Power* examines China's development of second-generation nuclear weapons and special operations troops, the buildup of naval and air capabilities, and the economic aspects of Deng Xiaoping's military reform.[45] Hiramatsu noted the possibility of China using its navy to threaten other claimants in territorial disputes in the South China Sea and warned about the possibility of the Chinese navy advancing into the Sea of Japan.[46]

MIDDLE KINGDOM SYNDROME

In the introduction to his book, Hiramatsu argued that the goal of Deng Xiaoping's military reforms was to restore China's status as "the great power at the center of the world," which it enjoyed before the decline of the Qing dynasty.[47] He is not the only Japanese who views China's actions and ambitions through the lens of China's imperial history.

In a more recent book, with the even more shocking title *China's Annexation of Japan*, Hiramatsu argued that China seeks to restore the glory and territorial claims of the Qing dynasty under the emperors Kangxi,

Yongzheng, and Qianlong.[48] These territorial claims were the most extensive in the history of Chinese empires. He argues, in other words, that irredentism is one of the motivations driving China's policy and points out that its historical claims include current Kazakhstan, Kyrgyzstan, part of Tajikistan, the Pamir Mountains, Nepal, Burma, Vietnam, Laos, Cambodia, Taiwan, Okinawa, the Korean Peninsula, and parts of Russia (including Khabarovsk, Primorsky, and Sakhalin).[49] He also points out that many of these states and territories were once tributary states of China, and that China uses the concept of "historical water" to imply that the Yellow Sea, East China Sea, and South China Sea are all "Chinese seas." Citing the wars China has fought since 1949 and evidence of aggressive maritime expansion, he warns, "Left unchecked, it is only a matter of time before the East China Sea and South China Sea become 'Chinese Seas.' If the East China Sea and South China Sea are controlled by China, Taiwan will lose the sphere of its existence and be absorbed by China. The next targets will be Japan's southwestern islands, such as the Sakishima and Okinawa Islands. The Korean Peninsula will also be absorbed. Restoration of the largest territorial expanse of the Chinese Empires is progressing gradually."[50]

Another vocal advocate of China threat arguments, journalist Yoshiko Sakurai, has argued, "What China pursues is the status and power of a superpower. What Mao and others must have thought concretely was probably the recovery of the territory of the Great Chinese Empire established by Emperors Kangxi, Yongzheng, and Qianlong at the height of the Qing dynasty. For that purpose, they pursued a powerful military state. After becoming a nuclear power, they turned their attention to the oceans and outer space. . . . Their ambition is now being realized."[51] The implication of this for Japan, according to her, is that "China is steadily moving toward superpower status. However, before it realizes that ambition, it must solidify its foundation as a regional power. The biggest and only obstacle is the existence of Japan."[52]

These views are extreme and do not represent mainstream opinion. But many Japanese are familiar with the idea of a Middle Kingdom syndrome (*chuka shisou*, in Japanese), and this provides fertile ground for public acceptance of the kind of arguments summarized here.[53] The term *Middle Kingdom syndrome* means different things to different people, but the basic idea is that China is the center of world culture and politics and superior to all other nations. Thus, it is natural and appropriate for China to seek an order with a central civilization surrounded by peripheral barbarian states or a tributary relationship like that during the heyday of China's imperial period. Such an idea is obviously incompatible with the strategic interests of neighboring countries, including Japan.

Japan became the world's second-largest economy through rapid economic growth in the 1960s and 1970s and, because of this, was expected to play a role commensurate with its economic status. In the 1980s, Japan fulfilled this role primarily by serving as the largest contributor of official developmental assistance. Expectations and demands of the international community continued to escalate, and in the 1990s, Japan had to respond to increasing pressures for international contributions involving the Self-Defense Forces. The expectation that Japan would contribute to military operations became particularly salient after the 1990–1991 Gulf War. Japan had contributed $13 billion to the multinational forces, increasing taxes to pay for the contribution, but instead of appreciation, the financial contribution was criticized as "checkbook diplomacy." Japanese people were shocked that Japan was not included on the list of countries to which Kuwait expressed gratitude for the help that contributed to the recovery of its sovereignty.

It was in this context that Japan enacted the UN Peace Cooperation Law to enable the Self-Defense Forces (SDF) to participate in UN peacekeeping operations. Chinese media criticized this legislation as a significant step toward dispatching troops abroad.[54] Chinese criticism was not generally seen at the time as intended to limit Japan's participation in international undertakings because opposition to the legislation from groups within Japan made arguments similar to those in Chinese media. But when Japan passed, with little domestic opposition, the Anti-Terrorism Special Measures Law in late October 2001, which enabled the Self-Defense Forces to assist multinational forces participating in Operation Enduring Freedom to defeat the Taliban and Al-Qaeda in Afghanistan, Chinese media again sounded alarm and decried both the speed of the process and the fact that it was the first time the Self-Defense Forces had participated in an overseas conflict since World War II.[55] Prime Minister Junichiro Koizumi visited Beijing in early October to explain to President Jiang Zemin and Premier Zhu Rongji that the bill under deliberation included several restrictions on the operation of the Self-Defense Forces, the most significant of which was that it would not engage in combat operations. The Chinese accepted his explanation.[56] Once again, Chinese criticism was explained away and did not lead to concern in Japan that China was trying to block Japan's international engagement.

Japanese perceptions of Chinese intent changed in 2005, when Japan, Germany, Brazil, and India sought to become permanent members of the UN Security Council. China worked actively to prevent this from happening. Chinese diplomats lobbied Southeast Asian and African nations to persuade them to vote against the motion. Their efforts to block Japan were justified by arguing that Japan's alleged refusal to accept responsibility for the invasion of China and other Asian countries before August 1945 made it ineligible for a permanent seat on the Security Council. It was widely suspected in Japan that the real reason the Chinese opposed a seat for Japan was that China was reluctant to lose its position as the only Asian permanent member. After Japan's prospects seemed enhanced by a supportive statement by UN Secretary-General Kofi Annan, huge anti-Japanese demonstrations occurred in major cities of China.[57] These demonstrations made Japanese realize that China would oppose anything that would enhance Japan's international standing.

Increasing Assertiveness

As noted earlier, even though Prime Minister Koizumi's annual visits to the Yasukuni Shrine elicited harsh criticism from China, he did not subscribe to the China-threat theory, and Japan's economic relations with China continued to expand during his administration. Bilateral trade grew from $89.2 billion in 2001 to $211.2 billion in 2006. Japan's trade with China surpassed that with the United States in 2006, making China Japan's number-one trading partner. China's share of Japan's total trade in that year was 20.1 percent; the US share was 18.6 percent. Japan's direct investment in China also continued to increase through 2005 but declined in the following two years as Japanese investors sought to broaden their portfolios in what was called a "China plus one" approach. The search for investment locations outside of China was a response to heightened concern about the "China risk" triggered by violent anti-Japanese demonstrations in the spring of 2005. Investment by Japanese firms resumed its upward trajectory in 2008.

The most recent phase of China's rise seems to contradict Japan's expectation that engagement would lead to a more cooperative, if not democratic, China. It is now widely accepted that China began to act more assertively and in defiance of existing norms in 2009–2010.[58] Japan became the target of this assertiveness in September 2010, when a Chinese fishing boat rammed two Japanese coast guard ships near the Senkaku Islands. The Japanese coast guard detained the boat and the crew. The ship and the crew, except for the captain, were released after a few days; the captain was detained for possible indictment. China predictably berated the Japanese government with harsh words and took measures considered pressure tactics by the Japanese. In September, China halted exports of rare earth materials, for which Japan was dependent on China for about 90 percent of total supply. In October, China arrested Japanese citizens working in Shanghai and charged them with having filmed military installations.

Though serious, the incidents had relatively little impact on the economic relationship. Firms attempted to diversify the supply of rare earth materials to reduce dependence on China, but trade in 2010 reached a record high of $301.9 billion. The following year, it climbed to $344.9 billion. There was no significant decline in direct investment in China.

However, the perception of China's high-handed approach to the Senkaku issue and assertive actions toward other East Asian neighbors made many Japanese feel that China was finally revealing its "true color" of seeking regional hegemony.[59] The change in perception had consequences. The National Defense Program Guideline (NDPG), issued on December 2010, which updated the version issued in 2004, listed China's increasing defense expenditures, rapid military modernization, greater power projection capability, increased maritime activities, and lack of transparency as matters "of concern for the regional and global community."[60]

In response to China's greater assertiveness, the Japanese government took measures to adjust its military posture and to strengthen the alliance relationship with the United States. Severe budget constraints limited the scope of military posture changes, but the fact that they were made at all is significant. For example, the 2010 NDPG reaffirmed the significant shift in the characterization of Japan's defense capability that had been introduced in the 2004 NDPG. Earlier characterizations, known as the concept of base defense force, had emphasized the importance of avoiding a power vacuum in Japan rather than actual use of defense capability. The 2004 and 2010 formulation emphasized ways to use military force. The 2010 NDPG characterized the shift as transformation into the "dynamic defense force," which emphasizes "readiness for immediate and seamless response to contingencies" and "regular intelligence, surveillance, and reconnaissance activities (ISR)" during peacetime.[61] The 2010 NDPG also specifically listed response to attacks on offshore islands as one of the major roles of the nation's defense forces.[62] Reflecting the new posture, the three services of the Self-Defense Forces conducted an integrated exercise with about thirty-five thousand soldiers in mid-November 2011. The scenario called for recovering offshore islands after they had been invaded.[63]

Japan's alliance with the United States was reaffirmed for the post–Cold War era in 1996 and gradually strengthened through subsequent measures such as the Acquisition and Cross-Servicing Agreement, revision of the Defense Cooperation Guideline, and joint research for missile defense systems. After the 9/11 terrorist attacks on the United States, alliance cooperation deepened further with Japan's provision of oil to the multinational forces fighting in Afghanistan and contributions to postwar reconstruction of Iraq. The process of adjusting the alliance to the post-9/11 strategic situation progressed smoothly from the agreement to start the Defense Policy Review Initiative in December 2002 to the identification of the common strategic objectives in February 2005, to the mission, role, and capability of each side in October 2005, and to the road map for base realignment in May 2007.

The historic change of party in power from the Liberal Democratic Party to the Democratic Party of Japan in September 2009 led to disturbances in alliance cooperation because of the failed attempt by the first DPJ prime minister, Yukio Hatoyama, to renegotiate relocation of the US marine air base in Okinawa. The relationship was put back on an even keel after Hatoyama's resignation in June 2010. When conflict arose between Japan and China over the Senkaku Islands in September of that year, Japan sought and obtained Secretary of State Clinton's reaffirmation that article 5 of the Japan-US Security Treaty applied to the Senkakus. In return for this reaffirmation, Japan promised to release the fishing boat captain who had been detained.[64]

At the time, many in Japan believed that the disturbance in the alliance relationship had allowed China to act in a high-handed way at the time of the fishing boat incident. In response to that belief, the 2010

NDPG specifically mentioned the importance of bilateral cooperation to "strengthen the US forces' deterrent and response capability in regional contingencies."[65] The editorial of a major newspaper explicitly endorsed this policy by arguing that Japan had to restore the alliance with the United States in order to persuade China to play the role appropriate for a major power, and noting that the influence of Japan acting alone was limited.[66]

When the triple disaster occurred in March 2011, the US forces in Japan deployed sixteen thousand troops to the Tomodachi (Friends) rescue and recovery operations. This assistance provided the backdrop for the June 2011 meeting of foreign and defense secretaries and ministers (the US-Japan 2+2 Meeting) at which they issued a joint statement restating common strategic objectives, which included urging China to play a responsible role in regional stability and prosperity, to abide by international norms, and to enhance openness and transparency about military modernization and activities. The joint statement issued upon conclusion of the 2+2 meeting in April 2012 acknowledged that the deterrent capabilities of the alliance would be strengthened through Japan's development of a dynamic defense force and enhancement of defense posture in Japan's Southwest Islands as well as through bilateral "dynamic defense cooperation," including joint training, joint reconnaissance and surveillance activities, and joint and shared use of facilities.[67]

Relations Deteriorate

Japanese perceptions of China had become increasingly negative by early 2012, when the simmering dispute over ownership of the Senkaku Islands erupted anew. The proximate cause—Tokyo governor Shintaro Ishihara's announcement that the Tokyo metropolitan government would purchase privately owned islands to underscore Japan's sovereignty—was unnecessarily provocative, but his grandstanding and the ensuing chain of events were symptoms of an already-deteriorating relationship.[68] Both sides mishandled the situation, but policy makers' errors were less important than the changes in perception and relative power that shaped attitudes, actions, and outcomes. The remainder of this section focuses on developments that shaped Japanese perceptions of China's goals and the means used to achieve them.

Japan's decision to purchase islands that previously had been leased from private owners triggered demonstrations in China that quickly surpassed those of 2005. On September 11, 2012, anti-Japanese demonstrations took place in Beijing, Shanghai, Guangzhou, and other cities. The protest movement quickly spread across the country, with boycotts, violence against Japanese people and installations, and government acquiescence.[69] Targets included Japanese citizens in Shanghai, a Japanese supermarket in Qingdao, a Japanese department store in Changsha, and Panasonic electronics factories in Qingdao and Suzhou. The fact that in some cities demonstrators carried pictures of Mao and, in Shenzhen, attacked the building housing the local communist party committee suggest that demonstrators were motivated by more than just anger at Japan.[70]

The protests started to dwindle after September 18 and ended by September 24. But the decline in anti-Japanese demonstrations was more than offset by incursions of Chinese official vessels, mostly of China Marine Surveillance (CMS), into the territorial waters around the Senkaku Islands. The incursions began on September 14. There were two more incursions by CMS vessels in September, five in October, four in November, eight in December, and four in January 2013.[71] There were also several incursions into Japanese air space, and on February 5, 2013, Defense Minister Itsunori Onodera announced that a Chinese frigate had locked its fire-control radar on a Japanese destroyer in the East China Sea on January 30 and that, two weeks earlier, a Chinese ship had targeted a Japanese helicopter in the same way.

Chinese actions around the Senkaku Islands strengthened Japanese conviction that China was pursuing a long-term maritime strategy with far-reaching implications for the region. According to one commentator, the first step of the strategy was to bring the area from the Yellow Sea to the East and South China Seas within China's sphere of influence. Then China would extend its military influence to the western Pacific and Indian Oceans. Such an "expansionist strategy" is a serious threat to Japan's security and will lead to confrontation with the United States and the breakdown of the post war international order in the region.[72]

The developments summarized here led to an important change in the Japanese government's approach to the Senkaku Islands problem. One facet of the new approach was to shift from the simple declaration that Japanese sovereignty over the islands was indisputable to a more vigorous defense of Japan's claim. The government prepared documents justifying Japanese sovereignty over the islands, refuting the Chinese arguments, and justifying the recent decision on the government ownership of those islands.[73]

A second part of the approach was to take small but significant steps to strengthen alliance cooperation with the United States. In the last phase of the DPJ government, Defense Minister Satoshi Morimoto and Defense Secretary Leon Panetta agreed to revise the Defense Cooperation Guideline of 1997. Later that month two thousand US marines and forty Japanese soldiers conducted a joint exercise in Tinian and Guam. The scenario for that exercise was to recover an island taken over by an enemy.[74] In mid-September, Defense Secretary Panetta visited Tokyo and reaffirmed that the security treaty applied to the defense of the Senkaku Islands.

The House of Representative election on December 16, 2012, resulted in the landslide victory for the LDP. The results reflected public frustration with the DPJ government, including the way it had managed relations with China. The day after he was elected, the new prime minister, Shinzo Abe, laid out the key elements of his external strategy, including more alarmist expressions of concern about China's maritime influence than had been made by other leaders of the party.[75] He warned about the danger of the South China Sea becoming "a Lake Beijing" and argued that Japan should not yield to China's "daily exercise in coercion" around the Senkaku Islands, which he maintained was intended to establish China's jurisdiction in waters surrounding the islands as a fait accompli. He also said the South China Sea would become fortified and that freedom of navigation there would be seriously hindered.[76]

The Abe government continued, and rapidly expanded, measures to cope with China that had been initiated by the DPJ government. One such measure was to revise the 2010 NDPG, to permit expansion of the Self-Defense Forces.[77] The draft budget for fiscal 2013 included a slight increase (0.8 percent) in defense expenditures, which had been slowly but steadily decreasing over the previous eleven years, and a very small increase in personnel.[78] The Maritime Safety Agency decided to establish a six-hundred-person unit to patrol waters near the Senkakus and to redeploy twelve ships by 2015.[79]

Japan is mindful that its efforts to enhance the capability of the Self-Defense Forces and the alliance with the United States could fuel a classic security dilemma with China. To avoid or ameliorate such an outcome, the Japanese government had sought to cooperate with China on as many issues as possible and attempted to persuade China to establish a mechanism for the management of maritime uncertainties. China had agreed to establish a "communication mechanism between the two defense authorities" to "prevent the occurrence of unforeseen circumstances at sea" in April 2007 and to establish a joint working group the following August.[80] In June 2012, Beijing and Tokyo achieved basic agreement on the aim, structure, and mode of communication, but the Senkaku flare-up impeded its implementation.[81] With a greater sense of urgency caused by the fire-control radar incident of late January 2013, the Japanese government sent a high official of the Defense Ministry to Beijing in April for consultation, but no progress was achieved. Other areas of cooperation include negotiations for a free-trade agreement among Japan, China, and the Republic of Korea, as well as active participation in regional security forums such as the Association of Southeast Asian Nations (ASEAN) Regional Forum, the Shangri-La Dialogue, and the ASEAN Defense Ministers' Meeting-Plus with the goal of promoting rule-based maritime order in Asia.

Conclusion

The trends and examples examined here, especially the consistently high percentage of Japanese who do not feel affinity with China since 2004, suggest that this development is less a direct reaction to the rise of China per se than a response to unfriendly or even hostile Chinese actions toward Japan. They also suggest that reliance on people-to-people friendship to provide stability to the relationship, which could have been effective in the 1980s, would not be effective now. However, the somewhat lower percentage of those who explicitly dislike China indicates that many who do not feel affinity with China are not strongly hostile, and that political leaders would not encounter strong resistance if they adopted a more positive approach to China, especially if it were incremental.

The findings summarized here also indicate that Japanese increasingly perceive China's ambitions and behavior as threatening to Japan. This is particularly true of those who are better informed about international affairs. The public's vague but widely felt sense of unease about China is reinforced by the notion of *chuka shisou*, the idea that China's behavior is driven by a Middle Kingdom syndrome that links contemporary Chinese actions to patterns of behavior found in China's dynastic history.

The third noteworthy finding is the importance of the alliance with the United States as a part of Japan's strategy to cope with China's rise. Indeed, the alliance may temper Japan's response to provocative actions by China.

For example, the credibility of the US commitment to defense of the Senkakus increases the potential cost and reduces the likelihood of an armed clash between Japan and China. Moreover, even though the United States shares many of Japan's concerns about a more assertive China, Washington is unlikely to abandon its long-standing policy of engagement. Although the United States is expected to discourage and deter China's provocations, it is also expected to constrain Japan's provocative pursuit of a nationalistic agenda with respect to China.

Notes

1. Ezra F. Vogel, *Japan as Number One: Lessons for America* (Cambridge, MA: Harvard University Press, 1979).

2. In late December 1978, the Chinese Communist Party reached a critical decision to emphasize economic development through "reform" of the economic system from central planning to reliance on market mechanisms and to "opening" of the system for external trading and foreign investment. For the background and early development of the reform and opening, see Harry Harding, *China's Second Revolution: Reform After Mao* (Washington, DC: Brookings Institution Press, 1987).

3. One of the thorny issues in the negotiations for the establishment of diplomatic relations in September 1972 was how the Sino-Japanese War should be treated in the joint communiqué to announce the agreement. The Chinese side demanded an explicit declaration of the end of the war in the document; the Japanese maintained that the declaration had already been made in the Japan–Republic of China Peace Treaty of 1952. The compromise was to declare the "end of the abnormal state" in bilateral relations in the joint communiqué and to begin negotiations for the Peace and Friendship Treaty. For the texts of the joint communiqué and the Peace and Friendship Treaty in Japanese, Chinese, and English, with additional relevant documents, see Minoru Takeuchi, ed., *Nitchu Kokko Kihon Bunkenshu* [Compilation of Documents on Japan-China Diplomatic Relations] (Tokyo: Sososha, 1993), 2:174–225 and 2:257–284.

4. On the renunciation of reparations, see article 5 of the "Joint Communiqué of the Government of Japan and the Government of the People's Republic of China," September 29, 1972, http://www.mofa.go.jp/region/asia-aci/china/joint72.html.

5. For details of the process, see Seiichiro Takagi, "Human Rights in Japanese Foreign Policy: Japan's Policy Towards China After Tiananmen," in *Human Rights and International Relations in the Asia Pacific Region*, ed. James T. H. Tang (London: Pinter, 1995), 97–111.

6. For more on Deng's southern journey, see Ezra F. Vogel, *Deng Xiaoping and the Transformation of China* (Cambridge, MA: Belknap Press of Harvard University Press, 2011), 664–690.

7. "Jiang Zemin zai Zhongguo Gongchandang Dishisici Quanguo Daibiao Dahui de Baogao" [Jiang Zemin's Report to the 14th National Congress of the Chinese Communist Party], October 12, 1992, http://cpc.people.com.cn/GB/6416 2/64168/64567/65446/4526308.html.

8. "Zhonghua Renmin Gongheguo Linghai ji Pilianqu Fa" [People's Republic of China Territorial and Contiguous Waters Law], http://www.law-lib.com/law/ law_view.asp?id=227.

9. Japanese official developmental assistance consists of three kinds of programs: the Yen-Loan, a long-term, low-interest loan that is the mainstay of ODA and has the highest monetary commitments; grant-in-aid; and technical assistance.

10. On the decision to suspend this program, see Jo Kenfun (Xu Xianfen), *Nihon no Taichu ODA Gaiko* [Japan's ODA Diplomacy Toward China] (Tokyo: Keiso Shobo, 2011), 193–201.

11. For the details of Clinton's visit to China, see "The Trip of the President to the People's Republic of China," White House, http://clinton2.nara.gov/WH/ New/China/.

12. Ryosei Kokubun, "Shiren no Jidai no Nitchu Kankei: Koutakuninn Hounichi Kijitu" [Sino-Japanese Relations in a Trial Era: A Historical Record of Jiang Zemin's Visit to Japan], *Hogaku Kenkyu* 73, no. 1 (January 2000): 65–81.

13. Ministry of Foreign Affairs, "Japan-US Joint Declaration on Security: Alliance for the 21st Century," April 17, 1996, http://www.mofa.go.jp/region/ n-america/us/security/security.html.

14. See, for example, Aaron L. Friedberg, *A Contest for Supremacy: China, America, and the Struggle for Mastery in Asia* (New York: W. W. Norton, 2011), 88–119, and the sources cited therein.

15. Prime Minister Junichiro Koizumi, "Asia in a New Century—Challenges and Opportunity," speech at the Boao Forum for Asia, April 12, 2002, http:// www.kantei.go.jp/foreign/koizumispeech/2002/04/12boao_e.html.

16. In fact, the Chinese side was not enthusiastic about this expression at the time, and it was not used in the joint press communiqué issued after the summit. It was explained later that the expression in the communiqué meant the "mutually beneficial relationship based on common strategic interest," which was somewhat different from the connotation of the Japanese expression. It did appear (defined in this way) in the joint press communiqué issued when Wen Jiabao visited Japan in the following year. For more details, see Seiichiro Takagi, "Nitchu 'Senryakuteki Gokei Kankei': Shinten to Kadai" [Japan-China "Strategic Relationship of Mutual Benefit": Progress and Problems], *Kokusai Mondai*, no. 569 (March 2008): 1–10.

17. For a description of the trip, see James J. Przystup, "Japan-China Relations: Ice Breaks at the Summit," *Comparative Connections* 8, no. 4 (2007): 125–128.

18. For the descriptions of the trips, see the following articles by James J. Przystup: for Wen's trip, "Wen in Japan: Ice Melting But . . . ," *Comparative Connections* 9, no. 2 (2007): 131–135; for Fukuda's trip, "Politics in Command: Part 2," *Comparative Connections* 9, no. 4 (2007): 116–118; for Hu's trip, "Progress in Building a Strategic Relationship," *Comparative Connections* 10, no. 2 (2008): 119–124.

19. For Japan's relationship with the United States during the Hatoyama administration, see the following four articles by Michael J. Green and Nicholas Szechenyi: "Interpreting Change," *Comparative Connections* 11, no. 3 (2009): 17–28; "Adjusting to Untested Political Terrain," *Comparative Connections* 11, no. 4 (2010): 15–24; "Many Issues, a Few Bright Spots," *Comparative Connections* 12, no. 1 (2010): 13–22; and "New Realism," *Comparative Connections* 12, no. 2 (2010): 21–32. For Japan-China relations in the same period, see the following four articles by James J. Przystup: "Old Issues Greet a New Government," *Comparative Connections* 11, no. 3 (2009): 111–120; "Gathering Momentum," *Comparative Connections* 11, no. 4 (2010): 107–116; "All's Well That Ends Well," *Comparative Connections* 12, no. 1 (2010): 99–108; and "Troubled Waters to Calm Sea?" *Comparative Connections* 12, no. 2 (2010): 117–126.

20. See, for example, Japan Forum on International Relations, "'Senkaku Shoto-oki deno Gyosen Shoutotsu Jikenn' nikansuru Ikennkoukan notameno Kakudai Kinkyu Teigen Iinkai—Sokkiroku" [Minutes: The Enlarged Emergency Meeting for Policy Recommendation concerning the 'Fishing Boat Collision Incident off the Senkaku Islands], October 6, 2010, 30–38.

21. At 14:46 on March 11, 2011, an earthquake that registered 9.0 on the Richter scale (the largest in the history of modern earthquake measurement) occurred offshore from the northeastern prefectures of Japan's main island. The highest seismic intensity was 7.0, which was followed by a huge tsunami more than ten meters high. These disasters caused the death of almost sixteen thousand people and economic losses between 16 trillion and 30 trillion yen. Under the impact of the earthquake and tsunami, three nuclear reactors in a power plant in the prefecture of Fukushima had core meltdown and a hydrogen explosion, which led to widespread diffusion of radioactive material.

22. Hisayoshi Ina, "Nitchuu Gyakuten nimo Nibui Nihon" [Japan Dull to the Japan-China Reversal], *Nihon Keizai Shimbun*, September 10, 2010.

23. Jim O'Neill, "Building Better Global Economic BRICs" (Global Economics Paper No. 66), Goldman Sachs, November 30, 2001, S.07, http://www.gold mansachs.com/our-thinking/archive/archive-pdfs/build-better-brics.pdf.

24. Ibid., S.04.

25. "2010nen ni GDP ga Nitchuu Gyakuten mo" [It Is Possible That There Would Be a Reversal of the GDP Standing Between Japan and China], *Nikkei Bijinesu Henshubu*, September 21, 2008, http://business.nikkeibp.co.jp/article/manage/20070920/135510/?rt=ncont.85.

26. Ibid.

27. Until 1985 the survey was conducted in different months, but since 1986 it has been conducted in October.

28. BBC World Service poll, May 10, 2012, 9, http://www.worldpublicopinion.org/pipa/pdf/may12/BBCEvals_May12_rpt.pdf.

29. "Nitchu-kankei, Fukamaru Mizo: Asahi Shimbun-sha Yoron-chosa" [Deepening Gap in Japan-China Relations: The Public Opinion Poll of the Asahi Shimbun Company], *Asahi Shimbun*, September 24, 2012, 13.

30. Kenneth Lieberthal and Wang Jisi, "Addressing US-China Strategic Distrust," John L. Thornton China Center at Brookings, March 2010, 20, https://www.brookings.edu/wp-content/uploads/2016/06/0330_china_lieberthal.pdf.

31. Ibid., 21.

32. This is an adaptation from the definition of "mutual strategic trust" by Niu Xinchun, who defines it as mutual confidence between two countries with conflicting national interest, such that the other side does not pursue national goals violating one's core national interests. See Niu Xinchun, "Zhongmei Zhanlue Huxin: Gainian, Wenti yi Tiaozhan" [China-US Mutual Strategic Trust: Concept, Problems, and Challenges], *Xiandai Guoji Guanxi*, 3 (2010): 1. The Lieberthal-Wang paper mentioned earlier uses basically the same definition (5).

33. For the fluctuation of China's military budget, see Boueishou (Ministry of Defense), "Heisei 24 nendoban Nihon no boouei—Boueihakusho" [Defense of Japan for 2012—Defense White Paper], 29–30.

34. For recent information on weapons deployment and space capabilities, see Office of the Secretary of Defense, *Military and Security Developments Involving the People's Republic of China 2013, Annual Report to Congress*, 28–43.

35. Ministry of Defense, *Defense of Japan 2008*, 55–56, http://www.mod.go.jp/e/publ/w_paper/pdf/2008/11Part1_Chapter2_Sec3.pdf.

36. Ministry of Defense, *Defense of Japan 2009*, 56–57, http://www.mod.go.jp/e/publ/w_paper/pdf/2009/11Part1_Chapter2_Sec3.pdf.

37. *Nihon Keizai Shimbun*, April 23, 2010.

38. Ibid.

39. Ministry of Defense, *Defense of Japan 2015*, http://www.mod.go.jp/e/publ/w_paper/pdf/2015/DOJ2015_1-1-3_web.pdf.

40. *Yomiuri Shimbun*, December 16, 2006, and November 9, 2010. In both polls respondents were asked to choose from a list of countries and regions those

they thought constituted a "military threat to Japan." They were allowed to choose as many as they wanted, but the lists were not identical. The 2006 poll listed thirteen countries and regions, whereas the 2010 list contained only the United States, China, Russia, North Korea, South Korea, and India.

41. *Asahi Shimbun*, September 24, 2012.

42. The "knowledgeable" include "enterprise managers, scholars, media people, civil servants, and others" who had participated in the activities of the not for profit organization.

43. Available at the Genron NPO website, at http://www.genron-npo.net/world/archives/4347.html. The full results of surveys in other years are not available at the website.

44. Hiramatsu holds a PhD in political science from Keio University.

45. Shigeo Hiramatsu, *Gunjitaikoku-ka suru Chuugoku no Kyoui* (Tokyo: Jiji Tsushinsha, 1995).

46. On the South China Sea, see ibid., 149–152. On the Sea of Japan, see ibid., 164.

47. Ibid., 11.

48. Shigeo Hiramatsu, *Chugoku wa Nihon wo Heigou suru* (Tokyo: Kodansha International, 2006). The translation of the title here is by Hiramatsu.

49. Ibid., 19.

50. Ibid., 10–11. It should be noted that what he means by "annexation" is not as provocative as might be suggested. He says, "It is an unquestionable 'aggression' to freely collect the data on seabed and steal resources from Japan's exclusive economic zone and continental shelf. These were done without firing a shot, and most Japanese people are unaware or reacted calmly and matter-of-factly. Aggression and annexation do not always accompany the use of force" (ibid., 17–18).

51. Yoshiko Sakurai, *Igyou no Taikoku Chugoku—Karerani Kokoro wo Yurusitewa Naranai* [China, a Monstrous Big Power—We Should Never Lower the Guard Against Them] (Tokyo: Shincho-sha, 2010), 287–288.

52. Ibid., 288.

53. The Chinese translation of the term is *Zhonghua Sixiang*, but Chinese do not use that term. Although commonly used in Japan, the meaning of the term is not always clearly defined. However, the following explanation of the term in the electronic Japanese edition of the *Britannica International Encyclopedia* is close to the common understanding of the term:

> The consciousness or the thought that China is the center of the world culture and politics and is superior to the others. . . . This thinking starts in ancient Zhou dynasty and has been used continuously until the modern era.

It describes a unique worldview of the Chinese people and has greatly influenced their history and culture. As long as superiority of the Han Chinese is acknowledged, China is relatively open and tolerant, but once the superiority is denied, Chinese attitudes tend to become a extremely narrow and conservatively anti-foreign.

This way of thinking can mutate into a belief that there is an unstoppable traditional impetus among the Chinese to secure a superior position vis-à-vis their neighbors and, as its concrete manifestation, to establish a civilization-barbarian order or a tributary relationship like those in the imperial period. Thus, it can become the basis of strategic distrust of China. For elaboration of this point, see Kunihiko Miyake, "'Chuka-shiso' wo gokaisuru nihonjin" [Japanese Misunderstanding of the "Middle Kingdom Syndrome"], *PHP Online Shuchi*, http://shuhi .php.co.jp/article/1657.

54. See, for example, Zhang Dalin, "Ping Ribende 'Lianheguo Weichi Heping Xingdong Hesuo Faan'" [Critiques on Japan's "UN Peacekeeping Operations Cooperation Bill"], *Guoji Wenti Yanjiu* 2 (1992): 18–24, 54.

55. See, for example, Zi Chu, "Weixiande Yibu you Yibu—Riben Jiweidui jie Fankonbu zhi ming Zouxiang Shijie" [Dangerous Step by Step—With the Excuse of Anti-Terrorism Japanese Self-Defense Force Is Expanding (Its Operations) Toward the World], *Shijie Zhishi* 23 (2001): 20–22.

56. Ministry of Foreign Affairs, "Visit to the People's Republic of China by Prime Minister Junichiro Koizumi: Meeting with Premier Jiang Zemin," http:// www.mofa.go.jp/region/asia-paci/china/pmv0110/meet-2.htm; and Ministry of Foreign Affairs, "Visit to the People's Republic of China by Prime Minister Junichiro Koizumi: Meeting with Premier Zhu Rongji," http://www.mofa.go.jp/ region/asia-paci/china/pmv0110/meet-1.htm.

57. See, for example, Edward Cody, "New Anti-Japanese Protests Erupt in China," *Washington Post*, April 16, 2005, http://www.washingtonpost.com/wp -dyn/articles/A58567-2005Apr16.html.

58. For a detailed examination of China's assertiveness, see Michael D. Swaine and M. Taylor Fravel, "China's Assertive Behavior—Part Two: The Maritime Periphery," *China Leadership Monitor 2011*, September 21, 2011, 1–29.

59. See, for example, "Senkaku Shoto-oki," 30–38.

60. Ministry of Defense, *National Defense Program Guidelines for FY 2011 and Beyond*, 4, http://www.mod.go.jp/e/d_act/d_policy/pdf/guidelinesFY2011.pdf.

61. Ibid., 6.

62. Ibid., 10.

63. *Sankei Shimbun*, May 9, 2012.

64. Jeffrey A. Bader, *Obama and China* (Washington, DC: Brookings Institution Press, 2012), 107.

65. *National Defense Program Guideline for FY 2011 and Beyond*, 8.

66. "Shasetu: Nichi-Bei de Chuugoku no Sekinintaikoku-ka wo dou Unagasuka" [Editorial: How Japan and the US Should Urge China to Become a Responsible Power], *Nihon Keizai Shimbun* [Japan Economic Journal], January 8, 2011, 2.

67. "Joint Statement of the Security Consultative Committee, April 27, 2012, by Secretary of State Clinton, Secretary of Defense Panetta, Minister for Foreign Affairs Gemba and Minister of Defense Tanaka," obtained through Ministry of Foreign Affairs website, pp. 1–2, at http://wwwmofa.go.jp/region/n-america/us/security/scc/pdfs/joint_120427_en.pdf.

68. For chronology and analysis of developments, see, for example, Ryoichi Hamamoto, "Senkaku Kokuyuka de Chuugoku ga Gekikou, Toutaikaimae no Jinji-kousou mo gekika" [The Nationalization of the Senkaku Led to China's Outrage, Conflict over Personnel Intensifies], *Toa* 544 (October 2012): 43–56; and Gaimushou (Ministry of Foreign Affairs), "Senkaku-shotou wo meguru jousei to Kongo no Nitchuu-kankei" [The Situation Surrounding the Senkaku Islands and the Japan-China Relations Hereafter], February 2013.

69. On September 15, the first weekend after the formal decision, large-scale demonstrations took place in at least fifty-seven cities, including Beijing, Shanghai, Chongqing, Xian, Changsha, Qingdao, and Nanjing. On September 16, demonstration took place in eighty to one hundred cities including cities just mentioned, in addition to Shenyang, Changchun, Xiamen, Shenzhen, Foshan, and Zhuhai. On September 18, the eighty-first anniversary of the Liutiaohu Incident, which touched off the Manchurian Incident, demonstrations took place in between 100 and 125 cities. For further details, see Ministry of Foreign Affairs, "The Situation Surrounding the Senkaku Islands."

70. Ryiochi Hamamoto, [Nationalization of the Senkaku].

71. Gaimusho, "Senkaku-shotou," 3–5.

72. Takakazu Kuriyama, "Senkaku Shotou to Nitchuu-kankei" [The Senkaku Islands and Japan-China Relations], *Ajia Jiho*, no. 482 (December 2012): 8.

73. The documents are available on the Ministry of Foreign Affairs website in three languages: Japanese, English and Chinese. The English version is available at http://www.mofa.go.jp/region/asia-paci/senkaku/index.html.

74. *Asahi Shimbun*, August 23, 2012.

75. Shinzo Abe, "Asia's Democratic Security Diamond," *Project Syndicate*, http://www.project-syndicate.org/print/a-strategic-alliance-for-japan-and-india-by-shinzo-abe. According to the note to the article it was written in mid-November.

76. Ibid.

77. *Asahi Shimbun* (evening edition), January 7, 2013.

78. *Asahi Shimbun*, January 30, 2013.

79. *Yomiuri Shimbun*, January 29, 2013.

80. "Japan-China Joint Statement," April 11, 2007, item 5(1)(iv), http://www.mofa.gojp/region/asia-paci/china/pvo704/joint.html.

81. Boueishou, "Nitchu Bouei-Toukyoku-kan no Kaijo Renraku Mekani-zumu nikansuru Dai3kai Kyodo-Sagyo-Grupu-kyogi (Kekka Gaiyo)" [The Consultation at the Third Joint Working Group for the Maritime Communication Mechanism Between Defense Authorities of Japan and China (Outline of the Results)], June 29, 2012. This document is embedded in a more comprehensive document, "Kaijou Renraku mekanizumu nituite" [On the Maritime Communication Mechanism (Between the Defense Authorities of Japan and China)], http://www.mod.go.jp/j/approach/exchange/nikoku/asia/china/kaijou_mechanism.html. See the item "Dai 3-kai kekka gaiyou" [The Outline of the Results of the Third (Joint Working Group meeting)].

SIX

China and Korea
Proximity, Priorities, and Policy Evolution

Thomas Fingar

For thousands of years, China's relationships with the Korean Peninsula were shaped primarily by geography. Proximity facilitated economic and cultural interchange beneficial to both but on terms largely dictated by China by virtue of its much greater size, wealth, and population. During much of this long history, China viewed Korea as a vassal state whose primary importance derived from its location between Japan and the Chinese capital. This characterization is, of course, a gross oversimplification of the long and rich history of relations between peoples and polities with much in common but also a powerful sense of their distinctive identities and different interests.[1] Moreover, and more important, the region, China, and Korea have changed dramatically in the past century and a quarter. So, too, have China's priorities and judgments about potential Korean threats and contributions to the achievement of Chinese objectives.[2] This chapter examines some of the factors that changed and shaped Chinese perceptions of and policies toward the Korean Peninsula, especially those that have occurred during the era of reform and opening that began in 1979.

Though oversimplified, the characterization of how China views Korea given here contains three elements of continuing importance. The first is proximity. Korea is more salient to China than are most countries because

This chapter examines how perceived changes in security risks and economic opportunities on the Korean Peninsula shaped the evolution of Chinese perceptions of and policies toward the Republic of Korea and the Democratic People's Republic of Korea.

the two share an 880-mile land border adjacent to one of the most populous and prosperous regions of China, and because North Korea is only a few hundred miles from Beijing. Proximity gives China both the incentive and the ability to monitor and to affect what happens on the peninsula.

Proximity magnifies Korea's geopolitical significance because it intensifies the extent to which Korean policies and actions can enhance or endanger China's security. For obvious reasons, successive Chinese regimes have paid close attention to real and imagined threats perceived either as originating on the peninsula or to be more dangerous because of Korea's relationships with China's rivals. This geography-based fact causes Chinese strategists and policy makers to view what happens on the peninsula through a security-focused lens and to develop policies intended to reduce the threat to China's interests.[3]

The third continuing element is also linked, albeit less closely, to Korea's proximity. That element is Korea's ability to contribute to China's economic well-being and, indirectly, to domestic tranquillity and the legitimacy of the regime. Korea's status as a tributary state was sometimes more nominal than real, but tribute was a form and facilitator of trade, and trade contributed to the prosperity of adjacent regions and ruling elites.[4] The ability of Korea and Koreans to contribute to economic growth and prosperity, and thereby to the derivative consequences of economic performance, has been and still is an important part of China's policy calculus.

The ways in which proximity, security, and economic well-being are conceived and their relative importance have changed over time, but all have been critical to the way in which China has interacted with the peninsula since the founding of the People's Republic in 1949. Some of the changes were triggered and/or shaped by developments internal to China or one of the Korean states; others were made possible, necessary, or desirable by changes beyond the region. The remainder of this chapter describes and explains the evolution of China's relationships with the Democratic People's Republic of Korea (DPRK, or North Korea) and the Republic of Korea (ROK, or South Korea).

Setting the Stage: 1949–1978

When Mao Zedong proclaimed the establishment of the People's Republic of China (PRC) on October 1, 1949, the Korean nation had already been divided by the United States and the Soviet Union and transformed into two new states by Syngman Rhee (the ROK) and Kim Il Sung (the DPRK). Mao and other leaders of the Chinese Communist Party (CCP) had not yet completed the "liberation" of territories controlled by the Nationalist government of Chiang Kai-shek or the recovery of areas that had drifted beyond the orbit of the Middle Kingdom during the period of dynastic decline, warlord rule, and Japanese aggression. They faced daunting challenges of political consolidation, economic reconstruction, and the perceived need to reduce PRC vulnerability to attack by "capitalist" and "imperialist" forces. To address these challenges, Mao and the PRC made fateful choices that almost immediately drove and constrained their relationships with North and South Korea.[5]

Shared ideology and the history of party-to-party ties between the CCP and the Communist Party of the Soviet Union alone might have been sufficient to persuade Mao to "lean" to the side of the Soviet Union in the early days of the Cold War, but in the event he also had other reasons for doing so. One reason was to secure Soviet protection from what he (and other Chinese leaders) judged to be the threat of military attack by the United States. Another was the seeming efficacy of the Soviet model of reconstruction and development and Stalin's willingness to provide the technology and training necessary to build a highly autarkic modern economy. At the time Mao cast his lot with the Soviet Union, it seemed a reasonable, if not necessary, choice for a country with China's perceived security and developmental challenges.[6]

The first consequences of that decision began to be felt almost immediately. After long and difficult negotiations, China and the Soviet Union concluded the "Sino-Soviet Treaty of Friendship, Alliance, and Mutual Assistance" on February 14, 1950. Less than five months later, North Korean troops invaded the South, President Harry Truman committed US forces to the defense of the ROK and ordered the US Seventh Fleet to prevent military action in the Taiwan Strait (thereby precluding PRC "liberation" of Taiwan and injected the United States into China's civil war), and the UN Security Council (with the Soviets boycotting) authorized assistance to the ROK. To demonstrate China's commitment to the international communist movement (and to ensure continued Soviet protection and support), Mao ordered Chinese troops to enter the war in support of the DPRK as UN forces neared the DPRK-PRC border.[7] China's intervention preserved the DPRK but prolonged the war and perpetuated division of the peninsula.

The Korean War had profound consequences for China. In addition to the human toll (China alone suffered almost a half million casualties; one of those killed was Mao's son), China incurred an enormous war debt to the Soviet Union, which it had to repay; lost the ability to end quickly Nationalist rule on Taiwan; and deepened and prolonged American hostility to the PRC.[8] China's Korean War decisions were carefully calculated to mitigate what Beijing judged to be the most dangerous threats to the newly declared PRC and to solidify China's position in the socialist camp and the Sino-Soviet alliance. In the short term and viewed narrowly, China's calculus made sense and its actions achieved the desired results. But the ancillary costs and long-term consequences proved more important. Those costs and consequences included prolonging the Chinese civil war; subjecting China to sanctions, embargoes, and other measures designed to "contain" the Soviet Union; initiating changes in US policy that transformed Japan from the Pacific War villain into a Cold War ally; and establishing the US alliance with the Republic of Korea. Taken together, these and other Korean War–related developments changed the global and regional situations in ways that constrained China's options for decades.

The Korean War also determined and locked in China's priorities, policies, and possibilities with respect to the peninsula. The DPRK became first a de facto and then a formal ally (in 1961), but it also became an ideological rival (Kim Il Sung's *Juche* ideology versus Mao Zedong Thought) and skillful exploiter of the political competition between Beijing and Moscow during the 1960s.[9] The relationship was forged on the battlefield and is generally characterized as especially close, but closer examination suggests that it amounted to little more than acknowledgment that proximity gave each an interest—and a stake—in what happened on the other side of the border, incentives to protect one's own interests by protecting those of the partner, and the ability of each to manipulate the other when it seemed useful to do so.

China's relationship with South Korea was also determined and constrained by the war. Alignment with Pyongyang made China the enemy of the ROK and the ROK's ally, the United States. The threat from the North brought US troops back to the southern part of the peninsula, deepening China's sense of threat and contributing to Mao's decision to disperse economic activity away from the more vulnerable northeast and coastal regions during the Great Leap Forward (1958–1962) and the Cultural Revolution (1966–1976).

China's objectives vis-à-vis North and South Korea solidified during and immediately after the Korean War and remained relatively unchanged until the late 1970s. Relations with the DPRK were often fractious and at times shaped by developments in Moscow, but for both sides there seemed to be no alternative to making the best of a difficult situation while taking advantage of opportunities to pursue mutual or compatible interests and doing what seemed necessary to address perceived threats to their regimes. Beijing's relationship with the ROK was in many ways the converse of that with the DPRK. Excessively positive rhetoric about the North was complemented by unrelievedly negative rhetoric about the South and its alleged subservience to the United States. In contrast to China's relationship with the North, which included a wide range of activities but was often fraught, that with the South was virtually nonexistent. China had no desire or ability to explore—let alone develop—economic or diplomatic ties, and the anti-communist ROK certainly was not pressing to do so.

China's relationships with the DPRK and the ROK during this period were also influenced by the state of relations between the two Koreas. Beijing's "one Korea" policy impeded dealings with Seoul and it was difficult to imagine how the PRC-ROK relationship might have become less hostile without improvement in ROK-DPRK relations. For a brief period in 1971–1972, there were signs that long-frozen relationships might be beginning to thaw as a result of the visits to Beijing by Henry Kissinger and Richard Nixon and the initial stage of US-China rapprochement. The shift in US-China relations caught both Kim Il Sung and ROK president Park Chung-hee by surprise, and both had reason for concern about what it might mean for relations with their principal international partners. They initiated secret talks and signed a joint declaration on pursuing reconciliation, which possibly reflected concern that their allies might decide the fate of Korea without their concurrence. In the event, however, their concern about a behind-the-scenes Korea deal between Beijing and Washington was misplaced, and the inter-Korean contacts produced no lasting consequences.[10]

Though the secret talks yielded little, the episode underscores two recurring themes in China's relationship with the peninsula. One is the extent to which China's aspirations and opportunities on the peninsula are constrained and shaped by the interests and objectives of Koreans in the North and the South. The second is Korean worry, in both North and South, that "big powers," in this case China and the United States, will pursue their own interests in ways that affect adversely the interests of Korea.

Dawn of a New Era: 1979–1991

The parameters and possibilities of China's interaction with the Korean Peninsula changed little during the first three decades after June 1950, but the genesis of later changes can be traced to 1969–1971, when concern about the threat posed by the Soviet Union prompted Mao and Nixon to begin the process of rapprochement that culminated in the establishment of diplomatic relations in January 1979. The process had barely moved beyond the "enemy of my enemy is my friend" stage while Mao was alive, but his death in 1976 made possible—and for some Chinese imperative—the adoption of new priorities, a new framework for deciding what was possible and desirable, and a wholly new strategy of development. These changes had far-reaching but not immediate consequences for China's relationships with the ROK and the DPRK.[11]

The central element in the strategy initiated by Mao (and Zhou Enlai) was to reduce the threat to China's security by improving relations with the United States. Doing so would diminish the direct threat from the United States and its capitalist allies while at the same time using the United States and its allies to counterbalance the greater threat posed by the Soviet Union. This was the advent of what became known as the "strategic triangle." Although initially limited to a tacit partnership against the Soviet Union, diminished hostility between Pyongyang's principal backer and its primary adversary had immediate and mostly negative implications for DPRK security. Neither Beijing nor Washington was especially concerned about how rapprochement would affect the peninsula, but Pyongyang and Seoul responded almost immediately. Kim Il Sung initiated the unsuccessful contacts with his South Korean counterpart as noted earlier. That effort had little impact, but at approximately the same time he launched the program to develop nuclear weapons that continues to bedevil leaders in China and the United States.[12] In South Korea, Park Chung-hee staged a coup against the constitutional system, declared martial law, initiated steps to acquire nuclear weapons, and adopted a range of authoritarian measures that he claimed were necessary to protect the country from external threats.[13] The responses to US-China rapprochement by Pyongyang and Seoul did not have immediate consequences for China, but they would later become central to the way in which Beijing viewed both Koreas.

When Mao died, China was in political disarray, economically backward, and losing ground to neighboring and rival states. Deng Xiaoping, Chen Yun, and other "veteran cadres" determined that drastic action was required to restore party legitimacy, resuscitate the economy, and reduce China's vulnerability to external threats.[14] Key elements of the strategy they adopted to achieve these objectives were the redefinition of the international environment from Mao's assessment that war was inevitable and imminent to one positing the possibility of avoiding the inevitable conflict for at least twenty years. This new assessment created a window of opportunity during which China could devote fewer resources to the military and restore and modernize the economy.[15] Having defined the strategic environment as less threatening made it possible for China to abandon the failed search for a uniquely Chinese approach to development with methods that had enabled Japan, Taiwan, and the ROK to become more prosperous and more modern through export-led growth and participation in the "free world" economic system.[16] To pursue this strategy, China had to gain access to the US-led economic order. To do that, rapprochement had to move beyond the stage reached by Mao and Nixon. Doing so entailed both direct and indirect consequences for the two Koreas.

Although the model or path of development Beijing had decided to follow was often described as "the Japanese model," the key to being able to follow that path was the United States' willingness to allow China to participate in what, at the time, was still essentially the "free world club," limited to democratic countries aligned, if not formally allied, with the United States. The Communist Party of China had no intention of reforming itself out of existence, so if China were to be admitted to the club, it would have to be as a Communist Party–led authoritarian state. By mid-1978, the Carter administration had signaled its willingness to do so. It is not a coincidence that the "normalization" of relations with the United States, symbolized by the exchange of diplomatic recognition, was announced at the same plenum at which was announced what became known as the policy of reform and opening to the outside world. At that time, the outside world that mattered most to China comprised countries able to provide the technology, training, capital, and markets needed to achieve export-led growth and comprehensive modernization of the country, that is, those in North America, Western Europe, and Japan.

Available evidence does not clarify whether Deng's judgment that war could be deferred was based on objective analysis of the international situation or opportunistic calculations that such a judgment was necessary for adoption of the reform and opening program.[17] Nor does it indicate whether or how Korea-related developments might have shaped Deng's perception of the situation. Those developments included Jimmy Carter's announced intention to withdraw most US troops from South Korea. Beijing viewed the presence of US troops in the ROK as a direct threat to China's security; if the number decreased, so might the threat. Carter's planned reductions were highly controversial in Washington and were not implemented, but the possibility remained alive that they would be until after the decision to normalize relations with the United States and to launch the policy of reform and opening.[18]

Even if Carter's desire to withdraw US troops from the peninsula played a larger role in Beijing's decision to follow the path to wealth and power pioneered by Japan and pursued by other Asian tigers than is indicated by available evidence, the fact remains that the prospective roles the DPRK and the ROK were expected to play in China's renewed quest for rapid modernization and sustained economic growth were much less important than the projected roles of more advanced economies.[19] Neither of the Koreas had much to contribute to the initial phases of China's effort to jump-start its economy and to modernize as much as possible before the posited short-lived window of opportunity closed. Beijing concentrated its attention and efforts on the countries able to do the most for China in the shortest time.

The Koreas were not a primary target of China's new priorities and foreign policy focus, but Pyongyang and Seoul recognized that China's policy shift could have significant implications for both of them.[20] Kim Il Sung perceived both a need and a possible opportunity to compensate for greater uncertainty about China's commitment to support the DPRK by exploring the possibility of better relations with the United States and, later, with the ROK. It also reinforced determination to press ahead with the nuclear weapons program launched after Nixon's visit to Beijing in 1972. Domestic developments in the ROK limited the interest and ability of Seoul to explore possibilities for better relations with Beijing for several years after 1978, but it is doubtful that Beijing would have been willing to jeopardize its relationship with Pyongyang by pursuing improved relations with the ROK until the South (and China) had developed to a point at which deeper interaction promised tangible benefits to both. The time was not ripe for exploring possibilities for closer relations between China and the ROK until the latter part of the 1980s.[21]

Proximity and initiatives by both Koreas required responses by Beijing and episodic interaction throughout the 1979–1991 period, but relatively little of what transpired during the 1980s was initiated by China to achieve the goals of its post-1978 strategy to manage threats to security and modernize as quickly as possible. Neither Korea posed a direct threat to China. Winning DPRK support in the ideological competition with the Soviet Union had become far less important to China after the death of Mao and the adoption of developmental policies unpalatable to both Pyongyang and Moscow. The indirect threat from the ROK was being managed via the improving relationship with the United States. Moreover, at this stage of PRC development, the DPRK did not have what China needed, and what it did have, namely raw materials, did not yet have to be imported in order to sustain high rates of growth. The ROK was developing more rapidly than China, but South Korean companies were not yet seeking overseas venues for production, and the ROK did not yet have the markets, capital, or technology sought by the PRC.

Four developments in the late 1980s changed both the context and the range of possibilities for Chinese policy toward the Koreas. One was the rise of Mikhail Gorbachev and the unraveling of the Soviet empire. Gorbachev's efforts to save the Soviet Union by pursuing changes even more radical than those undertaken by China were unsuccessful but triggered consequences that transformed the international system. The long-frozen conditions of the Cold War began to thaw in ways that made it possible— and for states in the communist camp, necessary—to devise new strategies to achieve their security, economic, and political objectives. This meant, inter alia, that China was less constrained in what it could do vis-à-vis the DPRK and the ROK.

The second development that changed the Chinese calculus with respect to the peninsula was the cumulative effect of ROK growth and development in the 1980s. By the end of the decade, the ROK was substantially better able to contribute to China's quest for modernization than it had been at the beginning. Despite the absence of formal diplomatic relations, the two sides began informal talks aimed at exploring possibilities for economic cooperation. Beijing saw potential for other benefits from better relations with Seoul (e.g., greater leverage for dealing with Pyongyang and Taipei), but economic considerations were at the core.[22]

A third development was political change in the South that produced the transition to a far more democratic government and the election of Roh Tae-woo, whose policy of *Nordpolitik* was intended to improve ROK relations with all communist countries, including the DPRK. Improvement of relations between South and North was a prerequisite for US exploration of better relations with the DPRK; the South's willingness to pursue exploratory talks with the North created possibilities for Washington to respond more positively to DPRK initiatives than had been the case previously.[23] As with Gorbachev's initiatives, political changes in the South were creating new possibilities for diplomatic interchange on the peninsula.

Cumulative progress in China was the fourth development that changed the possibilities available to Chinese policy makers. After nearly a decade of reform and investment by overseas Chinese, United States–based companies, and a growing number of other Organization for Economic Cooperation and Development member countries, China had developed to the point that firms operating there wanted to enter the growing ROK market and that Chinese firms were better prepared to accept inputs from the South. Economic possibilities were beginning to influence PRC policy decisions affecting relations with the peninsula.[24]

Together, these developments changed the geopolitical landscape and produced a number of enduring changes, including decisions by Beijing and Moscow to establish formal diplomatic and economic relations with the ROK, admission of both Koreas to the United Nations (the North having been pressed by the PRC to accept dual admission), and dramatic increases in Sino–South Korean trade.[25] Over slightly more than a decade, China's posture toward the Koreas had moved from tight alignment with the North and considerable hostility toward the South to a "two Koreas" policy that leaned increasingly away from Pyongyang and toward Seoul. Geopolitical changes made this shift possible, but perceived economic opportunities were the primary drivers. The ROK could, and was willing to, do more to assist China's quest for development, China was increasingly able to utilize the kinds of assistance the South was willing to provide, and the United States supported the rapprochement between Seoul and Beijing. Over the same period, the DPRK became less important to China's security, ideological pretensions, and international standing.

Further Evolution of Chinese Priorities and Policy: 1992–2006

When the Cold War ended with the demise of the Soviet Union in December 1991, the global order that had sustained the division of Korea and political alignments in Northeast Asia for more than four decades gave way to new alignments and international arrangements with remarkable speed and remarkably little violence. North Korea was commonly depicted as a political dinosaur that could not long survive the collapse of communism in the Soviet Union and Central Europe, and many questioned whether a China still reeling from the prodemocracy movement and Tiananmen crackdown of 1988–1989 could avoid the kinds of political transformation occurring elsewhere, including next door in the Republic of Korea. China, of course, did much better than merely survive. It maintained double-digit rates of growth, lifted hundreds of millions of people out of abject poverty, and became one of the world's largest economies and trading nations. The policy of reform and opening was proving to be a very effective strategy of development.

The demise of the Soviet Union fundamentally changed China's security situation, mostly for the better. Most of the causes of hostility between Moscow and Beijing dissipated almost immediately, as did what had long been regarded as the most dangerous threat to China's security. But it also eliminated what had once been the principal reason for Sino-American rapprochement, namely the shared interest in deterring a common enemy.[26]

Chinese leaders worried that the demise of the Soviet threat might make it harder to manage the possibly now greater threat from the United States, and that even if the threat could continue to be managed through diplomatic means, Washington might become less willing to support China's quest for modernity.[27] These concerns caused Beijing to be more attentive to US interests and objectives with respect to third countries and transnational issues, and to solidify China's ties to other countries that could provide factors needed to sustain Chinese growth to offset possible conditions and obstacles imposed by the United States.[28] The changed international situation and China's compensatory moves also affected its relations with both Koreas.

One element in the changed international environment was North Korea's increased efforts to counterbalance first China and later both China and the Soviet Union through a two-prong strategy to improve relations with the United States, if possible, and to acquire nuclear weapons. Both prongs were intended to ensure regime survival, and at the time, Pyongyang did not know which might succeed first. During the first half of the period examined here, Pyongyang managed to improve its relations with the United States, the ROK, and Japan. The most concrete manifestation of the new relationship was the Agreed Framework between the United States and the DPRK, which entailed the participation of South Korea and Japan in the funding and construction in North Korea of two light-water power reactors.[29]

Pyongyang's priorities and focus of attention were not overtly hostile to China, but pursuit of those priorities did not envision or require significant improvement in the still nominally close relationship with the PRC. For the most part, Pyongyang was careful about trying to entice the United States and its Northeast Asian allies to do more for the DPRK by implying that failure to do so would cause it to turn instead to China. The North probably did so because it recognized that the simultaneous improvement in its own relationships with Beijing and China's declining interest in using its relationship with Pyongyang to put pressure on the countries it most needed for sustained development doomed any such effort to failure.

China did not try particularly hard to improve its relationship with the DPRK or to counterbalance Pyongyang's growing ties with the United States, the ROK, and Japan, probably because it assessed that it would be difficult to do so and, more important, because it did not wish to do anything that might jeopardize its more important relationship with the United States and its allies. The United States was perceived to "need" China less after the demise of the Soviet Union, but China was increasingly dependent on the US-led global order for the success of its modernization strategy. These important considerations were reinforced by the fact that the DPRK still could provide little of what China needed to maintain high rates of growth. Moreover, Beijing judged that it had a freer hand to improve relations with the United States and its regional allies because they were deepening their own relationships with the North and eager to expand their own economic and other ties to the PRC.

Many of the developments and dynamics that caused Beijing to regard the DPRK as less important to China's security and to view it increasingly as an economic burden, particularly after drought, floods, and famine further weakened the North's economy, also made it more attractive and important to expand economic ties with the ROK. Year by year, ROK firms were more interested in access to Chinese labor to manufacture or assemble their products, and at roughly the same pace PRC firms were able and eager to become integrated into ROK (and other) production chains. Cultural similarities and geographic proximity made each a more attractive partner for the other than were most third countries. Initial successes paved the way for additional and more extensive forms of engagement in a self-reinforcing process that produced mutual benefit but also deepened corporate and national interdependencies.

China's stake in its relationship with South Korea increased as its stake in the North was eroded by developments elsewhere. More accurately, the nature of China's stake in the DPRK was transformed from one based heavily on the North's putative value as a buffer protecting China from US troops, democratic ideas, and capitalist economics in the South into one based primarily on Pyongyang's ability to put at risk the regional stability Beijing considered essential to its continued ability to attract investment and contracts.

China began to perceive the North more as a wild card or potentially disruptive factor with the capacity to undermine the stability, predictability, and relationships that were increasingly important to China's quest for modernity. The DPRK could not do much to help China on either the security or the development front, but it could do things that would jeopardize both. As a result, a priority objective of PRC policy toward and affecting the North was to minimize the danger and consequences of DPRK actions with the potential to impede attainment of China's objectives. This gave Pyongyang considerable leverage in its dealings with Beijing.[30] It exercised this leverage to secure food, fuel, and other forms of assistance, and to obtain Chinese diplomatic backing at the United Nations and in other forums.

From 1992 through 2000, developments on and affecting the peninsula were mostly favorable to China's interests. Pyongyang and Seoul were talking, as were Pyongyang and Washington. The Agreed Framework was being implemented and the Korean Peninsula Energy Development Organization (KEDO) was constructing two light-water reactors in the DPRK.[31] Russia was sitting on the sidelines, and prospects appeared favorable for greater stability and reduced tensions in the region. With developments moving in a positive direction, the goal of Chinese policy was to keep them on track. But preserving the status quo proved more difficult than Beijing anticipated.

Though positive (from Beijing's perspective), recent developments and evolving relationships in the region were very fragile. Few at the time appear to have recognized how fragile they were and how easily they could be derailed. Factors contributing to the fragility included low levels of trust among all the players, Republican animosity to almost everything accomplished by the Clinton administration, especially the Agreed Framework, and Pyongyang's decision to maintain its drive for nuclear weapons and delivery vehicles as a hedge against the failure of diplomacy to provide the security, recognition, and assistance it craved. The unraveling occurred quickly.

Developments that both symbolized and contributed to the unraveling included indications that the newly installed Bush administration did not intend to build on Clinton administration policy toward the DPRK, and the contretemps that ensued when the United States accused Pyongyang of failing to honor its nuclear commitments and pursuing a covert program to enrich uranium.[32] Beijing did not initiate or contribute to the events that produced the rapid deterioration of the situation on the peninsula, but it could not avoid the consequences.

One set of consequences derives, again, from proximity. As Chinese officials have stated many times, maintenance of a peaceful international environment is critical for achieving their country's security and developmental objectives.[33] Actions of the DPRK interpreted as provocations by the ROK and the United States invited retaliatory responses with the potential to escalate to a level of conflict that, at a minimum, would undermine the attractiveness of China as a place for foreign investment or producer of key intermediate goods or final products. This made it imperative for Chinese policy makers to attempt to constrain the DPRK (thereby underscoring the extent to which Pyongyang enjoyed leverage over Beijing) but also to persuade Seoul and Washington to exercise restraint and avoid actions that might trigger escalatory behavior by the North. This also meant that China had to be attentive to US bilateral concerns and concerns about Chinese behavior elsewhere in the world and on transnational issues.

Another consequence derived from China's proclaimed special relationship with the DPRK. The legacy of the Korean War, the actual volume of Chinese assistance to the North, and imputed DPRK dependence on China for key commodities and diplomatic support caused Washington and many other capitals to judge that China had greater ability to influence decisions in Pyongyang than did anyone else. Beijing regularly asserts that it has less influence than others assume but is stuck with the perception that less than is commonly assumed is still regarded as more than anyone else. Taking on responsibility for DPRK actions was certainly unwelcome in Beijing but its own self interest in maintaining stability and desire for recognition as an influential global player gave it no choice except to accept greater responsibility for "managing" or "controlling" the North.

The most visible symbol of China's special responsibility was its chairing of the Six-Party Talks on North Korea's nuclear program. The purpose of the talks, attended by the DPRK, China, the United States, the ROK, Japan, and Russia, was to prevent the DPRK from acquiring nuclear weapons.[34] Beijing may have viewed its task as an impossible mission, but criticism that it viewed its role as merely persuading the DPRK to return to the negotiating table each time the talks broke down is unfair. PRC officials tried hard to bridge gaps that proved unbridgeable (e.g., the North's demand for direct talks with the United States, the initial US refusal to talk without prior agreement on nuclear issues), but the talks ultimately failed.[35] Perhaps ironically, the fact that they agreed to chair the talks helped them in the US-China arena. Although President Bush was criticized for "outsourcing" the DPRK nuclear problem to the Chinese, his administration was able to deflect criticism of other Chinese actions by saying that they were, however, helping the United States to manage the difficult Korea problem.[36]

China's increasingly important economic ties with the ROK increased Beijing's stake in the maintenance of good relations with Seoul. As the ROK became a more important source of technology, investment, and training, and market for Chinese goods, China found that it had less freedom of action to manage the threat to its developmental strategy posed by DPRK actions with the potential to undermine stability or embroil China in hostilities with its most important economic partners. South Korea is more dependent on trade with the PRC than China is vis-à-vis the ROK, but South Koreans expect more from the relationship than just mutual economic benefit. They also want China to use the leverage it does have with Pyongyang to improve relations between North and South and to facilitate eventual unification. Economic ties give Seoul some amount of leverage, but certainly not as much as trade volumes might suggest. Nevertheless, Beijing is conscious that it must pay more attention to ROK political objectives in order to protect its own economic interests.

Higher Stakes, Diminished Leverage: 2006–Present

On October 9, 2006, the DPRK exploded its first nuclear device. The test was not fully successful, but it introduced a new level of complexity and challenge into China's policy calculations vis-à-vis the Korean Peninsula. Prior to the test, Chinese (and Russian) officials had been dismissive of US and ROK concerns about the ability of the North to build nuclear weapons, and they appear to have been caught by surprise. Among the new challenges they had to confront was the possibility that possession of nuclear weapons by the North would induce Japan and/or the ROK to seek a nuclear deterrent of its own. This challenge was exacerbated by subsequent, more successful DPRK nuclear tests in 2009, 2013, and 2016, and tests of longer-range missiles that eventually may be capable of delivering nuclear warheads.[37]

For either Japan or the ROK to possess nuclear weapons would increase the threat to China's own security, but it would be almost as unpalatable to China if the United States restrained its allies from acquiring the bomb, because that would entail moves to reassure the allies by taking steps to buttress the alliances. In fact, the United States did so, and its actions indeed were interpreted in China as increasing the indirect threat to China's security and a possible harbinger of the delayed but "inevitable" US military action to thwart China's rise before it could seriously challenge US hegemony.[38] China's diplomatic agenda came to include needing to contain, and hopefully roll back, the acquisition of nuclear weapons by the DPRK, dissuading the ROK and Japan from pursuing independent nuclear weapons programs, dissuading the United States from taking military action against the North to preempt acquisition of a meaningful arsenal of nuclear weapons, and limiting both the reality and the domestic political fallout of high-profile US efforts to reassure its allies.

The way in which the North conducted nuclear tests was a slap in the face of its longtime ally and protector. Quite apart from what the tests have to say about Pyongyang's lack of confidence in its alliance with the PRC and disregard of possible consequences for China's security, they put China in the position of having to choose between its relationship with the DPRK and concerns about maintaining stability in the region, and its obligations as a permanent member of the UN Security Council. Forced to choose, China determined that its international image, relationship with the United States, and interest in preventing further nuclear and missile proliferation made it more costly to continue to shield Pyongyang from international opprobrium and UN Security Council sanctions. The sanctions imposed were probably less severe than they might have been because of China's intervention, but the more important fact is that China did not veto and actually voted in favor of increasingly strong sanctions.[39]

Although Beijing condemned the North's nuclear and missile tests with increasing vehemence and voted to approve sanctions, it was not willing to exacerbate the risk of destabilizing DPRK actions by curtailing deliveries of food and fuel or taking other steps that could be construed as attempts to engineer regime change. Beijing feels it must strike a delicate balance between punishing and pressuring Pyongyang to avoid high risk and seriously destabilizing actions, and preventing regime collapse. Thus far it has managed to do so, but the situation is becoming worse, not better, with the passage of time.[40]

Beijing has expressed its unhappiness with DPRK behavior in culturally symbolic ways as well, namely by refusing to host a visit to Beijing by Kim Jong Un, who succeeded his father in December 2011, and by severely limiting the number of high-level visits to the DPRK. These rebuffs stand in stark contrast to the fact that Chinese president and party leader Xi Jinping has visited the ROK and met with ROK president Park Geun-hye on several occasions.[41] The disparity in the way Beijing now treats Pyongyang and Seoul is more than a simple expression of disapproval of DPRK actions; it is also a reflection of the importance of economic ties between China and the ROK, and a part of China's attempt to extract political leverage from South Korea's economic dependence on the PRC. The clearest manifestation of this effort to date is Beijing's ultimately unsuccessful attempt to dissuade Seoul from agreeing to deployment of the Terminal High Altitude Area Defense (THAAD) missile defense system by telling South Koreans that

Beijing considers the US system a threat to the viability of China's nuclear deterrent and reminding them that their economy is now more closely tied to China's than to that of the United States. This approach ignores that the perceived need for the ROK to have a missile defense capability is the fact that China's treaty ally in the north has acquired both nuclear weapons and the means to deliver them. Nevertheless, the fact that many South Koreans openly discuss the perils of being caught between the United States and China and having to choose between their most important security partner and their largest economic partner attests to the effectiveness of China's diplomacy.[42]

Conclusion

China's priorities and policies toward North and South Korea have changed dramatically during the past forty years. Before the advent of the reform era, Chinese rhetoric and policy toward the peninsula reflected and were shaped by geography, ideology, the Korean War, and the personalities and convictions of Mao Zedong and Kim Il Sung. The DPRK was China's closest ally, buffer against ideas and troops in the ROK, and sometime partner in ideological contests with the Soviet Union. South Korea was treated as the forward bastion of US efforts to contain, and ultimately invade, China, and contacts between the ROK and PRC were minimal to nonexistent. Four decades into the reform era, Beijing's relationships with the ROK are far deeper and more extensive than those with the DPRK, and Pyongyang arguably poses the greatest external threat to the continued success of China's strategy to attain wealth, power, and influence through participation in the US-led global system.

These changes came about partially as a result of changes in the international system, most notably the demise of the Soviet Union and end of the Cold War, but also because of changes in China and the ROK, and the actions of the DPRK. Rapprochement between China and the United States, beginning with the tacit united front against the Soviet Union endorsed by Mao and Nixon, and the revolutionary changes in China made possible by Mao's death and the determination of his successors to abandon experimentation in favor of a proven path to sustained development and economic growth changed Beijing's perception of what was possible and facilitated the adoption of new priorities and policies to achieve them.

Concerns about security and stability as well as development and modernization were, and continue to be, the most important determinants of the way China views and interacts with other nations. Those perceived to threaten China, directly or indirectly, must be deterred and counterbalanced through combinations of national strength and diplomatic skill. Those best able to contribute to China's quest for modernity, prosperity, and power command the most attention and those with little to contribute or posing no significant danger are much less central to Beijing's policy calculus. Application of this calculus has produced dramatic change in the way Beijing perceives and interacts with the DPRK and the ROK during the decades of reform and opening. China and the ROK have changed more than has the DPRK. One could make a case that engagement with the United States and the possibilities that engagement has created for Chinese and South Koreans have been critical to their transformations, and that the absence of engagement between the United States and the DPRK produced an equally significant but opposite outcome. It is much more difficult to make a convincing argument that interaction with China has had a major impact on the evolution of the two Koreas.

Increased interaction between the PRC and the ROK has brought economic benefits to both, but it does not appear to have had much effect on either's domestic politics. Where it does seem to have had an impact is in the realm of foreign and security policy. Mutual benefit has deepened interdependence and decreased the ability of both to act in disregard of the other's interests and concerns. Whether or how that will give one or both leverage over one another or with third countries remains unclear.

The evolution of Chinese perceptions, priorities, and policies summarized in this chapter suggests that many of the reasons often adduced to explain China's past actions and to predict what it will do in the future to protect its interest on the Korean Peninsula have become much less important than they were in the past.[43] China's economic and political stakes in its relationship with the ROK are now much greater than those it has in the DPRK, and North Korea's location and ideological similarities are much less relevant than they were in the 1950s and 1960s. Given China's priorities and alternatives, there is little that the North can do to facilitate China's quest for security, modernity, and economic growth, especially in comparison to the South and many other nations. Pyongyang's importance to Beijing derives primarily from its ability to undermine regional stability through provocations with the potential to trigger conflict on China's borders and to diminish China's attractiveness as a destination for foreign investment. Continued division of the peninsula no longer helps China to achieve its security or economic objectives, but there is no easy path to reunification. Beijing would probably welcome reunification under terms acceptable to the South, but it does not know how to achieve that outcome without unacceptable risk to its own more important priorities. Essential continuity of PRC policy is likely, therefore, not because it is desirable or even highly effective, but because the short-term risks of attempting to change the status quo appear unacceptably high.

Notes

1. See, for example, Evelyn S. Rawski, *Early Modern China and Northeast Asia: Cross-Border Perspectives* (Cambridge: Cambridge University Press, 2015).

2. This chapter employs a unitary actor approach for all countries because its focus is on the outcome of policy deliberations, not on the often complex and contentious processes that generate and assess alternative courses of action.

3. On the importance of geography, both in general and specifically with respect to China, see Robert D. Kaplan, *The Revenge of Geography* (New York: Random House, 2012).

4. On the relationship of China's tributary state system and trade, see John King Fairbank, ed., *The Chinese World Order* (Cambridge, MA: Harvard University Press, 1968).

5. See Thomas W. Robinson, "Chinese Foreign Policy from the 1940s to the 1990s," in *Chinese Foreign Policy: Theory and Practice*, ed. Thomas W. Robinson and David Shambaugh (New York: Clarendon Press, 1994), 555–602.

6. See, for example, Mao Zedong [Mao Tse-tung], "On the People's Democratic Dictatorship" June 30, 1949, in *Selected Works of Mao Tse-tung* (Beijing: Foreign Languages Press, 1961), 4:411–424; and Sergei N. Goncharov, John W. Lewis, and Xue Litai, *Uncertain Partners: Stalin, Mao, and the Korean War* (Stanford, CA: Stanford University Press, 1993), chaps. 2–4.

7. Ibid., chaps. 5–6. See also Henry Kissinger, *World Order* (New York: Penguin Books, 2014), 288–295.

8. Goncharev, Lewis, and Xue, *Uncertain Partners*; Zhang Xiaoming, "China, the Soviet Union, and the Korean War: From an Abortive War Plan to a Wartime Relationship," *Journal of Conflict Studies* 22, no. 1 (2002): https://journals.lib.unb .ca/index.php/jcs/article/view/368/582#a61; and Nancy Bernkopf Tucker, *Patterns in the Dust: Chinese-American Relations and the Recognition Controversy, 1949–1950* (New York: Columbia University Press, 1983).

9. See, for example, Dae-Sook Suh, *Kim Il Sung* (New York: Columbia University Press, 1988), chap. 10.

10. See Scott Snyder, *China's Rise and the Two Koreas* (Boulder, CO: Lynne Rienner, 2009), 27–28; and Don Oberdorfer and Robert Carlin, *The Two Koreas: A Contemporary History*, 3rd ed. (New York: Basic Books, 2014), 18–25.

11. See, for example, Harry Harding, *A Fragile Relationship: The United States and China Since 1972* (Washington, DC: Brookings Institution, 1992), chaps. 2–3; Henry Kissinger, *On China* (New York: Penguin, 2011), chaps. 5–10; and Ezra F. Vogel, *Deng Xiaoping and the Transformation of China* (Cambridge, MA: Belknap Press of Harvard University Press, 2011), chap. 11.

12. See Jonathan D. Pollack, *No Exit: North Korea, Nuclear Weapons and International Security* (New York: Routledge, 2011), chap. 3.

13. Oberdorfer and Carlin, *Two Koreas*, 30–33.

14. See Vogel, *Deng Xiaoping*, chaps. 7–12; and Harry Harding, *China's Second Revolution: Reform After Mao* (Washington, DC: Brookings Institution, 1987).

15. Thomas Fingar, "China's Quest for Technology: Implications for Arms Control II," in *Arms Control II: A New Approach to International Security*, ed. John H. Barton and Ryukichi Imai (Cambridge, MA: Oelgeschlager, Gunn and Hain, 1981), chap. 10.

16. See, for example, Eun Mee Kim, ed., *The Four Asian Tigers: Economic Development and the Global Political Economy* (Bingley, UK: Emerald Group, 1998).

17. See, for example, Thomas Fingar, "China and South/Central Asia in the Era of Reform and Opening," in *The New Great Game: China and South and Central Asia in the Era of Reform*, ed. Thomas Fingar (Stanford, CA: Stanford University Press, 2016), chap. 1.

18. For details on Carter's troop reduction plans and their impact on the peninsula, see Oberdorfer and Carlin, *Two Koreas*, chap. 4.

19. In 1978, the ROK was still at an early stage of development. It did not become eligible for OECD membership until 1995. The DPRK's per capita gross domestic product was higher than that of China until 1994, but it did not have the technology, capital, or other factors central to China's reform and opening strategy.

20. See, for example, Samuel S. Kim, "The Making of China's Korea Policy in the Era of Reform," in *The Making of Chinese Foreign and Security Policy in the Era of Reform*, ed. David M. Lampton (Stanford, CA: Stanford University Press, 2001), chap. 12.

21. See Jae Ho Chung, *Between Ally and Partner: Korea-China Relations and the United States* (New York: Columbia University Press, 2007), chap. 4; Snyder, *China's Rise*, chap. 2; and Oberdorfer and Carlin, *Two Koreas*, chap. 6.

22. Snyder, *China's Rise*, 30–38.

23. Oberdorfer and Carlin, *Two Koreas*, 146–153.

24. See, for example, Barry Naughton, *Growing Out of the Plan: Chinese Economic Reform 1978–1993* (Cambridge: Cambridge University Press, 1996), chaps. 5–7.

25. Oberdorfer and Carlin, *Two Koreas*, chaps. 9-10; Chung, *Between Ally and Partner*, chaps. 3–5.

26. See Thomas Fingar and Fan Jishe, "Ties That Bind: Strategic Stability in the US-China Relationship," *Washington Quarterly* 36, no. 4 (Fall 2013): 125–138.

27. See Thomas Fingar, "China's Goals in South Asia," in *The New Great Game: China and South and Central Asia in the Era of Reform*, ed. Thomas Fingar (Stanford, CA: Stanford University Press, 2016), chap. 2.

28. See David Shambaugh, "China and Europe: The Emerging Axis," *Current History*, September 2004, 243–248.

29. See Joel S. Wit, Daniel B. Poneman, and Robert L. Gallucci, *Going Critical: The First North Korean Nuclear Crisis* (Washington, DC: Brookings Institution, 2004); and Rust Deming, "US-North Korea Agreed Framework and KEDO," Testimony Before the Senate Foreign Relations Committee, Subcommittee on East Asian and Pacific Affairs, July 14, 1998, http://www.state.gov/1997 -2001-NOPDFS//policy_remarks/1998/980714_deming_north_korea.html.

30. See Charles K. Armstrong, *Tyranny of the Weak: North Korea and the World, 1950–1992* (Ithaca, NY: Cornell University Press, 2013).

31. Charles Kartman, Robert Carlin, and Joel Wit, *A History of KEDO, 1994– 2006* (Stanford, CA: Center for International Security and Cooperation, 2012).

32. These developments are summarized in Oberdorfer and Carlin, *Two Koreas*, chap. 17.

33. See, for example, "China Needs Peaceful, Stable International Environment: Senior Official [Vice Foreign Minister Li Baodong]," *Xinhuanet*, April 28, 2015, http://news.xinhuanet.com/english/2015-04/28/c_134189709.htm.

34. For more on the Six-Party Talks, see Charles L. Pritchard, *Failed Diplomacy: The Tragic Story of How North Korea Got the Bomb* (Washington, DC: Brookings Institution, 2007), chaps. 5–9; and Jayshree Bajoria and Beina Xu, "The Six Party Talks on North Korea's Nuclear Program," Council on Foreign Relations, September 30, 2013, http://www.cfr.org/proliferation/six-party-talks -north-koreas-nuclear-program/p13593.

35. See, for example, Mike Chinoy, *Meltdown: The Inside Story of the North Korean Nuclear* Crisis (New York: St. Martin's Griffin, 2009); and Yoichi Funabashi, *The Peninsula Question: A Chronicle of the Second Korean Nuclear Crisis* (Washington, DC: Brookings Institution, 2007); and Joseph Kahn, "China Says US Impeded North Korea Arms Talks," *New York Times*, May 13, 2005, http://

www.nytimes.com/2005/05/13/world/asia/china-says-us-impeded-north-korea
-arms-talks.html.

36. See, for example, Michael Abramowitz, "Bush Says It's 'Important to Engage' China," *Washington Post*, August 5, 2008, http://www.washingtonpost.com/wp-dyn/content/article/2008/08/04/AR2008080402460.html.

37. Articles describing the tests and summarizing reactions to them can be found in "North Korea's Nuclear Program," *New York Times*, http://topics.nytimes.com/top/news/international/countriesandterritories/northkorea/nuclear_program/index.html. On the possibility that Japan and/or the ROK might seek nuclear weapons, see Stephen J. Cimbala, *Nuclear Weapons and Cooperative Security in the 21st Century: The New Disorder* (New York: Routledge, 2010), chap. 7.

38. See Michael D. Swaine, "Chinese Leadership and Elite Responses to the US Pacific Pivot," *China Leadership Monitor*, no. 38 (Summer 2012): 1–26.

39. UN sanctions imposed on North Korea beginning in 2006 can be found at the website Security Council Report, at http://www.securitycouncilreport.org/un-documents/search.php?IncludeBlogs=10&limit=15&tag=%22Security%20Council%20Resolutions%22+AND+%22DPRK%20(North%20Korea)%22&ctype=DPRK%20(North%20Korea)&rtype=Security%20Council%20Resolutions&cbtype=dprk-north-korea.

40. See, for example, Siegfried S. Hecker, "The Real Threat from North Korea Is the Nuclear Arsenal Built over the Last Decade," *Bulletin of the Atomic Scientists*, January 7, 2015, http://thebulletin.org/real-threat-north-korea-nuclear-arsenal-built-over-last-decade7883.

41. See, for example, Jeremy Page and Alastair Gale, "China President's Visit to South Korea Before North Seen as Telling," *Wall Street Journal*, June 27, 2014, http://www.wsj.com/articles/chinas-president-xi-to-visit-seoul-1403858327.

42. See, for example, Choe Sang-Hun, "South Korea Tells China Not to Meddle in Decision over Missile System," *New York Times*, March 17, 2015, http://www.nytimes.com/2015/03/18/world/asia/south-korea-tells-china-not-to-meddle-in-decision-over-missile-system.html; and John K. Warden and Brad Glosserman, "China's THAAD Gamble Is Unlikely to Pay Off," *The Diplomat*, April 2015, http://thediplomat.com/2015/04/chinas-thaad-gamble-is-unlikely-to-pay-off/.

43. Summaries of conventional wisdom analyses of Chinese views on Korea can be found in Isabella Francisca Uria, "The Devil You Know: The PRC's Strategic Calculus Regarding Korea Since the Korean War" (Honors thesis, Center for International Security and Cooperation, Stanford University, Stanford, CA, 2014); and Kwangdeok Ahn, "The Chinese Security Perspective on Unification of the Korean Peninsula Considering the Implications of US-China Relations" (MA thesis, Center for East Asian Studies, Stanford University, Stanford, CA, 2015).

SEVEN

South Korea's Approach to a Rising China
Pragmatic Opportunism

Myung-Hwan Yu

For most of its history, China has dominated the Asia-Pacific region. Koreans are very aware of this history, which is why even though China's rise provides the Republic of Korea (ROK, or South Korea) with an opportunity for even greater economic prosperity, Koreans are also confronted with a perceived need to position their country diplomatically and strategically between the two superpowers, the United States and China. The regional security order is changing, and all countries, certainly including Korea, need to make adjustments in response to the changing balance of power. The changes do not simply involve displacement of one dominant power by another.

The United States remains the preeminent power in the global system, and US primacy is deeply embedded in the fabric of relations in the Asia-Pacific region. The presence and power of the United States, the importance of the US-ROK alliance to South Korea's security, and Washington's own adjustments to China's rise have been, and must be, factored into the equation as Seoul calculates how best to respond to the opportunities and hazards resulting from China's economic growth and increasing military power. This chapter examines the principal geopolitical, historical, security, and economic considerations shaping Seoul's response to a rising China.

This chapter complements Chapter 6 by providing Seoul's perspective on opportunities and perils resulting from China's rise and changed policies toward South and North Korea.

Geopolitics and History

Korea is located in a strategic but bellicose neighborhood and has been invaded many times during its long history as a nation. Its neighbors include three great powers—China, Japan, and Russia—but of the three, China has had by far the greatest influence on every aspect of Korean society, particularly with regard to culture. When thinking about China, most Koreans frame their observations about the relationship in terms of the two peoples' five-thousand-year history of interaction between good neighbors that are closer to each other than either is to any other country. But they also remember that China claimed suzerainty over and demanded tribute from Korea for several hundred years. China did not surrender its claim to suzerainty over the Korean kingdom until 1895, after it had lost a war to Japan.[1]

The Russo-Japanese War of 1904–1905 was another conflict for control of the Korean Peninsula.[2] Japan's victory in the war made it the new dominant power on the Korean Peninsula, which it eventually colonized in 1910. As the then new superpower in East Asia, Japan started to extend its influence into Manchuria and China. Its vigorous pursuit of colonial expansion in Southeast Asia led inevitably to war with the United States, in the 1940s. Japan's defeat and surrender to the Allied forces led by the United States freed Korea from Japanese rule but resulted in the division of the peninsula, because, during the final days of the conflict, the Soviet Union declared war on Japan and sent its troops into Korea to capture industrial machinery and establish a communist government. The Soviet occupation was limited to the northern part of the country, but this led to the establishment in 1948 of both the Republic of Korea (ROK, or South Korea) and the Democratic People's Republic of Korea (DPRK, or North Korea) and the nation's enduring division along roughly the thirty-eighth parallel.

When North Korea invaded South Korea on June 25, 1950, for example, President Harry Truman immediately sent US forces to the Korean Peninsula to repel the invasion by Soviet-equipped North Korean troops and to rescue the fragile South Korean government. The war lasted three years, during which American and South Korean forces fought side by side and the United States and South Korea became military allies. The reason the war lasted so long and produced so many casualties and so much destruction is that the People's Republic of China (PRC) dispatched hundreds of thousands of "volunteers"—in reality, battle-hardened veterans of the Chinese civil war—to assist the North. Doing so helped the North Korean army to recover from its defeat at Inchon and the subsequent victories of the United Nations forces moving northward. The UN forces captured Pyongyang and had occupied almost the entire northern half of the divided peninsula when China intervened.[3]

If China had not intervened in the Korean War, Korea could have been reunified more than half a century ago. Perpetuating the division of Korea was not the only consequence of China's intervention; it also forestalled resolution of what has become known as "the Taiwan issue," perhaps through the unification of China, and delayed the PRC's normalization of relations with the United States for more than two decades. The Korean people are acutely aware that for more than sixty years strategic and ideological factors have been central aspects of China's relationship with the Korean Peninsula. In retrospect, it is clear that China did not want the Korean Peninsula to fall within the sphere of influence of the United States, which had become the new dominant power in the region after the Pacific War ended in 1945.

Much has changed in the decades since the end of the Korean War, but the peninsula is of course still located where it always has been and many Koreans view their geopolitical situation with a strong sense of déjà vu. After a hiatus of more than two hundred years, China has regained strength and ambitions for regional dominance and is becoming increasingly assertive in its diplomacy, particularly toward the Korean Peninsula. Koreans may be overly sensitive and suspicious, but history has taught us to be attentive to seemingly innocuous Chinese actions. That is why the research project "History and Current State of the Northwest Borderland," launched by the Chinese Academy of Social Sciences in 2002, sparked concern and caused tension in the relationship. The project was perceived as intended to build a case for arguing that Korea's ancient kingdom of Goguryeo (37 BC–AD 668) was part of the Chinese empire.[4]

A New Setting

South Korea and China, situated just across the West (Yellow) Sea from each other, again became trading partners in the 1980s as China attuned its foreign policy to gain access to the external sources of capital, markets, and technology required to achieve and sustain rapid economic development. Korea's successful hosting of the Seoul Olympic Games in 1988 attracted worldwide attention, including from the Soviet Union and other Eastern bloc countries. Hungary was the first communist country to establish formal diplomatic ties with South Korea.[5] South Korea had long hoped to establish normal relations with China despite the Cold War confrontation in the region. Chinese participation in the Seoul Olympic Games brought a sense of euphoria to many South Koreans, who enthusiastically cheered the Chinese athletes in the games as if enjoying a reunion with old friends whom they had not seen for a long time. The desire for more normal relations with China was not simply a matter of sports or nostalgia; the ROK government hoped that better relations would help South Korea to cope with the dangerous military threat from North Korea. The threat was real, and widely perceived by Koreans to be imminent. Over the years, Pyongyang had launched many provocative actions, including assassination attempts against President Park Chung-hee in 1968 and President Chun Doo-hwan in 1983.[6] South Koreans also recognized that the ROK could not join the United Nations and become a full member of the international community without the consent of the PRC, which, as a permanent member of the UN Security Council, enjoyed veto power. The collapse of the Soviet bloc in the later part of the 1980s, and with it, the end of the Cold War, soon gave South Korea a chance to normalize relations with most former Soviet bloc countries.

In the late 1980s, South Korea was more eager than the PRC to end the almost four decades of animosity between them. Although China became increasingly interested in economic ties with South Korea, it remained cautious. It insisted on a clear-cut separation of politics and economics, largely because North Korean leaders were very sensitive about China's increasingly frequent contacts with South Korean officials, contacts Pyongyang regarded as acts of betrayal. Beijing worked hard to persuade Kim Il Sung to understand and accept that the reasons for the changes in China's approach to the Korean Peninsula were primarily economic. By the start of the Seoul Olympic Games, Sino–South Korea trade volume had grown to $3.1 billion; meanwhile, South Korea's trade with the North remained stagnant, at roughly $500 million per year, much of which was heavily subsidized by China. In May 1991, during Premier Li Peng's official visit to North Korea, he informed Kim Il Sung of China's decision not to veto South Korea's long-standing bid to enter the United Nations.[7] Recognizing that it had no choice, North Korea then entered the United Nations along with the South.

Seoul's new official status as a full member of the international community provided a rationale for upgrading its relationship with China. For its part, Beijing had the delicate and difficult challenge of managing its new diplomatic relationship with South Korea in a way that would not antagonize the North.[8]

China's decision to normalize diplomatic relations with South Korea was motivated not only by the attraction of economic ties but also by a strategic consideration surrounding the Korean Peninsula. Russia and other countries of the former Soviet Eastern bloc had normalized their relationships with South Korea partly in response to South Korea's *Nordpolitik*.[9] To achieve diplomatic normalization with China, Korea had to sever its formal and friendly relationship with Taiwan, which was making a concerted effort to gain increased international recognition. Breaking diplomatic ties with Taiwan as demanded by China was far from easy for South Korea. In fact, however, China's decision to normalize relations with Seoul might have been motivated, in part, by a desire to penalize Taiwan for its efforts to broaden support for its independence.[10] In other words, Beijing may have seen the establishment of diplomatic relations with South Korea as a way to retaliate against Taiwan. When Seoul broke ties with Taiwan, the island was deprived of its last remaining full-fledged diplomatic foothold in Asia.

In August 1992, South Korea announced the historic agreement to restore a formal relationship with China after an eighty-seven-year hiatus.[11] The Qing dynasty had opened a diplomatic mission in Seoul when the Choson dynasty of Korea changed the country's name to "Imperial Korea" in August 1898. The Chinese legation was closed in 1905, when Japan took over the entire Korean Peninsula and assumed control of the diplomacy of the Imperial Korean government. But the diplomatic rapprochement in 1992 was made without addressing the unfortunate history of China's involvement in the Korean War. In the course of negotiations for normalization, Chinese negotiators adamantly refused to allow the inclusion of any reference to the Korean War in the joint declaration. The Chinese argued that they had had to intervene in the war to deter the American forces advancing toward their border, and that they had fought against the United States, not against South Korea. Chinese leaders' characterization of the Korean War as a "righteous war" stirred the emotions of many South Koreans, who were also tremendously disappointed about the PRC's apparent lack of reflection and repentance.

For North Korea, the new ties between Seoul and Beijing must have been hugely upsetting, even though China took great pains to help North Korea save face by sending high-level delegations to Pyongyang. North Korea accepted the apparent shock with official silence, a clear contrast to the response it had showed two years earlier when Soviet foreign minister Eduard Shevardnadze visited Pyongyang on an analogous mission.[12] The change in the great power alignments around the Korean Peninsula mattered even more to North Korea because it still had not established relations with the United States or Japan. North Korea hoped that China would withhold official relations with South Korea until a package deal could be arranged to achieve cross-recognition by the two Koreas and the four surrounding powers. However, China could not ignore the strategic situation and the tenacious approach of South Korea, which offered a variety of friendly gestures, such as an offer to cooperate for the success of the 1990 Asian Games in Beijing. China wanted to use the games to showcase domestic stability and restore confidence after the Tiananmen Square incident.

Economic Dependency

The bilateral relationship between South Korea and China has been transformed beyond what anyone could have imagined at the time of normalization. First and foremost, economic ties have become far more important than the political aspects of the relationship owing to the pragmatic willingness of both sides to separate economics from politics. Bilateral trade between the two countries leaped from $19 million in 1979 to $462 million in 1984, and from $3.1 billion in 1988 to $190 billion in 2010 and $229 billion in 2013.[13] South Korea's total trade volume with China now exceeds that with the United States and Japan combined. More than 25 percent of South Korea's exports go to China. Also, China has become Korea's favorite investment and tourist destination. Korean businesses have invested at least $40 billion in China, and more than six million people travel between the two countries each year. Without the Chinese market, Korea could not maintain its current level of exports, now the world's sixth largest.[14] If the Chinese economy faltered, Korea would suffer the first shock wave. This interdependency offers major benefits but also entails substantial risks for South Korea, whose economy is only one-fifth the size of China's. China's gross domestic product is now the second largest in the world, amounting to $9.24 trillion.[15]

South Koreans believe that economic interdependency in the age of globalization is an inevitable concomitant of robust economic exchanges. Nevertheless, they worry not only about becoming dependent on China but also about losing the ability to compete successfully against it. During the financial crisis in the late 1990s, many South Koreans anticipated that their country would find itself sandwiched between Japan, with its high-tech industry, and China, with its low labor costs. Over the years, however, Koreans found that trade between South Korea and China developed in a very complementary fashion. For South Koreans, the ever-expanding Chinese market provided many opportunities to revitalize their own economy. For Chinese, the fact that almost 60 percent of Korea's exports to China were reexported to other countries paved China's road to becoming an export-oriented economy.[16]

South Koreans want to believe that neither side will exploit such economic interdependence for political or security reasons. Thus, many Koreans were upset when Chinese media criticized South Korea for daring to act contrary to China's interests by enhancing American military power despite the ROK's economic dependence on China.[17] Moreover, some Korean investors have complained that Chinese authorities' attitudes have made it difficult to engage in small business in China. South Koreans are very aware of the change in the way Chinese treat them, especially compared to the situation in the 1990s. To some extent, such a change may be considered "natural" as China has achieved a higher level of economic development and become a global economic powerhouse.

Recognizing the difficulties and constraints in doing business in China, leaders from both countries agreed to negotiate a bilateral free-trade agreement (FTA) intended to further increase trade volume and deepen their economic relationship. China was eager to conclude an FTA with South Korea for both economic and political reasons, and the agreement was signed on June 1, 2015.[18] However, the initial impact of the FTA will not be as great as was expected, because the concession rate on major export items is lower than that of the FTAs Korea signed with the United States and the European Union.

Two Schools of Thought

Their rejuvenated relationship with China has presented Koreans with a dilemma: can they maintain close and cooperative relations with both China and the United States? Most South Koreans agree that Korea needs to develop much closer relations with China, but they also want to maintain the traditional alliance relationship with the United States to deter North Korean military threats. If relations between the United States and China are good, South Korea should be able to maintain good relations with both. If, however, the United States and China antagonize each other and engage in a strategic competition, Korea will find it extremely difficult to side with either.

After South Korea and China normalized diplomatic relations in 1992, they were able to develop their bilateral relationship without being hampered by North Korean–related factors. This was due in part to Chinese insistence on maintaining a clear line between the economy and politics. Thus, while ROK-PRC economic relations were hot, the political relationship was cold. However, China also signaled that, owing to growing PRC-ROK economic interdependence, it expected Korea to eschew acting in ways inconsistent with Beijing's strategic interests. Indeed, mindful of Chinese strategic interests, the South Korean government had already responded carefully and prudently to a suggestion from the United States that it join the US missile defense system. The previous Korean and US administrations had agreed to limited operational flexibility on the part of US forces stationed in South Korea, for fear that full operational capability would provoke a negative reaction from China toward South Korea in a time of crisis in the Taiwan Strait. South Korea did not want to see American forces stationed in South Korea deployed outside the Korean Peninsula to fight against Chinese forces.

South Koreans are divided about how to address the apparent dilemma. One school of thought suggests that South Korea must acknowledge China's new role with respect to security issues on the Korean peninsula and reevaluate the traditional ROK-US alliance in order to accommodate Chinese strategic interests. Thus, at the outset of President Lee Myung-bak's administration in 2008, some South Koreans suggested he visit China before visiting the United States. This, they argued, would highlight the importance of South Korea's relationship with China and show that Seoul recognized the new situation in Northeast Asia created by China's rise. (President Lee did not agree; he visited the United States first.) Those espousing this view insist that Beijing's annual double-digit increases in defense spending will soon give China the capability to deny American intervention in the western

Pacific. American analysts themselves frequently mention that China's anti-access/area-denial (A2/AD) strategy along its periphery concerns many US allies in the region.[19] Some Koreans, though they are the minority, even believe that Korea can play the role of a "balancer" in Northeast Asia when troubles occur between China and the United States.[20] It is true that without Chinese help and support, South Korea cannot maintain peace and stability in the peninsula. Moreover, a considerable number of nationalists in South Korea are sympathetic to North Korea's situation. They tend to be critical of the United States and favorably inclined toward China.[21]

The other school of thought argues that South Korea needs to strengthen its alliance with the United States as China becomes more powerful and assertive both economically and militarily. Adherents of this view are concerned that China will once again try to bring the Korean Peninsula into its sphere of influence and that it will be more aggressive in its diplomacy, which is backed by a blue-water navy and strategic nuclear weapons. They believe that the rise of China will pose a security threat to the Korean Peninsula and undermine the balance of power in the region.[22] They welcome President Obama's renewal of American attention to Asia, the so-called pivot or rebalance, and hope that his stance will check China's ever-increasing influence.

Some Korean supporters of the US alliance worry about the United States' long-term ability to meet its security commitments in view of its recent financial and economic troubles and the resultant major defense budget cuts.[23] Reflecting concerns about China similar to those of South Korea, several Southeast Asian countries have tried to realign their relationships with the United States to counter Chinese moves to control the waters of the South China Sea. Some in the region have expressed concern that China would use its economic advantage to influence the diplomacy of governments involved in the territorial disputes over islets in the South China Sea. Indeed, China appears to have pursued a strategy in Southeast Asia that relies on economic carrots to increase the stake of some countries in maintaining good relations with it.[24] If China uses coercive economic diplomacy to compel countries to alter their policies, however, it will prove counterproductive in the long term. The concerns of China's neighboring countries may be a tactical asset to the United States in its diplomatic competition with China, but they may also increase the risk of a military confrontation with China, something the United States hopes does not occur.

Koreans will continue to debate the two different approaches to dealing with China. Their views will be shaped by their assessment of the relationship between China and the United States, perceptions of the two countries' relative power and influence, and their feeling about which side more sincerely espouses and supports universal values. Such a debate is normal and healthy in a democracy such as South Korea. But South Koreans are fully aware that China has often complained that the United States is trying to contain it and prevent it from becoming a new superpower able to say no to the United States. For its part, the United States has never acknowledged the validity of these Chinese assertions. In fact, the United States has proposed that China become a "stakeholder" in keeping peace and stability in the world and that it assume commensurate responsibility for maintenance of the system from which all benefit. China, however, seems reluctant to endorse an international order shaped by the Western countries, even though China has been the greatest beneficiary of the existing international order.

A Stumbling Block

Relations between South Korea and China have become more robust and closer in every respect, while those between North Korea and China have remained static and become more burdensome to China. Rather than stressing the value of its traditional close ("lips and teeth") relationship, China has evinced increasing concern about the political and economic situation in the North since the collapse of the Soviet bloc in the early 1990s. China has had to provide continuing economic assistance to sustain the North's failed economy and to prevent the regime's collapse, which could result in the North's absorption by South Korea. Nevertheless, the North Korea–China relationship was forged in the 1940s and strengthened during the Cold War era, and it will not fundamentally change until China no longer views the situation on the Korean Peninsula as a zero-sum game.

China's strategic interest in keeping North Korea within its sphere of influence still outweighs the diplomatic and economic burdens Beijing has to bear as a result of Pyongyang's erratic and provocative behavior. In particular, Pyongyang seems determined to continue its missile and nuclear program regardless of how much the programs cost in terms of both actual expenditures and opportunity costs. All indications, including the North's own official statements, are that it has no intention of giving up its nuclear weapons through negotiations with the United States. The North Korean leadership apparently believes that it can retain its nuclear weapons and missile capabilities and yet eventually improve ties with the United States. But Washington seems to have concluded that the only way to stop the North Korean nuclear program is through a transformation of the North Korean regime.

During twenty years of nuclear negotiations with the United States, North Korea repeatedly cheated and lied to its American interlocutors. In 2010 the DPRK surprised not only the United States but also the entire world when it revealed to an American nuclear scientist an advanced uranium enrichment facility at Yongbyon.[25] The North Koreans had vehemently denied the existence of such a program since 2002, when US assistant secretary of state James Kelly visited Pyongyang and raised concerns about just such a covert North Korea program for uranium enrichment.[26]

The North Korean regime seems to believe that China will not allow South Korea or the United States to intervene militarily to solve the nuclear conundrum and bring about unification, even in the event of a regime collapse in North Korea. In fact, since the armistice agreement in 1953, North Korea has conducted numerous military provocations against South Korea, including a 2010 torpedo attack on a naval vessel and the unprovoked shelling of an island near the border, killing fifty South Koreans in total.[27] Unfortunately, North Korean leaders may have assessed that South Korea would not respond in kind for fear that doing so would escalate into war and that the United States would intervene to dissuade South Korea from taking retaliatory military action. So far, North Korea has enjoyed immunity from retaliation or punishment by either South Korea or the United States. In the future, all of North Korea's neighbors should coordinate their policies to make the DPRK understand clearly that it has already crossed a red line and further murderous provocations will not be tolerated.

With only a few exceptions, North Korea has rejected South Korean offers to enter into bilateral negotiations on security issues. One of the exceptions produced the Basic Agreement between North and South in 1991 and the 1992 Joint Declaration on the Denuclearization of the Korean Peninsula, which Pyongyang soon after renounced.[28] North Korea has since insisted that any negotiations to settle peace and security matters should be conducted primarily between the United States and the DPRK because, according to North Korea, the Korean War was a war fought against so-called invading US forces, not against the people of South Korea. For a long time, the PRC supported this contrived assertion. North Korea claims it has the only legitimate government on the Korean Peninsula and that the ROK is a US puppet.[29]

North Korea thus remains a stumbling block impeding the ability of both China and South Korea to broaden their bilateral relationship beyond an economic partnership to include substantial cooperation on security and political issues. Unfortunately, this inherent constraint on South Korea–China relations will continue to exist into the foreseeable future.

Frustration

For South Korea, the purpose of its alliance with the United States is to deter military provocations from North Korea, not to contain China. But China apparently perceives the alliance as a potential threat to its own security as well as that of its ally North Korea. Until the Soviet Union collapsed and Soviet documents regarding the Korean War were released, China had insisted that it was the United States and South Korea that initiated the war in 1950. It retreated from this position only in 2010.[30]

The South Korean government has been frustrated by China's policy toward North Korea, particularly since North Korea conducted nuclear tests in 2006, 2009, 2013, and 2016. While Seoul and Washington have accorded highest priority to the denuclearization of North Korea, China seems to regard that goal as secondary to preserving stability in the North. The dilemma for China is that North Korea's continuing pursuit of the development of nuclear weapons and long-range missiles will undermine the regime's stability. Under the current circumstances, the international community will not provide economic and food assistance to North Korea, despite the evident need. Even South Korea and the United States, which used to provide the majority of food and other international aid to North Korea, have become reluctant to provide further help.[31]

If North Korea continues to build nuclear weapons, China may eventually decide that the strategic value of keeping Pyongyang as an ally is not worth the reputational price it must pay in the international community for continuing to back the regime. China also may change its strategic calculation if North Korea continues to provoke South Korea and risk dragging the region into a military conflict. However, as shown by the Chinese response to the sinking of the corvette *Cheonan* and the shelling of Yeon-pyeong Island in 2010, Beijing's tolerance level is extremely high.[32]

Unfortunately, if China is anxious and concerned about US strategic intentions toward it, it will feel less reason to help the United States and South Korea solve the North Korean nuclear problem. The announcement of the US pivot to Asia has intensified Chinese suspicions; China views the announcement as a step taken specifically to counter its rise. Dissuading China of this view will not be easy, but Washington should make increased efforts to engage in strategic dialogue with Beijing about this and other Chinese concerns.

The Chinese response to the North Korean military provocations reminded the Korean people that the peninsula remains caught in a Cold War situation and reinforced their belief in the continuing need for their military alliance with the United States. China claims that the United States and South Korea point to the North Korean threat to justify the existence and strengthening of the military alliance. Actually, however, if the North Korea issue were solved, the alliance would lose much of its raison d'être.

South Korea wants China to play a more active role in persuading North Korea to give up the nuclear option and refrain from engaging in military provocations. What the South wants from the North is peaceful coexistence. At the very least, China should play the role of an umpire if North Korea makes a foul play. Instead, China has turned a blind eye to North Korean military provocations. China's unconditional support for North Korea in the UN Security Council debate on the sinking of the *Cheonan* in 2010, blocking a strong condemnation by the international community, shocked many South Koreans who had maintained a favorable attitude toward China.[33]

The issue of North Korean refugees in China has also been a stumbling block for South Koreans who want to cultivate a deeper friendship with China. Chinese authorities have maintained the position that North Korean refugees are illegal migrants who cross the border for economic reasons. South Koreans believe those fleeing the North should be considered refugees who deserve protection by the international community. The Chinese government has at times been quite helpful in allowing North Korean refugees to travel to South Korea, but there have been several unfortunate incidents in which the PRC forcibly returned refugees to North Korea, where they must have faced punishment.

These incidents have caused many South Koreans to judge that China failed to treat the issue as the serious humanitarian concern. Instead, they believe, China treated the refugees as pawns in its political relationship with North Korea. As a result, many Koreans believe that China follows a political and value system quite different from that of South Korea. A particularly egregious example was the case of a South Korean human rights activist who helped refugees; he accused Chinese security officials of torturing him while he was detained in China.[34]

Finally, China has always professed support for the peaceful and democratic unification of the Korean Peninsula, but South Koreans find it difficult to believe that China would actually endorse unification of Korea on terms agreeable to the South.

Given the dire situation in the North, South Korea and the United States must find a way to coordinate with China on how to deal with North Korea. It would be a mistake for China to continue to view Korean issues purely in the strategic context of US-China relations. North Korea is a failed state that needs immediate help from the outside. In the event of regime collapse or some other kind of crisis there, China might consider military intervention to prevent refugees from flooding across the border. That could provide China an excuse to again dispatch troops to the Korean Peninsula, putatively to control access to DPRK nuclear facilities. That alone would provide the primary rationale for US forces to intervene. To avoid an unintended military confrontation between the two superpowers, both sides must be prepared to discuss the North Korea situation in official channels, including possible joint action to secure nuclear weapons and fissile material.

A Strategic Cooperative Partnership

Reflecting changes in the character of their bilateral relationship, South Korea and China agreed in 2008 to establish a "strategic cooperative partnership" when President Lee Myung-bak visited China at the outset of his administration. Ten years earlier, during President Kim Dae-jung's visit to China, the two governments characterized their relationship as a "cooperative partnership toward the twenty-first century." In 2003, during President Roh Moo-hyun's visit to China, the relationship was further upgraded, to a "comprehensive cooperative partnership."[35] The aim of South Korea's decision in 2008 to propose including the word *strategic* in describing its relations with China was to broaden the scope of security dialogue on a regional and global level, even though it might be premature to discuss military issues involving North Korea. China welcomed the idea of renaming the bilateral relationship with South Korea but seemed reluctant to engage in a substantive discussion on North Korean issues, including the nuclear program.

The South Korean government has made clear through various bilateral channels that it does not oppose a closer or better relationship between China and North Korea. The South Korean government has also tried hard to convince China that South Korea has never sought to bring about regime change or collapse in North Korea. The ROK government believes that China's close ties and friendly gestures toward North Korea will play an important role in persuading the North to give up its nuclear program and eventually take a more conciliatory attitude toward the South. Many South Koreans believe that China wants to keep North Korea under its influence in order to use it as a buffer zone to prevent a US military presence closer to its border. China, they argue, would not want to see a unified Korea, under American influence, which continued to host US forces on the Korean Peninsula. To put it bluntly, they feel that China does not support unification and prefers that the Korean Peninsula remain divided because it sees no possibility that North Korea would prevail in the course of unification.

However, China did play an important role in chairing the Six-Party Talks on the denuclearization of North Korea, even though the talks failed to bring about a resolution. The talks could provide a useful forum for discussion of regional peace and stability in the future but, practically speaking, only after the North Korean nuclear issue is resolved. The Six-Party Talks began with a common understanding among the parties concerned that stability in Northeast Asia cannot be maintained without solving the nuclear issue.

The bottom line is that South Korea wants to maintain a traditional security alliance with the United States while developing closer friendly relations with China. In a twenty-first century of globalization and interdependence, a new strategic paradigm is required to maintain peace and stability on the Korean Peninsula. A win-win strategy should replace the Cold War legacy of a zero-sum game. In other words, maintaining a strong relationship with the United States should not prevent South Korea from developing a strategic cooperative partnership with China. Likewise, South Korea's strong bilateral ties with China should not prevent it from maintaining its existing relationship with the United States.

The Republic of Korea wants to remove North Korea as a factor in its effort to strengthen strategic cooperative relations with China. Whether or not that will prove possible, convincing China that a unified Korea led by South Korea will not be a strategic loss but rather a possible asset, will be a difficult, long-term task. Most Koreans want to have a friendly and reliable relationship with China, a feeling that derives from their tendency to hold China in awe as well as reverence and fear throughout the long history of their relationship. Such aspirations will remain a long-term goal. Now and for the foreseeable future, the relationship remains an uneasy partnership.

Notes

1. See, for example, Michael J. Seth, *A History of Korea: From Antiquity to the Present* (Lanham, MD: Rowman and Littlefield, 2011); and S. C. M. Paine, *The Sino-Japanese War of 1894–1895: Perceptions, Power, and Primacy* (New York: Cambridge University Press, 2003).

2. See, for example, Geoffrey Jukes, *The Russo-Japanese War, 1904–1905* (Oxford, UK: Osprey, 2002).

3. On China's involvement in the Korean War, see Sergei N. Goncharov, John W. Lewis, and Xue Litai, *Uncertain Partners: Stalin, Mao, and the Korean War* (Stanford, CA: Stanford University Press, 1993).

4. The project is described in "Brief Introduction to the Northeast Project," published by the Research Center for Chinese Borderland History and Geography of the Chinese Academy of Social Sciences (2014) (in Chinese), at http://bjzx.cass .cn/news/129976.htm. For a summary of Korean concerns, see Jae Ho Chung, "China's 'Soft' Clash with South Korea: The History War and Beyond," *Asian Survey* 49, no. 3 (May–June 2009): 468–483.

5. See Susan Chira, "South Koreans Woo Communists; Move to Full Ties with Hungary," *New York Times*, September 14, 1988.

6. For a more comprehensive list of DPRK provocations, see Dirk K. Nanto, "North Korea: Chronology of Provocations, 1950–2003," Congressional Research Service, March 18, 2003, http://fas.org/man/crs/RL30004.pdf.

7. See Don Oberdorfer and Robert Carlin, *The Two Koreas: A Contemporary History*, 3rd ed. (New York: Basic Books, 2014), chap. 10.

8. See, for example, Jae Ho Chung, "China's Ascendency and the Korean Peninsula: From Interest Reevaluation to Strategic Realignment?," in *Power Shift:*

China and Asia's New Dynamics, ed. David Shambaugh (Berkeley: University of California Press, 2005), 151–169.

9. For more on *Nordpolitik*, see Dan C. Sanford, "ROK's *Nordpolitik:* Revisited," *Journal of East Asian Affairs* 7, no. 1 (Winter–Spring 1993): 1–31.

10. See Shih-shan Henry Tsai, *Lee Teng-hui and Taiwan's Quest for Identity* (New York: Palgrave Macmillan, 2005).

11. Nicholas D. Kristof, "Chinese and South Koreans Formally Establish Relations," *New York Times*, August 24, 1992, http://www.nytimes.com/1992/08/24/world/chinese-and-south-koreans-formally-establish-relations.html.

12. See Oberdorfer and Carlin, *Two Koreas*, chap. 9.

13. Trade data provided by Korea International Trade Association (KITA; http://www.kita.org).

14. World Trade Organization, "International Trade and Market Access Data," 2015, https://www.wto.org/english/res_e/statis_e/statis_bis_e.htm?solution=WTO&path=/Dashboards/MAPS&file=Map.wcdf&bookmarkState={%22impl%22:%22client%22,%22params%22:{%22langParam%22:%22en%22}}.

15. Figures on China's gross domestic product are available at the World Bank website, at http://data.worldbank.org/indicator/NY.GDP.MKTP.CD/countries.

16. The high percentage of South Korean goods reexported from China underscores the fact that China is not yet the end destination for much of the production there. South Korea and other countries that supply intermediate products to the global production chain that runs through China ultimately remain dependent on the large import markets of North America, Europe, and Japan.

17. See, for example, Han Suk-Hee, "South Korea Seeks to Balance Relations with China and the United States," Council on Foreign Relations, November 2012, http://www.cfr.org/south-korea/south-korea-seeks-balance-relations-china-united-states/p29447.

18. See "China Headlines: China, ROK Sign Free Trade Agreement," *Xinhuanet*, June 1, 2015, http://news.xinhuanet.com/english/2015-06/01/c_134288195.htm.

19. See, for example, Michael D. Swaine, Mike M. Mochizuki, Michael L. Brown, Paul S. Giarra, Douglas H. Paal, Rachel Esplin Odell, Raymond Lu, Oliver Palmer, and Xu Ren, *China's Military and the US-Japan Alliance in 2030: A Strategic Net Assessment* (Washington, DC: Carnegie Endowment for International Peace, 2013).

20. See, for example, Jae Ho Chung, *Between Ally and Partner: Korea-China Relations and the United States* (New York: Columbia University Press, 2007), chap. 9.

21. See, for example, Kang Jin-kyu, "Jail Time Slashed for Lee Seok-ki," *Korea JoonagAng Daily*, August 12, 2014, http://koreajoongangdaily.joins.com/news/article/Article.aspx?aid=2993387.

22. See, for example, Han Suk-hee, "South Korea Seeks to Balance"; and Kim Jiyoon, "Can't Buy Me Soft Power (With Hard Power): China's Appeal to South Koreans," *Asan Forum*, April 15, 2016, http://www.theasanforum.org/cant-buy-me -soft-power-with-hard-power-chinas-appeal-to-south-koreans/.

23. See, for example, Thom Shanker, "Assessment Criticizes Pentagon Plan for Asia Shift," *International Herald Tribune*, August 2, 2012, http://ihtbd.com/ ihtuser/print/old%20THT/August-2012/02-08-2012/a0208x03xxxxxxxxx.pdf; and Michael Auslin, "Asian Anxiety," *International Herald Tribune*, October 26, 2011, http://www.nytimes.com/2011/10/26/opinion/26iht-edauslin26.html?_r=0.

24. See Donald Emmerson, ed., *The Deer and the Dragon: China and Southeast Asia in the Era of Reform* (forthcoming).

25. See David E. Sanger, "North Koreans Unveil New Plant for Nuclear Use," *New York Times*, November 20, 2010, http://www.nytimes.com/2010/11/21/world/ asia/21intel.html?_r=0; and Siegfried S. Hecker, "A Return Trip to North Korea's Yongbyon Nuclear Complex," Center for International Security and Cooperation, Stanford University, November 10, 2010, http://iis-db.stanford.edu/pubs/23035/ HeckerYongbyon.pdf.

26. See Charles L. Pritchard, *Failed Diplomacy: The Tragic Story of How North Korea Got the Bomb* (Washington, DC: Brookings Institution, 2007), chap. 2.

27. See Scott Snyder and See-Won Byun, "Cheonan and Yeonpyeong: North-east Asian Response to North Korea's Provocations," *RUSI Journal* 156, no. 2 (April–May 2011): 74–81, https://asiafoundation.org/resources/pdfs/201104 SnyderandByun.pdf.

28. For discussion of these agreements, see Tae-Hwan Kwak, "Basic Issues in the Peace Process on the Korean Peninsula," in *The Major Powers of Northeast Asia: Seeking Peace and Security*, ed. Tae-Hwan Kwak and Edward A. Olsen (Boulder, CO: Lynne Rienner, 1996), chap. 10.

29. For typical North Korean characterization, see "DPRK Exposes True Colors of US-South Korean Alliance," *KCNA*, March 31, 2015, http://www.kcna.co.jp/ item/2015/201503/news31/20150331-24ee.html.

30. See Malcolm Moore, "China Rewrites History of Korean War," *The Telegraph*, June 25, 2010, http://www.telegraph.co.uk/news/worldnews/asia/south korea/7853746/China-rewrites-history-of-Korean-War.html.

31. During the ten years of the Kim Dae-jung and Roh Moo-hyun administrations (1998–2008), Seoul provided North Korea with economic assistance totaling $6.9 billion, including $2.9 billion in cash.

32. See, for example, Willy Lam, "Beijing's Stance on North Korea Challenged by Yeonpyeong Island Incident," *China Brief* 10, no. 24 (December 3, 2010): http://www.jamestown.org/single/?tx_ttnews%5Btt_news%5D=37242&no _cache=1#.VYRz7uuTTlc.

33. See, for example, the polling data in *South Koreans and the Neighbors, 2015* (Seoul: Asan Institute for Policy Studies, 2015), http://sinonk.com/2014/05/15/yongusil-34-kei-panel-on-public-opinion-in-south-korea/.

34. See Choe Sang-Hun, "South Korea Repeats Call to Investigate Torture Claim," *New York Times*, July 31, 2012, http://www.nytimes.com/2012/08/01/world/asia/seoul-demands-that-china-respond-to-torture-allegation.html.

35. See South Korea and China Form Strategic Partnership," *The Hankyoreh*, May 28, 2008, http://english.hani.co.kr/arti/english_edition/e_international/290102.html.

EIGHT

Geography and Destiny
DPRK Concerns and Objectives with Respect to China

Thomas Fingar and David Straub

Even in today's world, geography creates and constrains the options of people and their institutions everywhere. Powerful neighbors can provide protection, but their strength also makes them a potential—if not necessarily actual—source of danger. Wealthy neighbors can provide markets for indigenous goods and capital for domestic projects, but greater wealth also gives them the capacity to limit the options and foster the dependence of their less prosperous neighbors. The potential benefits and perils of living next to a powerful and wealthy country are magnified when that neighbor is many times larger, has cities with larger populations than one's entire country, and historically treated neighbors as vassal states. For millennia, China has been just such a looming presence and inescapable fact of life for Koreans that cannot be ignored and that always must be managed.[1]

Although "China" is an ever-present factor in Korean security calculations and judgments about how best to pursue Korea's national interests, the ways in which China affects Korean perceptions and policies vary over time. The most important causes of the variance are the situation in China, the situation in North and/or South Korea, and the perceived situation in the international system. This generalization applies to both the Republic of Korea (ROK, or South Korea) and the Democratic People's Republic of Korea (DPRK, or North Korea); this chapter focuses on the DPRK.

This chapter examines DPRK thinking and actions in response to changes in the international system and China's moves to achieve its own security and developmental goals.

Geography and situational variables shape DPRK concerns and objectives with respect to China, but perceptions of what is necessary and what is possible are also influenced by history and personalities. Stated another way, the lens through which DPRK officials view developments and assess possibilities magnifies, reduces, or distorts the significance of particular developments, and it is shaped by perceived lessons from history and the idiosyncratic views of particular leaders. Each of these observations is developed at greater length in the pages that follow.

Setting the Stage

China and Korea are contiguous countries with boundaries that have changed many times over the past millennium, not to mention in the more distant past. Korean culture has been strongly influenced by China, and for long periods the leaders of the Chinese empire considered Korea a vassal state. But Koreans do not now and never did consider themselves to be Chinese, and, in fact, linguistically, culturally, and governmentally, they are clearly distinct peoples. Moreover, the tremendous disparity in size between the two has made Koreans fiercely protective of their identity and their autonomy. Most of the time, Koreans regarded their huge neighbor to the west as the greatest challenge to their national integrity. At other times, they have considered it prudent to solicit China's support and protection, but their gratitude was always tempered by concern about Chinese intentions.[2] That remains true today.

Disparity in size and the long history of real and imagined Chinese attempts to dominate the Korean Peninsula influence the way Chinese and Koreans view and interact with one another. The net result is that DPRK officials are always wary of and often worried about the actions and intentions of their Chinese counterparts. Ritualistic declarations on both sides that the relationship is "as close as lips and teeth" do little to assuage North Korean concern that China's pursuit of its own interests could have undesirable consequences for the DPRK. Pyongyang often finds it difficult to determine whether adverse implications are merely the result of Beijing's disregard for its interests or represent a deliberate intent to pressure and constrain.[3] The problem is so endemic and the implications so consequential that DPRK officials devote much time and attention to anticipating, forestalling, and responding to what they perceive as harmful decisions by

Beijing.[4] As a result, they need to know more, and do know more, about China than they know about any other country.

Geography and history are thus fundamental and omnipresent, but they are not the only factors that shape DPRK perceptions of and policies toward China. To a degree that may be unequaled anywhere else in the modern world, DPRK perceptions and policies have also been shaped by the personalities, experiences, and priorities of the three men who have headed the Kim family regime since the DPRK's founding: Kim Il Sung (ruled 1948–1994), Kim Jong Il (ruled 1994–2011), and Kim Jong Un (ruled 2011–present).[5] All three presided over, ruled through, and were constrained by individuals and institutions with stakes and experiences in the relationship with China. But this institutional or systemic ballast has generally been less decisive than the wishes and whims of North Korea's three paramount leaders.[6]

The DPRK's relations with China are also shaped by high politics and geopolitics involving interests and actors beyond the peninsula. Pyongyang's ability to manage its relationship with the People's Republic of China (PRC) changed fundamentally when Beijing broke with Moscow in the late 1950s and again when the Soviet Union ceased to exist in 1992. Other important changes include Beijing's increasing dependence on the United States after adoption of Deng Xiaoping's reform and opening policy in 1978 and China's increasingly important economic relationship with the Republic of Korea, especially since diplomatic relations were established with Seoul in 1992.[7] These and similar developments changed the priorities of other nations and the range of possibilities within which DPRK leaders had to manage the relationship with China.[8]

The remainder of this chapter examines the influence and interplay of recent history, the roles of key individuals, geopolitical developments that have shaped China's behavior toward the DPRK, and DPRK efforts to take advantage of its relationship with China without suffering constriction of its autonomy, much less the loss of its unique political system.

Past Events That Shaped Later Decisions and Perceptions

History—or, more accurately, historical memory—affects current perceptions and decisions in both general and specific ways. The overarching impact of history on Korean perceptions and expectations about China was noted earlier and can be summarized as a persistent wariness and determination to minimize vulnerability to Chinese pressure and blandishments. This general or "background" impact of historical memory has been reinforced by a series of specific developments in China, in the DPRK, and in DPRK-China relations. The next few pages summarize some of the most important ones.

INDEPENDENT ORIGINS AND OBJECTIVES

North Korea's "socialist" ruling party and the system it leads has both indigenous and external origins, but Korean nationalism and Kim Il Sung's triumph over rival individuals and factions during the decade from 1946 to 1956 increased both the independence of the regime and the determination of its leaders to resist efforts by Moscow or Beijing to influence the DPRK. Concern about attempts to constrain and manipulate the Korean Worker's Party and the DPRK was based on more than mere paranoia. Groups of Korean communists had spent time in Russia and China during the anti-Japanese war and immediately after the war, and both Stalin and Mao Zedong had dispatched members of these groups to North Korea to protect Soviet and Chinese interests during the establishment of a regime there. Although Kim Il Sung had served militarily under both the Chinese and the Soviets, he was not a member of either the pro-Soviet faction or the pro-Chinese "Yanan" faction. In fact, he regarded the members of both as agents of influence of the Soviet Union and communist China and a threat to his own authority.[9]

Kim's conviction that China and the Soviet Union had different priorities from his own and were willing to subordinate Korean goals to their own interests was reinforced by Stalin and Mao's reluctance to support his plan to reunify Korea by military means. Although Kim ultimately won the consent of Stalin, who in turn pressed Mao to acquiesce, the experience doubtless reinforced his wariness about them and underlay his reluctance to comply with later requests from Moscow and Beijing that he judged inimical to North Korea's own interests.[10]

CHINESE ASSISTANCE DURING THE KOREAN WAR

China's decision to send troops (the "Chinese People's Volunteers") to Korea in October 1950, only one year after the PRC's establishment, saved the Kim Il Sung regime even though that was not the PRC's primary motivation.

Rather, it acted from a perceived need to deter the United States from attacking the PRC, intervening in the Chinese civil war, or using Korea as a base from which to apply military pressure on the PRC. Saving the Kim Il Sung regime was a by-product.[11]

Kim understood this reality and appears to have judged that the best way to enlist China's assistance while deterring Beijing from undertakings inimical to DPRK interests was to frame issues in terms of their prospective impact on China's own priority objectives. He also understood, or quickly discovered, that Mao was prepared to leverage China's heroic sacrifices in the Korean War (more than 180,000 combat deaths) to exercise long-term influence in Pyongyang. National bonds forged and obligations incurred during the Korean War (bonds cemented in blood were and remain important, but they are not sufficient to explain DPRK perceptions of and policies affecting the PRC. Moreover, Kim Il Sung personally learned probably even more important lessons from his interactions with Chinese leaders before and also immediately after the war.

CHINA TEACHES BY NEGATIVE EXAMPLE

China's relative stability and sustained high rates of economic growth during the past two and a half decades are in stark contrast to the situation during the PRC's first three decades and even during the first decade of its period of reform and opening.[12] Similarly, the DPRK's enormous economic problems, especially since the mid-1990s, and the increasingly glaring shortcomings of the Kim family regime may obscure the fact that the North Korean system performed relatively well—indeed, much better than China's—for at least the first two decades of its existence. Thus, North Koreans' current views of China are informed by the memories and assessments of what worked and what did not work well in earlier periods.

In the early 1950s, both the DPRK and China adopted variants of Stalin's "socialism in one country" model of development. This was designed to make each socialist country as economically self-reliant as possible, to avoid becoming dependent on foreign trade and thus vulnerable to external interference. Sometimes called the multiple autarky model, the approach was almost the complete opposite of the liberal order that relied on comparative advantage and resulted in increasing interdependence and what we now refer to as globalization. Pyongyang stuck with the model and made it work reasonably well despite its inherent limitations; in fact, most experts believe that the North's economy performed better than that of the South for the first two decades after the war.[13]

China, however, began to tinker with the model almost immediately and abandoned it completely in the late 1950s.[14] Mao's repeated dramatic policy swings to induce change and better economic performance through mass campaigns and the disruption of state and party mechanisms left China almost as economically poor—and as poorly governed—as it had been on the eve of the communist victory. The contrast between the economic performance of the DPRK and the PRC during the first three decades of their existence was so striking that it would have been amazing if DPRK leaders had not concluded that their system was superior to that of China. Thus, for the North Koreans, the most important lessons to be learned from China's experience were negative ones, that is, practices to avoid.[15]

In the late 1970s, Deng Xiaoping and other Chinese leaders reached similar judgments about the Maoist era and launched China on yet another new path to wealth and power. This time, however, they eschewed experimentation in favor of emulating Japan's proven path to economic success.[16] Key elements included abandonment of the quest for autarky inherent in both the Stalinist and Maoist models of development, and the pursuit of positive relationships with the United States and its free-world partners.

The DPRK's leaders, however, took a jaundiced view of the PRC's new, pragmatic course, for two major reasons. First, it would make China more dependent on external actors in general. Kim Il Sung probably saw that as unwise even for China, but he almost certainly regarded it as completely inappropriate—indeed, dangerous—for the DPRK. The model Deng decided to pursue was not only fundamentally incompatible with Kim's *Juche* ideology of political independence, economic self-sustenance, and military self-reliance; it would also greatly increase Pyongyang's vulnerability to outside pressure and interference.[17] Second, Kim regarded Deng's path negatively because it was predicated on an improvement of relations with, and greater dependence on, the United States and Japan. Beijing was tying its fate to North Korea's enemies in a way that potentially increased the incentives for China to sacrifice DPRK interests. Moreover, there was no certainty that Deng's strategy would be more successful than China's previous experiments. Kim may not have been overly concerned about a potential policy failure that could leave his huge neighbor weaker and thus less capable of putting pressure on Pyongyang, but he would have been concerned that

desperation for success would incline Beijing to make additional concessions to the United States and Japan that could jeopardize DPRK interests,
security, and stability.

INDIVIDUALS MATTER

Geography and history are ever-present variables, but individuals and institutions always mediate their impact on perceptions and policy. In the
DPRK's case, such mediation is disproportionately in the hands and minds
of a tiny elite dominated by the head of the Kim family dynasty.[18] Throughout his life and military and political careers, Kim Il Sung interacted ex-
tensively with Chinese leaders. Different experiences and different contexts
sometimes caused his son and grandson to perceive and prescribe differently
than Kim Il Sung, even though their overarching considerations remained
essentially the same. In other words, all three were wary of and worried by
China, but they were concerned about different things and adopted different methods to address their concerns and the perceived threats to DPRK
interests.

Kim Il Sung understood but did not trust the Chinese. His confidence
that he understood Chinese thinking was based on his personal experience
as a member of the Chinese Communist Party (which he joined after the
Communist Party of Korea was expelled from the Comintern for being too
nationalistic), residence in China, and fluency in the Chinese language. He
knew Mao, Deng, and many other Chinese leaders from their days in the
anti-Japanese struggle. Like most of them, he was a nationalist first and an
internationalist second.[19] He put Korean interests ahead of abstractions like
proletarian internationalism and knew that his Chinese counterparts did as
well. This, in Kim's view, made the Chinese predicable; they would always
do what was in China's interest, and it would be foolish to pretend, or imagine, otherwise.

Kim's personal relationships with Chinese leaders were reinforced positively by their bond of blood forged during the Korean War and negatively
by their mutual recognition that each could seriously trouble the other. This
provided a floor to their ties, preventing a break and limiting deterioration
even when relations were badly strained. But again, both sides understood
the hard reality of the relationship. Over-the-top rhetoric about the nature of ties between the people, parties, and governments of China and the
DPRK glossed over substantive disagreements. Nevertheless, most of the

time each side was relatively confident that its counterpart would not intentionally jeopardize the interests of the other.

The Chinese understood, but did not like, Kim's use of the Soviet Union to pressure and constrain them. During the period 1949–1959, a decade of basically good relations between Moscow and Beijing, Kim exploited China's dependence on the Soviet Union for protection and assistance. He enlisted Moscow to pressure China to support DPRK undertakings, most notably in advance of and during the Korean War. After the Sino-Soviet rift, which was very unsettling to Pyongyang, Kim first sided with Beijing but later achieved rapprochement with Moscow so that he could continue to employ the classic techniques of balance of power and strategic triangle to protect and advance DPRK interests. He tilted further toward Moscow after the PRC normalized relations with the United States in 1979 as part of Deng's effort to use Washington as a strategic counterweight against Moscow as well as to secure American support for China's new developmental strategy.[20] Thus, when the Soviet Union ceased to exist in 1992, Kim had to develop a new strategy.

When Kim Il Sung died in 1994, his son, Kim Jong Il, succeeded him. Like his father, Kim Jong Il distrusted the Chinese, but unlike his father, he appears to have profoundly disliked the Chinese.[21] Kim Jong Il grew up as a possible heir to absolute power and thus was not in a position to have the intense relationships with Chinese that his father had had as a young man. Growing up as possible heir, Kim Jong Il was probably also more sensitive to perceived Chinese slights than his commoner father had been at the same age. Pyongyang's feeling of betrayal when China recognized the ROK in 1992 doubtless exacerbated Kim Jong Il's reasons for distrusting the Chinese.[22] This difference in background between father and son in regard to China made it difficult for Kim Jong Il's subordinates to manage the relationship with China on a day-to-day basis.

Unfortunately for Kim Jong Il, he ascended to power just as the DPRK economy shifted from slow decline to desperate straits. In the mid-1990s, a devastating famine arose due to the DPRK's command economy and autarkic policies and the end of fraternal socialist aid and trade following the collapse of the Soviet bloc, exacerbated by the coincidence of serious flooding and drought.[23] Industrial production also crashed. In the 1960s and 1970s, when Mao's policies created or worsened famine and economic deprivation in China, the DPRK had provided assistance. Thus, North Korea's economic distress in the mid-1990s contrasted mightily with China's sustained double-digit growth. By this time, the viability and success of Deng's reform and opening policy was undeniable. Indeed, in 1994 China's per capita gross domestic product surpassed that of North Korea for the first time.

Kim Jong Il's dislike of the Chinese may also have been fueled by pressure from Beijing to adopt Chinese-style economic reforms.[24] Although Chinese officials probably genuinely believed that it would be beneficial to the DPRK to reform and open up its economy, pressing the DPRK to do so in the midst of extreme economic problems while it was still adjusting to the demise of the Soviet Union and the loss of a reliable strategy to counterbalance the PRC was not well received in Pyongyang. Indeed, China's actions and approach were particularly grating because North Korea did not even criticize China, much less call for policy change, when the shoe had been on the other foot in earlier decades.

Kim Jong Il's unhappiness about Chinese pressure may have been exacerbated by the too-slow realization of benefits from a new policy approach adopted by his father in 1991. Reduced to its essentials, the policy called for improving relations with the United States to counterbalance risks resulting from China's success as well as the greater uncertainty about Soviet intentions.[25] Kim may also have felt an economic incentive to improve relations with the United States so the DPRK could follow something like Deng's path to prosperity.

Kim Il Sung began, and Kim Jong Il continued, a two-track strategy to address DPRK security requirements, including perceived threats from China. One track was to pursue the acquisition of an independent nuclear weapon capability that would give Pyongyang, they felt, the ability to deflect pressures from the United States, China, the ROK, Japan, and any other potential adversary. The second track was diplomatic: an effort to seek better relations with the United States as a way to counterbalance the PRC and to induce Washington to remove sanctions against the DPRK and distance itself from its South Korean ally.

When the Kims initiated this strategy in the early 1990s, it would have been difficult to predict which track, the nuclear or the diplomatic, was likelier to succeed, hence the pursuit of both. The DPRK's willingness to abandon the nuclear weapon program completely in exchange for a peace treaty and normal relations with the United States seemed unlikely but not impossible, at least until it became clear to the North that it could acquire nuclear weapons. Indeed, Kim Jong Il pursued the two-track strategy for more than a decade before it became clear that early normalization of relations with the United States was unlikely and that the DPRK could soon have a nuclear weapon.

The DPRK's successful detonation of nuclear devices in tests beginning in 2006 changed the equation decisively and prompted Kim Jong Il to adjust the North's strategy for managing the threat from China. The new strategy is described more fully later in this chapter, but the key elements were to address the North's severe economic problems through greater reliance on the PRC while continuing to eschew fundamental reform or opening to the outside world, and attempting to limit the risks of dependence on China by making clear to Beijing that Pyongyang was prepared to put at risk the continued success of China's own strategy to achieve power and influence through sustained growth if Beijing acted in ways contrary to DPRK interests.

After Kim Jong Il suffered a stroke in 2008, Pyongyang accelerated plans for the succession of Kim Jong Un.[26] Those plans included locking in the new China strategy while Kim Jong Il was still at the helm. A key feature of the new China strategy was the North's willingness to accept much greater Chinese involvement in the DPRK economy than ever before and the abandonment of efforts to counterbalance Chinese influence by improving relations with the United States. Thus, Kim Jong Il visited China many times over the following two years, including making a journey through northeastern China that retraced some of his father's footsteps.[27] China responded with alacrity to the new opportunities to build cross-border infrastructure and develop DPRK resources for export to the PRC. By the time of Kim Jong Il's death in December 2011, bilateral relations had rebounded and were quite good.

Kim Jong Un inherited his father's policy intended to increase DPRK prosperity and facilitate their transfer of power. The younger Kim does not appear to have tampered with the policy itself, but developments caused Pyongyang's relations with the PRC to deteriorate rapidly. In early 2012, just four months after the leadership succession, the North launched a long-range Taepodong-2 missile in violation of sanctions imposed by the UN Security Council after the North's initial nuclear tests in 2006 and 2009. China did not support new sanctions but did concur with a statement by the president of the Security Council censuring the launch.[28] China did, however, support additional sanctions after the DPRK tested a third nuclear device in 2013, an action that likely carried greater weight in Pyongyang than accompanying statements by Beijing that it would not forsake the North.[29]

From Pyongyang's perspective, Beijing compounded its affront to the DPRK by refusing to invite new leader Kim Jong Un to visit Beijing. Even worse, president and party leader Xi Jinping hosted a state visit by ROK president Park Geun-hye, and Xi later visited Seoul but has yet to visit the DPRK.[30] The symbolic importance of the visits—and the refusal to accept or make official visits—is clear, but the underlying causes are not. Much more is involved than personal pique or simple disapproval of specific actions by one side or the other. The best evidence of deeper causes is the execution, in December 2013, of Kim Jong Un's uncle Jang Song Thaek. Jang was widely viewed as "Beijing's man" in Pyongyang and was a key architect of the DPRK's opening to Chinese investment in 2009. His execution, and the litany of charges against him, including thinly veiled criticism of resource sales to China, is at least partially related to Jang's role vis-à-vis China.[31]

High Politics and Geopolitical Developments

Korea is often described by others, and sometimes by Koreans themselves, as a shrimp among whales. North Korean media and officials eschew such language, preferring to emphasize that the DPRK is the equal of or superior to all other nations. Such claims notwithstanding, the major powers in Northeast Asia generally pursue their own interests in and beyond the region with little thought to Pyongyang's interests. Pyongyang understands but resents this and employs a variety of tactics, many of them provocative, to make it more difficult for others to ignore its concerns.

Despite ritualistic declarations of special friendship, North Korean leaders have always believed their Chinese counterparts would sell them out if it were in China's interest to do so. This general conviction acquired new significance in 1978, when Beijing decided to improve relations with the United States to pursue Deng's strategy of reform and opening. Pyongyang had no way of knowing at that point precisely how the shift in PRC policy would affect DPRK interests, but Kim Il Sung recognized at once that if Beijing was willing to abandon Mao's demand for resolution of the "Taiwan issue" before fully normalizing relations with the United States, it would certainly be even less reticent about sacrificing the DPRK.[32] Thereafter, the North's foreign and security policies evolved iteratively in response to developments in several arenas.

One stream of developments shaping DPRK calculations was the steady expansion and intensification of relations between China and the United States. What began as a partnership of convenience to counter and contain the Soviet Union evolved into a multifaceted relationship in which the success of China's modernization strategy and the legitimacy of its party rule were increasingly dependent on maintaining good relations with the United States. The more China needed the United States to achieve its own priorities, the less likely it would be to defend the DPRK or its interests if doing so might jeopardize PRC-US ties. Pyongyang's recognition that this was the case meant that it had to develop new strategies to counter both China and the United States.

A second stream of developments occurred in the superpower arena. Moscow's attempts to improve relations with Washington in order to deal with its myriad problems at home and abroad made it increasingly apparent to Pyongyang that it could no longer rely as heavily on the Soviet Union, superpower rivalry, or competition between the Soviet Union and the PRC to protect its interests. The problem became more obvious and more serious after Mikhail Gorbachev became general secretary in 1985. Moscow had not yet done anything that specifically worked to DPRK disadvantage, but Kim Il Sung must have anticipated that the situation was likely to worsen, from his perspective, and concluded that it would be prudent to prepare for the worst. That apparently included pressing ahead with the quest for nuclear weapons.[33]

The third stream of developments affecting DPRK foreign and security policies involved the three major powers and the Republic of Korea. As noted already, during at least the first two decades after the Korean War, the DPRK rebuilt and achieved economic growth more quickly than did the ROK, but the advantage had clearly shifted to the South by the 1980s and the ROK began to pull ahead at an accelerating pace. The combination of DPRK problems and ROK success posed an increasing security problem for Pyongyang at a time when it judged that it must rely less than in the past on assistance from Beijing and Moscow. In addition to growing Chinese and Soviet dependence on the United States, both China and, to a much lesser extent, the Soviet Union increasingly saw the ROK as more important than the DPRK to the success of their own economic strategies. In other words, Pyongyang's longtime benefactors and protectors were beginning to have larger stakes in their relationship with the South than with the North.

Perhaps the clearest manifestation of the changing power dynamics among and policies of North Korea's neighbors was the fact that by 1991 Moscow and Beijing were no longer willing to continue blocking the ROK's admission as a full member of the United Nations. Until then, they had supported Pyongyang's position that neither Korean state should be admitted to the United Nations before reunification.[34] Thus it was that North Korea was left with no choice but to join the United Nations together with the South on September 17, 1991. That watershed development had been preceded by the Soviet Union's establishment of formal diplomatic relations with the ROK on September 30, 1990. By that time, Kim Il Sung had already concluded that Moscow's determination to forge a new relationship with the United States made it impossible for him to rely on Russia for either direct assistance or as a counterweight to the United States and China.[35] Kim also judged that China had become a less reliable protector and more uncertain partner even before it committed the ultimate betrayal, from Pyongyang's perspective, of according diplomatic recognition to the ROK on August 24, 1992.

Taken together, these three streams of developments made North Korea's strategic situation far more difficult and dangerous. Kim Il Sung responded by developing a new, multifaceted strategy to protect DPRK interests. This had both military and diplomatic components. Despite having concluded security treaties with the Soviet Union and the PRC in 1961, Kim Il Sung did not regard either of them as a reliable long-term solution to the DPRK's security problems. His assessment, doubtless shared by others in the leadership, was that the only way for the DPRK to protect itself and its interests was to acquire nuclear weapons and the means to deliver them. Programs to acquire these capabilities were under way before the new strategy was formulated. Although the programs may or may not have been ratcheted up in the early 1990s, the more important fact is that they were continued despite the adoption of a very different diplomatic strategy.

Beginning in 1991, Pyongyang downplayed the "hedgehog" aspects of its security policy, that is, tacit and explicit threats to make it very costly for any nation that attacked the DPRK or threatened its interests. Instead, it launched a charm offensive intended to reduce threats to its security by improving relations with all nations, especially its most dangerous adversaries. The most dangerous, in Pyongyang's view, was the United States. But improving relations with the United States was likely also to be the most difficult part of the strategy because of the magnitude of mutual hostility and the determination of Washington to foil DPRK attempts to drive a wedge between itself and its ROK ally. To some extent, Pyongyang recognized this and decided to take the even more politically unpalatable step of seeking to improve its relations with the South.

Inter-Korean rapprochement efforts began in 1991, slowly at first but accelerating to culminate in a series of bilateral agreements in late 1991 and early 1992 that included the Joint Declaration on the Denuclearization of the Korean Peninsula.[36] There were also symbolic but important developments, such as references to the official title of the ROK president. Unfortunately, relations soon soured. Major progress did not occur again until the inauguration of ROK president Kim Dae-jung's "sunshine policy" in 1998. The years since have been marked by swings between apparent progress and retrogression in inter-Korean relations, but Pyongyang's basic strategy of modulated rapprochement adopted in 1991 appears to be still in effect, albeit on hold as Kim Jong Un consolidates his position at home. Implementing that strategy has been made considerably more difficult by the North's nuclear detonations, missile tests, and murderous attacks on the South, and by great swings in ROK policy toward the North depending on whether the Blue House was occupied by progressives or conservatives.

Despite—or perhaps because of—the failure of the two Korea's to improve their relations significantly, the DPRK decided to seek a new, less hostile relationship with the United States. The centerpiece of the new relationship was supposed to be the 1994 Agreed Framework to freeze the North's indigenous nuclear program in exchange for US-facilitated construction of light-water reactor power plants.[37] To what extent the North intended to honor that agreement (or the joint declaration concluded with the ROK) is uncertain. It may always have depended on the interplay between progress toward the bomb and progress on the diplomatic front, but Kim Jong Il appears to have regarded the Agreed Framework as the first step toward a peace treaty and a more normal relationship with the United States.

To the DPRK, normal relations with the United States (i.e., a peace treaty ending the Korean War and formal diplomatic relations signifying that Washington fully accepted the DPRK's legitimacy) would enhance its security in several ways. Perhaps most important, it would reduce the perceived danger that the United States and its ROK ally would use either soft or hard means to oust the regime and achieve reunification by force. In the absence of what it considered an adequate independent deterrent (even though its thousands of artillery tubes arrayed just across the Demilitarized Zone from Seoul effectively constituted weapons of mass destruction) and reliable support from its own allies, this was a high priority for Pyongyang. Another DPRK objective in seeking normal relations with the United States was to counterbalance real and expected pressures from Beijing and reduce the danger that China would act against DPRK interests to placate Washington.[38]

Pyongyang's desire to counterbalance China, which was becoming more worrisome both because of Beijing's expanding power and influence and its increasing economic dependence on states hostile to the DPRK, also contributed to Pyongyang's decision to seek better relations with Japan. This decision may have been almost as unpalatable as the one to improve relations with the ROK, because of the strength of anti-Japanese sentiment in the North and the central role of the anti-Japanese struggle in the official mythology of the DPRK. It was made more palatable by the prospect of reparations on a scale similar to what the South had received as de facto compensation for Japan's forty-year colonialization and the presumed effect that normalization of DPRK-Japan relations would have on China.

Pyongyang assessed that, like the ROK, Japan coveted access to its resources and cheap and disciplined labor force. It thus hoped that normalized relations with both South Korea and Japan would lead to competition between them for access, which the North could exploit to obtain more favorable terms with fewer demands for reform than were being offered by the PRC. This would enable the North to open its own economy in ways that limited its dependence on China or any other single country. As noted already, Beijing had been pressing Pyongyang for years to adopt its own variant of China's reform and opening policy. Among the reasons the North was reluctant to do so was that, absent better relations with other countries, "opening up" would expose the DPRK to greater dependence on China than it wanted to incur.

The strategy adopted in 1991 also had a modest economic reform component, and there were episodic attempts to alter the balance between civilian and military industry, consumer and producer goods, and reliance on plans and markets.[39] But these attempts all proved ineffective and short lived, in part because they were not matched by increased engagement with other countries. In other words, for the reforms to gain traction by producing tangible benefits, they had to be linked to external markets and sources of technology, capital, and training. That, in turn, required greater success with the diplomatic strands of the strategy than the DPRK was prepared or able to achieve.

Despite only limited success, Kim Jong Il stuck with this strategy for almost two decades. It failed because the United States was never prepared to normalize relations with the DPRK on terms equivalent to those applied earlier to China, that is, engagement without regime change or abandonment of nuclear weapons. The discovery in 2002 that the DPRK had not abandoned its quest for the bomb, followed by the North's tests of nuclear devices in 2006 and 2009, caused Washington to abandon whatever lingering hope it had that Pyongyang might trade its nuclear weapons program for diplomatic recognition and economic assistance.

By 2015, China was looming ever larger on the DPRK's political radar. Sustained economic success had made China even wealthier, stronger, more influential, and in greater need of ensured access to resources available, among other places, in the DPRK. It had also changed public opinion in the PRC, making PRC leaders more attentive to China's international image.[40] None of these changes boded well for the DPRK. General discomfort about Chinese attitudes and intentions were given specific focus by Beijing's reaction to the North's nuclear and missile tests, especially its acquiescence to UN Security Council resolutions condemning and penalizing the DPRK.[41] At the same time, the North was becoming more dependent on fuel and food from China and less optimistic about possibilities to balance Chinese influence and demands by improving relations with the United States, Japan, and the ROK. In an act of geopolitical desperation, Pyongyang again tilted toward Moscow.[42]

Reduced to its essentials, the strategy Pyongyang adopted in 2009 calls for maintaining its nuclear "deterrent," increasing China's economic stake in the DPRK by permitting substantially more Chinese investment, and constraining China's scope for punitive measures against the DPRK by threatening provocations that jeopardize the peaceful international environment Beijing has declared necessary for its own strategy to succeed. In other words, the DPRK's current strategy, of necessity, depends on its ability to manage its much larger neighbor without reliance on other countries.[43]

Conclusion

Today, perhaps more than ever, Pyongyang is caught on the horns of a dilemma. Lacking reliable allies or normal relations with the countries it considers its most dangerous adversaries, it regards nuclear weapons as essential not only to its continued security but also to its very survival. But retention of nuclear weapons and the capability to produce them constitutes the greatest and most insuperable obstacle to the normalization of its relationships with other countries, the achievement of which would reduce the perceived threat they pose and also allow the DPRK to reduce its extreme external dependence on China. As a result, the gravest danger of all to the DPRK is that China will decide at some point that its own interests would be best served by curtailing aid and basic support for Pyongyang in an effort to force it to surrender its nuclear capabilities. Such a decision would certainly result in the DPRK's economic stagnation and could put its very survival at risk.

Notes

1. See, for example, Kyung Moon Hwang, *A History of Korea* (New York: Palgrave Macmillan, 2010).

2. See, for example, Evelyn S. Rawski, *Early Modern China and Northeast Asia: Cross-Border Perspectives* (Cambridge: Cambridge University Press, 2015).

3. See, for example, Ming Lee, "North Korea's China Policy," in *North Korea's Foreign Policy Under Kim Jong Il: New Perspectives*, ed. Tae-Hwan Kwak and Seung-Ho Joo (Burlington, VT: Ashgate Publishing, 2009), 161–178.

4. This judgment and others in the chapter that are not ascribed to a source should be read as analytical assessments rather than as statements of fact.

5. See, for example, Dae-Sook Suh, *Kim Il Sung: The North Korean Leader* (New York: Columbia University Press, 1988); and John H. Cha, with K. J. Sohn, *Exit Emperor Kim Jong Il* (Bloomington, IN: Abbott Press, 2012).

6. Bradley K. Martin, *Under the Loving Care of the Fatherly Leader: North Korea and the Kim Dynasty* (New York: Thomas Dunne, 2004).

7. See, for example, Andrei Lankov, "North Korea and the Fall of the Soviet Union and the Soviet Satellite States," in *Troubled Transition: North Korea's Politics, Economy, and External Relations*, ed. Choe Sang-Hun, Gi-Wook Shin, and David

Straub (Stanford, CA: Walter H. Shorenstein Asia-Pacific Research Center, Stanford University, 2013), chap. 12.

8. See Don Oberdorfer and Robert Carlin, *The Two Koreas: A Contemporary History*, 3rd ed. (New York: Basic Books, 2014).

9. See James F. Person, "New Evidence on North Korea in 1956," *Cold War International History Project Bulletin*, no. 16 (2007–2008): 447–454, http://www.wilsoncenter.org/sites/default/files/CWIHPBulletin16_p5_1.pdf.

10. Sergei N. Goncharov, John W. Lewis, and Xue Litai, *Uncertain Partners: Stalin, Mao, and the Korean War* (Stanford, CA: Stanford University Press, 1993).

11. Ibid.; and Allen Whiting, *China Crosses the Yalu: The Decision to Enter the Korean War* (Stanford, CA: Stanford University Press, 1960), 151–162.

12. See Andrew G. Walder, *China Under Mao: A Revolution Derailed* (Cambridge, MA: Harvard University Press, 2015).

13. Charles K. Armstrong, *The Koreas*, 2nd ed. (New York: Routledge, 2014).

14. Walder, *China Under Mao.*

15. See, for example, "The DPRK Attitude Toward the So-Called 'Cultural Revolution' in China," March 7, 1967, Wilson Center Digital Archive, http://digitalarchive.wilsoncenter.org/document/114570.pdf?v=9100c07716552633cc2ca1f1 57a64f9e.

16. Ezra F. Vogel, *Deng Xiaoping and the Transformation of China* (Cambridge, MA: Belknap Press of Harvard University Press, 2011).

17. See Jae-Jung Suh, *Origins of North Korea's Juche* (Plymouth, UK: Lexington Books, 2013).

18. Kim Hakjoon, *Dynasty: The Hereditary Succession Politics of North Korea* (Stanford, CA: Walter H. Shorenstein Asia-Pacific Research Center, Stanford University, 2015).

19. Suh, *Kim Il Sung*, chap. 1.

20. Yongho Kim, *North Korean Foreign Policy: Security Dilemma and Succession* (Plymouth, UK: Lexington Books, 2011), chap. 3.

21. See, for example, Jang Jin-sung, *Dear Leader: My Escape from North Korea* (New York: Atria, 2014). Deng Xiaoping's opposition to hereditary succession might also have contributed to Kim Jong Il's personal antipathy. See Adam Cathcart and Charles Kraus, "China's 'Measure of Reserve' Towards Succession: Sino-North Korean Relations, 1983–1985," *SinoNK.com China-North Korea Dossier*, no. 2 (February 2012): http://sinonk.com/wp-content/uploads/2012/02/sinonk _dossier_no_2.pdf.

22. Oberdorfer and Carlin, *Two Koreas*, 194–195.

23. See Andrew S. Natsios, "North Korea's Chronic Food Problem," in *Troubled Transition: North Korea's Politics, Economy, and External Relations*, ed. Choe

Sang-Hun, Gi-Wook Shin, and David Straub (Stanford, CA: Walter H. Shorenstein Asia-Pacific Research Center, Stanford University, 2013), chap. 6.

24. Ian Rinehart, "Nothing to Be Afraid Of?" *Joint US-Korea Academic Studies: Emerging Voices* 22 (2011): 7–20.

25. Oberdorfer and Carlin, *Two Koreas*, chap. 11.

26. Brent Choi and Mi Jeong Hibbitts, "North Korea's Succession May Go Smoothly After All," Nautilus Institute, 2011, http://nautilus.org/napsnet/napsnet -policy-forum/north-koreas-succession-may-go-smoothly-after-all/.

27. Thomas Fingar, "China's Growing Presence in the DPRK: Origins, Objectives, and Implications," in *Troubled Transition: North Korea's Politics, Economy, and External Relations*, ed. Choe Sang-Hun, Gi-Wook Shin, and David Straub (Stanford, CA: Walter H. Shorenstein Asia-Pacific Research Center, Stanford University, 2013), chap. 9.

28. Choe Sang-Hun, "UN Council to Expand North Korea Sanctions," *New York Times*, April 16, 2012, http://www.nytimes.com/2012/04/17/world/asia/north -korea-sanctions-expanded-by-united-nations.html?_r=0.

29. Jan Perlez, "China Says It Won't Forsake North Korea, Despite Support for UN Sanctions," *New York Times*, March 9, 2013, http://www.nytimes.com/ 2013/03/10/world/asia/china-says-it-will-not-abandon-north-korea.html.

30. See Zhao Jinglun, "Park Geun-hye Fever Sweeps China," *China.org.cn*, July 1, 2013, http://www.china.org.cn/opinion/2013-07/01/content_29281001.htm; Shannon Tiezzi, "No, Kim Jong Un's Not Visiting China (Yet)," *The Diplomat*, September 17, 2014, http://www.nytimes.com/2014/07/03/world/asia/chinas -president-to-visit-south-korea.html; and Jane Perlez, "Chinese President's Visit to South Korea Is Seen as Way to Weaken US Alliances," *New York Times*, July 2, 2014, http://www.nytimes.com/2014/07/03/world/asia/chinas-president-to-visit -south-korea.html.

31. See "Full Text of KCNA Announcement on Execution of Jang, Korean Central News Agency, December 13, 2013, http://www.northkoreatech.org/2013/12/ 13/full-text-of-kcna-announcement-on-execution-of-jang/.

32. Mao agreed to finesse Taiwan issues in the Shanghai Communiqué issued by Chinese premier Zhou Enlai and US president Richard Nixon in 1972, but Beijing maintained a firm position that prevented full normalization until 1978, when Deng Xiaoping decided that obtaining US support for China's policy of reform and opening was more important than an early resolution of Taiwan-related issues. See Henry Kissinger, *On China* (New York: Penguin, 2011), 267–274; and Vogel, *Deng Xiaoping*, chap. 11.

33. See Jonathan D. Pollack, *No Exit: North Korea, Nuclear Weapons and International Security* (New York: Routledge, 2011), chaps. 3–4.

34. Oberdorfer and Carlin, *Two Koreas*, 184–189; and Scott Snyder, *China's Rise and the Two Koreas* (Boulder, CO: Lynne Rienner, 2009), 34–37.

35. Sergey Radchenko, "Russia's Policy in the Run-Up to the First North Korean Nuclear Crisis, 1991–1993," Wilson Center, February 2015, http://www .wilsoncenter.org/publication/russias-policy-the-run-to-the-first-north-korean -nuclear-crisis-1991-1993.

36. Oberdorfer and Carlin, *Two Koreas*, 203–205.

37. See Joel S. Wit, Daniel B. Poneman, and Robert L. Gallucci, *Going Critical: The First North Korean Nuclear Crisis* (Washington, DC: Brookings Institution, 2004).

38. This argument is further developed in Thomas Fingar, "China's Goals in South Asia," in *The New Great Game: China and South and Central Asia in the Era of Reform*, ed. Thomas Fingar (Stanford, CA: Stanford University Press, 2016), 29–52.

39. See Robert L. Carlin and Joel Wit, *North Korean Reform: Politics, Economics and Security* (New York: Routledge, 2006).

40. See Jan Perlez, "Chinese Annoyance with North Korea Bubbles to the Surface," *New York Times*, December 20, 2014, http://www.nytimes.com/2014/12/21/ world/asia/chinese-annoyance-with-north-korea-bubbles-to-the-surface.html.

41. For list and texts of UN Security Council Resolutions and Presidential Statements criticizing DPRK actions, see UN Documents for DPRK (North Korea) at http://www.securitycouncilreport.org/un-documents/dprk-north-korea/.

42. See Georgy Toloraya, "Russia-North Korea Economic Ties Gain Traction," *38 North*, November 6, 2014, http://38north.org/2014/11/toloraya110614/; and Doug Bandow, "Friends with Benefits: Russia and North Korea's Twisted Tango," *National Interest*, March 6, 2015, http://nationalinterest.org/feature/friends-bene fits-russia-north-koreas-twisted-tango-12369.

43. This is developed at greater length in Fingar, "China's Growing Presence in the DPRK."

NINE

Soviet/Russian-China Relations
Coming Full Circle?

Artyom Lukin

For most of their history, Russia and China were separated—and for long periods subjugated—by nomadic tribes and the Mongol empire of Genghis Khan and his successors. The Mongols arguably had greater influence on both than either had on one another. This situation began to change in the seventeenth century, when the Russian empire expanded to the borders of China.[1] In a relatively short time, limited commercial contacts evolved into an imperial rivalry that tipped heavily in Russia's favor in the nineteenth century, when China was forced to cede vast territories to Russia during what the Chinese describe as the "century of humiliation."[2] The relationship was one of a dominant imperialistic power and a decaying empire until shortly after the communist victory in the October Revolution of 1917, when Moscow, via the Comintern, took a more active role in Chinese politics by supporting both the Nationalists, or Guomindang (Nationalist Party) of Sun Yat-sen, and later Chiang Kai-shek, and the Communist Party of Mao Zedong.[3]

Both countries declared that their relationship entered an entirely new stage in 1949, when the Chinese Communist Party (CCP) defeated the Guomindang and Mao proclaimed the People's Republic of China (PRC) on October 1. On the following day, the Soviet Union became the first nation to recognize the new government of China. The CCP had achieved

---

This chapter examines Soviet/Russian perceptions of China's rise and the implications for Moscow's economic and security interests.

victory in the long-running civil war thanks primarily to its own efforts to build a solid base of support among the country's predominantly peasant population and success in claiming credit for Japan's defeat. The Soviet Union did not install the CCP in Beijing, as it had the communist regimes in Eastern Europe, but Soviet support did play a role. For example, after the Red Army accepted the surrender of Japan's Kwantung Army in Manchuria in 1945, Moscow transferred confiscated Japanese weapons to the Chinese communist forces.

The CCP had attained power in China through its own efforts, but to maintain and solidify the new regime by ensuring its external security and jump-starting economic development, it desperately needed a strong partner. The Soviet Union was the only possible choice. Only Moscow was capable of providing security guarantees to counter American hostility, and only the Soviet Union was willing to provide much-needed assistance to rebuild the economy and achieve rapid modernization. The Stalinist model of "socialism in one country" offered a path to rapid recovery and achievement of a self-reliant modern economy that Mao was eager to adopt. Securing an alliance with the Soviet Union was the main purpose of Mao's two-month-long trip to Moscow from December 1949 to February 1950. Joseph Stalin made clear that it was Mao who was the supplicant and seemed in no hurry to start substantive negotiations with China's delegation. That said, Moscow had an enormous stake in the PRC. Without China, the communist bloc would have been limited to just the Soviet Union and the small Eastern European satellites whose communist regimes relied on the Soviet army to maintain their grip on power. Adding Asia's largest, and the world's most populous, country to the communist bloc geopolitically and symbolically strengthened the Soviet position in the incipient global contest with the West.[4] This consideration eventually prevailed over Stalin's less-than-full trust in Mao, whom the Soviet leader suspected of being a Chinese nationalist rather than a communist loyal to the Kremlin.

After weeks of sometimes-difficult negotiations, the Soviet-Chinese Treaty of Alliance, Friendship and Mutual Assistance was finally signed in Moscow on February 14, 1950. Stalin's economic assistance to China was hardly altruistic; China had to repay the loans provided by Moscow, and most of the money had to be used to purchase equipment and weapons from the Soviet Union. In addition, Moscow acquired 50 percent stakes in a number of joint stock companies established in the PRC, including those exploiting valuable natural resources such as oil, uranium, and nonferrous and rare earth metals. By 1952, the Soviet Union accounted for 53.4 percent of China's foreign trade.[5] An important limitation on Soviet economic aid to the PRC was Stalin's determination to limit the pace of China's industrialization; he understood that, if successful, China would soon be able to compete with or even surpass the performance of Soviet industries.[6]

To lock in China's membership in the Soviet-led bloc and preclude any possibility of rapprochement between Beijing and Washington, Stalin encouraged China's participation in the Korean War (1950–1953) while severely limiting direct Soviet involvement in the armed conflict.[7] This cynical game proved a success. Normalization of China's relationship with the United States, which did not seem impossible until the start of the Korean War, was delayed by two decades.[8]

The mid-1950s marked the high point of the Soviet-Chinese alliance. Nikita Khrushchev, who succeeded Stalin after his death in 1953, was much more generous to China than his cynical and calculating predecessor. Soviet financial and technical assistance was used to build or upgrade 156 modern industrial facilities in China. Thousands of Chinese youth received scholarships to study engineering and science in the best Soviet institutions. Moscow surrendered the Soviet shares in joint stock companies and provided substantial assistance in many fields of science and technology (including nuclear physics), and in the building of the People's Liberation Army (PLA) into a more modern force.[9]

Despite Khrushchev's largesse, cracks began to appear in the relationship that was still extolled by officials as "the eternal, unbreakable friendship and cooperation of Soviet and Chinese peoples." The first blow to the alliance came in 1956, when Khrushchev publicly denounced Stalin and exposed some of his political crimes. He did so without consulting with Mao (or with any other communist allies). The rift was exacerbated by increasing disagreements over the theory and practice of communist doctrine. Mao was particularly unhappy about Moscow's inclination to seek "peaceful coexistence" with the West and argued instead for much more robust efforts to spread communism around the world. The alliance was also undermined by a number of developments involving matters of foreign and security policy. Beijing was resentful that the Soviet Union failed to back China in the Taiwan Strait crisis of 1958. Mao was also offended by Moscow's decision to discontinue transferring nuclear technology that Beijing needed to build its atomic bomb. For its part, Moscow was increasingly concerned that the Chinese leadership might draw the Soviet Union into a war with the United States over Taiwan. The alliance failed another test when the Soviet Union refused to support China in its border conflict with India. In a tit-for-tat move, Beijing rejected Moscow's proposals to establish a Soviet naval facility on the Chinese coast and to create a joint Pacific fleet. By 1960, the split came into the open. Khrushchev recalled Soviet technicians and specialists from China, and Beijing and Moscow began a pitched campaign of public recriminations.

Why did Mao behave in a way that risked, and eventually produced, a complete break with the Soviet Union, China's main protector and benefactor? By the late 1950s, the Great Helmsman (Mao) was far more self-confident than he was at the time of his 1949–1950 pilgrimage to meet with Stalin. The CCP position inside China was unchallengeable, the PLA's performance in the Korean War against the Americans bolstered Beijing's confidence in China's ability to deter and defeat external aggression, and the general success of the First Five-Year Plan (1953–1957), especially in heavy industry, was cause to be upbeat about the PRC's economic prospects. China still depended on economic and technical assistance from the Soviet Union, but Mao apparently decided that if obtaining Soviet aid required China to be ideologically and geopolitically subordinate to Moscow, the price was too high. In the first half of the 1950s, Chinese used the slogan "Learn from the Soviet Union!" to describe the relationship; a decade later they declared that the PRC had become the beacon and standard-bearer of the global communist movement.[10]

The rupture in trade and technological ties with the Soviet Union was not without a cost, especially taking into account that China was still isolated from Western markets. However, given the relative autarky and primitive self-sufficiency of the PRC's economy at that stage, the damage was manageable.

Why did the Soviet Union allow the relationship with its most important communist ally to collapse? The Soviet superpower apparently was unwilling to accommodate China's desire for greater equality in the alliance. The Kremlin still saw itself as the only legitimate leader of the world's "progressive forces." Furthermore, Moscow, which strove for stability in its all-important relationship with Washington, was becoming more and more alarmed by China's "recklessness" and "adventurism" in its foreign policies.

China was increasingly viewed as more of a security liability than a strategic asset. In other words, the Soviet Union was unwilling to risk a third world war by yielding to Mao's ambitions. The commercial dimension of the relationship was not insignificant, but, just as in China's case, the Soviet Union was a largely self-contained economic system that could sacrifice links with the PRC at a time when China's economy was vastly inferior to Russia's.[11]

By the mid-1960s, Sino-Soviet conflict had escalated far beyond a mere ideological schism; it had become a full-blown and dangerous geopolitical confrontation. China's use of harsh rhetoric when discussing border issues proved a game-changing development. Even during the honeymoon of Sino-Soviet friendship, many Chinese remembered that the Soviet Union was the successor to tsarist Russia, the country that had used a blend of smart diplomacy and coercion to compel China to cede vast territories in the Amur River basin to Russia in the second half of the nineteenth century. In the 1960s, Chinese feelings of resentment were unleashed; indeed, they were whipped up by CCP leaders. For example, in 1964, Mao announced that China "had yet to settle its account" over territory ceded to tsarist Russia east of Lake Baikal.[12] China's pronouncements on "unjust" border treaties were taken at face value—and extremely seriously—by Moscow. The perceived territorial claims by China aroused the Russians' worst existential fear—the fear of a large-scale land invasion from a neighboring great power. Given the relative vulnerability of the Soviet Far East's land border, linked to the Soviet Union's main core by only tenuous communication lines, the threat from China seemed real and ominous.

The situation on the border grew increasingly tense and precarious, culminating, in 1969, in a bloody clash over Damansky (Zhenbao) Island on the Ussuri River. The two countries appeared to be edging toward war, with Moscow seriously considering preemptive air strikes to take out China's nuclear facilities. Washington made clear to Moscow that it should not make any such moves against China. This was one of the first signs of a coming rapprochement between the United States and the People's Republic. President Richard Nixon visited Beijing in 1972. The US-China alignment against the Soviet Union that took shape in the 1970s was another confirmation to Moscow of Beijing's hostility. The 1978 Sino-Japanese Treaty of Peace and Friendship was viewed with increasing alarm in the Kremlin because it seemed to provide proof of a US-China-Japan coalition encircling the Soviet Union from the east. At the same time, Beijing was worried about the Soviet penetration of Indochina (especially Vietnam) and Moscow's increasingly close strategic ties to India.

By the early 1970s the threat of war between the Soviet Union and the PRC had receded somewhat, but bilateral relations were virtually frozen and tensions still remained high. The Soviet Union was building up its military forces on its Far East border with China and in Mongolia. By the mid-1980s, some five hundred thousand Soviet troops were deployed on the border with China, a force concentration comparable to Soviet deployments in Eastern Europe. Another war scare happened in 1979 when China invaded the border areas of Vietnam, a Soviet ally, and a retaliatory response by Moscow appeared likely.

The Road to Normalization (1982–1991)

The death of Mao Zedong in 1976 did not lead to immediate improvement in Sino-Soviet relations. The fervor of ideological confrontation subsided somewhat, but geopolitical antagonism between the two powers was deeply entrenched. Deng Xiaoping, who became China's de facto leader in 1978, still saw the Soviet Union as the main threat. His top priority was to achieve rapid and sustained economic growth and modernization via a strategy of reform and opening that required dramatic improvement of relations with the West. The Soviet Union had little to contribute to the success of Deng's strategy. By the late 1970s the widening economic and technological gap between the decaying Soviet Union and the postindustrial West had become obvious.[13] However, Beijing was interested in reducing tensions, which led to the beginning of Sino-Soviet talks at the vice-ministerial level in 1979. They broke off after Soviet troops entered Afghanistan in December 1979.

The United States enthusiastically supported Deng's reformist agenda. Washington saw a twin opportunity to encourage China's domestic liberalization and to strengthen Sino-Western geopolitical collaboration against the Soviet Union. In 1979–1981, strategic relations between the United States and China reached their all-time peak. But their limitations were quickly revealed. China was unhappy about America's refusal to sever relations with Taiwan; even though Washington switched formal diplomatic recognition from Taipei to Beijing, the United States continued extensive ties with the island, including the sale of weapons. Beijing was also dissatisfied with what it saw as less than full US support of China's "punitive actions" against Vietnam in 1979. Washington was assisting China's modernization, but Beijing worried about becoming a dependent and junior partner in the political relationship with Washington.[14] This led the Chinese leaders to conclude that Beijing should pursue a more balanced and equidistant policy in the US-China-Soviet triangle. That assessment was supported by diminished perception of the Soviet military threat. After all, for two decades the Soviet Union had not attempted to invade China.[15] Furthermore, Beijing needed a peaceful external environment to focus on economic development and therefore had a stake in the reduction of tensions on its northern border. Moscow, sensing that it could no longer afford a two-front cold war, with the West and China, also wanted to normalize relations with China. Toward that end, Leonid Brezhnev made overtures aimed at confidence building along the Soviet-Chinese border in 1982. In the same year, Beijing and Moscow began diplomatic talks aimed at normalization. The progress was slow, partly because of the internal power transition and generational change in Moscow, which, in 1985, brought Mikhail Gorbachev to power.

Before Gorbachev, the Soviet leaders sought detente with China primarily for balance-of-power reasons. Moscow wanted to concentrate dwindling resources on countering what was perceived to be the greater foe: the United States. Gorbachev's "new thinking," which was the antithesis of realpolitik and distinctly idealistic, sought dramatic improvement of relations in all directions. Reconciliation with the West was the top priority for the Gorbachev team; China was not ignored, but it was accorded only second priority. This, again, had to do with both security and economic perceptions. By the mid-1980s, the arms race had reached a stage at which the Soviet Union probably could not keep up with the United States for much longer. In economic terms, the West was a far more attractive partner than China, whose economy was growing and modernizing thanks to Deng's reforms but was still in many respects regarded as inferior to that of the Soviet Union.[16]

That said, Gorbachev was eager to accelerate the normalization process with China. He stated Moscow's desire for better relations with Asian countries, above all the PRC. Gorbachev's overtures toward Asia and China were, to a large extent, spurred by the growing, albeit belated, realization by the Soviet leadership of the rising global importance of the Asia-Pacific.[17] In his Asia-Pacific policy speeches in Vladivostok (July 1986) and Krasnoyarsk (September 1988), Gorbachev announced a series of initiatives that, in effect, removed "the three obstacles" to normalization that China had insisted be removed before normalization could occur.[18] The Soviet Union agreed to significantly reduce the military deployments on its Far East border with China and in Mongolia, withdraw all troops from Afghanistan, and encourage Vietnam to end its military intervention in Cambodia. Gorbachev indicated that the Soviet Union wished to shift the main emphasis in its Asian policies from the military buildup to economic engagement.

Although Soviet-Chinese relations were rapidly warming, there was some mismatch regarding the priorities each side pursued in the rapprochement. As Gilbert Rozman points out, "China eyed geopolitical objectives, seeking a revival of the strategic triangle with itself at the pivot between the United States and the Soviet Union."[19] Gorbachev, in contrast, was not particularly interested in playing strategic triangle games.

There were also doctrinal differences about the way to reform socialism that grew more and more visible in the late 1980s and 1990. Deng Xiaoping was emphasizing market reforms and modernization while guarding the absolute political authority of the party-state. Reformers in Moscow appeared to be more interested in political democratization, experimenting with freedom of the press and free elections. This aroused alarm not only among the conservative circles in the Communist Party of the Soviet Union (CPSU) but also among hardliners in the CCP who feared that the Soviet reforms would set a dangerous precedent for the PRC. This concern was not completely unfounded, because China's liberal-leaning reformers, led by CCP general secretary Zhao Ziyang, drew some of their inspiration from Gorbachev.

In May 1989, Gorbachev traveled to Beijing to meet with Deng. This was the first Sino-Soviet summit since the days of Khrushchev and Mao; it signified the formal completion of the normalization process. The visit took place against the background of the student pro-democracy protests in Beijing that culminated in the Tiananmen tragedy of June 4. The turmoil he saw in Beijing and the ensuing bloodshed reinforced Gorbachev's conviction that China's way of putting market reforms ahead of democratization was flawed.[20] In China, supporters of political pluralism were purged, and the CCP took steps to fully restore the party-state monopoly of power.

Although, after Tiananmen Moscow and Beijing dramatically parted ways in terms of domestic reforms, their great power rapprochement continued. In April 1990, Premier Li Peng visited Moscow and concluded an agreement on demilitarization of the Soviet-Chinese border. The Soviet

Union agreed to sell China Su-27 fighter jets, a move that was especially significant at a time when the West was imposing an arms-sales embargo on Beijing as punishment for PLA actions near Tiananmen. The Su-27 deal proved to be the first manifestation of what would become a critical aspect of Sino-Russian strategic collaboration in the 1990s and beyond. As the final achievement of Sino-Soviet rapprochement, an agreement was signed during CCP general secretary Jiang Zemin's visit to Moscow in May 1991 that settled the long-contested eastern part of the border between the two countries.

The Post-Soviet Interlude (1991–1995)

In the immediate aftermath of the Soviet Union breakup, the Sino-Russian relationship experienced a period of uncertainty. The newly democratic Moscow was eager to join the West, to which it looked as the political and economic model. Russia's president, Boris Yeltsin, and his foreign minister, Andrey Kozyrev, were more than willing to act in lockstep with the United States, Western Europe, and the Western-led institutions. Understandably, this caused concern in Beijing, where the collapse of the Soviet Union was viewed as a serious blow to communist ideology with potentially adverse consequences for CCP legitimacy. Beijing also feared that, with Russia joining the Western liberal camp, China's semi-isolation in the wake of the Tiananmen Square events would become more complete. The Washington-Beijing-Moscow geopolitical triangle, which China had skillfully exploited since the early 1970s, threatened to reconfigure in a way that would leave Beijing out in the cold and facing the triumphant West. That would doom China to pariah status in the international community.

To the relief of Chinese leaders, the feared developments never materialized. The Kremlin had no intention of antagonizing or alienating China, even if doing so would bolster Russia's new democratic credentials. After a short time, Yeltsin continued Mikhail Gorbachev's drive to improve relations with Beijing.[21] Yeltsin visited Beijing in December 1992, and Jiang Zemin reciprocated with a visit to Moscow in September 1994. Yeltsin's maiden visit to Tokyo had been scheduled to take place before his trip to China, but it was abruptly canceled by the Russian side because the Kremlin was unwilling to make concessions on the South Kuril Islands dispute, which the Japanese saw as the main item on the bilateral agenda. This was an early indication that China, not Japan, was going to be Russia's main friend in Asia.

Sino-Russian trade was growing during this period, especially in border areas, but Russians still viewed China with condescension, as a supplier of cheap but low-quality consumer goods and a provider of manual labor. The West was regarded as a far more important economic partner, because it could provide the principal market for Russia's mineral wealth and the main source of investment and expertise.

The Birth of Strategic Partnership (1996–2000)

The mid-1990s marked a watershed in Moscow's foreign policy. Russia began to feel bitter disappointment, and even anger, with the West, and resented being treated as a defeated adversary that could at best be a junior partner in the Western-dominated global order. The list of Russian grievances included eastern enlargement of the North Atlantic Treaty Organization (NATO), failure to obtain the anticipated economic aid from the West, and refusal by the West to grant Moscow its "rightful place" in the international system. Toward the late 1990s, NATO's "humanitarian intervention" in Yugoslavia, the Western reaction to the war in Chechnya, and Washington's decision to withdraw from the Anti-Ballistic Missile Treaty further exacerbated the frictions.

Disenchantment with the West induced Moscow to seek closer ties with China. Beijing, in turn, was happy to embrace Russia. Aligning with Moscow could help balance America's unipolar predominance that, from Beijing's perspective, had achieved a level parlous for China. China's sense of vulnerability in the face of US preponderance grew especially acute after the 1995–1996 Taiwan Strait crisis, when Washington responded to China's firing of missiles that landed near Taiwan ports with a display of military might intended to serve as a humiliating warning to Beijing.[22]

Mutual desire to counterbalance the United States was manifested in Yeltsin's visit to China in April 1996, during which the two sides stated their intention to develop "relations of an equal trustworthy partnership aimed at strategic partnership in the 21st century."[23] Yeltsin declared that there were no more controversial questions between Russia and China, and from that time onward, the strategic partnership became official policy for the two countries.[24] Meeting in Moscow in April 1997, Yeltsin and Jiang Zemin signed the Declaration on a Multipolar World and Formation of a New International Order, which stated their common vision in clear opposition to the US-centered hegemony.[25]

Another reason for Russia's shift toward the PRC was the desire to obtain economic benefits by expanding trade with China's fast-growing economy. Whereas in the early 1990s China's economic weight was limited and the West appeared the only viable option for trade and investment, by the second half of the 1990s the rise of China and its potential was beyond doubt.

Evolution of the Sino-Russian Strategic Partnership (2001–2012)

Vladimir Putin, who succeeded Yeltsin in 2000, continued to emphasize good relations with China. In June 2001, Beijing and Moscow jointly launched the Shanghai Cooperation Organization (SCO), the successor to the Shanghai Five group (Russia, China, Kazakhstan, Kyrgyzstan, and Tajikistan) established at China's initiative in 1996.[26] The SCO added Uzbekistan as a sixth member and quickly became one of Eurasia's most important regional bodies and a major channel of Sino-Russian collaboration.

In July 2001, Putin and Jiang Zemin signed the Treaty of Good Neighborly Friendship and Cooperation, which became the legal foundation for a Sino-Russian strategic partnership. Inter alia, the parties affirmed their respect for joint borders and mutual support for their territorial integrity and national sovereignty. Beijing and Moscow declared that they did not have any territorial claims between themselves and vowed to turn the shared border into the "border of eternal peace and friendship." The treaty pronounced that it was not "aimed at any third country," and its wording was careful to avoid any phrases that could be interpreted as anti–United States.[27]

Unlike the 1997 declaration, the document did not even mention the idea of a multipolar world. This change in tone, as compared to the late 1990s, was partly attributable to Putin's desire for closer relations with the West. In his early years in office, Putin definitely saw the United States and Western Europe as Russia's top partners. This became especially apparent after September 11, 2001. While Putin was the first foreign leader to call George W. Bush and offer the United States all necessary help, he did not speak with Jiang Zemin until a full week later. As Alexander Lukin points out, "Russian contacts with China remained at the pre-9/11 level against the background of a radical intensification of Moscow's relations with the United States, NATO, and Western Europe."[28] This caused apprehension in China because it suggested the possibility that Russia might reorient its policies to favor the West. Chinese experts saw the Putin government as having lost enthusiasm for multipolarity because it feared offending the United States. Chinese security analysts were particularly alarmed by Moscow's decision to allow Central Asian countries to grant the United States access to their territory and airspace for the purpose of waging war in Afghanistan. The Chinese also took notice of Russia's increasing tolerance of NATO's eastward expansion.[29]

Moscow's somewhat reduced eagerness for engagement with Beijing was also evident in the economic sphere. In 2002 when a major state-owned company, Slavneft, was put up for privatization, the Russian government publicly refused to sell it to China National Petroleum Corporation even though the Chinese oil giant offered the highest bid. Another high-profile controversy involved the projected oil pipeline from Eastern Siberia to China. An agreement between Russia and China to build a pipeline from Russian Angarsk to Daqing in northeastern China was reached in 2001. But just a few months later, Moscow began negotiating with Tokyo for an alternative route to Nakhodka on the Pacific coast, targeting Japan and the United States, rather than China, as main consumers of the eastern Siberian oil. Not surprisingly, those about-faces by Moscow caused much consternation in Beijing.

This cooling in the relationship did not preclude Russia and China from signing, in 2004, an agreement that formally completed the long process of border settlement between the two countries. The agreement decided the ownership of several remaining islands and islets on the Amur River that had been left undetermined by the 1991 border treaty.[30]

By the mid-2000s, the Sino-Russian relationship began to pick up steam again. This was largely due to visible deterioration in relations between Russia and the West. Moscow felt that Washington did not reciprocate its goodwill and concessions. The George W. Bush administration would not recognize Russia as an equal partner and continued what the Kremlin perceived as a brazen encroachment on Russia's sphere of vital interests in its near abroad. The Putin government was especially alarmed by the color revolutions that took place in Georgia, Ukraine, and Kyrgyzstan, viewing them as engineered by the State Department. By then Russia, buttressed by strong economic performance on the back of high hydrocarbon prices, had enough confidence to stand up to the West. Putin's speech at the Munich Conference on Security Policy in February 2007 was a stark warning that Moscow was prepared to pick up the fight.[31] This necessitated a new closeness with Beijing. One of the initial signs of the stronger Russia-China partnership was the SCO's collective decision in July 2005 to call on the United States to withdraw its military bases from Central Asia.[32]

In a curious reversal of roles from the early 2000s, Russia began to act increasingly anti–United States, whereas China was quite cautious, reluctant to support the combative drive of Putin's Munich speech. China made clear that it was not ready to side with Russia in its tensions with the United States because it did not want to jeopardize Beijing's all-important relations with Washington. The Chinese leadership under Hu Jintao was also somewhat uncomfortable with Moscow's recalcitrant rhetoric and actions, since they obviously did not fit with Beijing's concept of the "harmonious world."[33] This stance was manifest in the wake of the August 2008 war that Russia waged against Georgia. Beijing conspicuously declined to approve of Moscow's actions and did not recognize the independence of Russian-backed South Ossetia and Abkhazia.[34] A temporary decline in the political dimension of the Sino-Russian partnership led some observers to conclude that, after having passed its peak in around 2005, the relationship would experience "growing distrust and complexity."[35]

However, Russian and Chinese views on the core issues of international politics had begun to converge again by 2012. Russia's posture remained more or less unchanged, so the shift occurred mainly in China's foreign policies. The 2008–2009 recession that wreaked havoc on the West seemed to have given Beijing confidence that the balance of power was inexorably moving in its favor. This coincided with a leadership transition in China. The cautious and uncharismatic Hu Jintao was succeeded by the much tougher and seemingly more nationalistic Xi Jinping, whose foreign policy bore discernible features of great power offensive realism.[36] China's growing geopolitical ambitions, particularly in East Asia, were clearly at odds with what the United States stood for. Russia and China had become almost equally hostile toward the United States. The reinvigorated Sino-Russian entente amply displayed itself in February 2012, when the two countries blocked the Western-backed vote on Syria in the UN Security Council.[37]

From 2013 Onward: Impact of the Ukraine Crisis

The Ukraine crisis, which started to develop in the fall of 2013, further consolidated the Moscow-Beijing axis, turning it into something approaching a
quasi alliance. Beijing refused to join the Washington-led campaign to ostra-
cize Moscow and displayed benevolent neutrality regarding Russian moves
in Crimea and Ukraine. Vladimir Putin's visits to Shanghai (May 2014) and
Beijing (November 2014), Xi Jinping's trip to Moscow (May 2015), and
many other high-level Russia-China meetings since the beginning of the
Ukraine trouble underscore the growing closeness between the two great
powers. In October 2014, during a meeting with Chinese premier Li Ke-
qiang, Putin declared that Russia and China were "natural partners and
natural allies," using for the first time the word *ally* with respect to Beijing.[38]

Russia and China concluded a host of agreements, substantially expanding and deepening bilateral cooperation in energy, finance, and high-tech
and other sectors. The biggest among them was a thirty-year $400 billion
contract to supply natural gas from eastern Russia to northeastern China
signed in May 2014. This was followed in November by a framework agreement that would allow China to receive gas from western Siberia. At the
same time, China's imports of Russian oil skyrocketed by nearly 40 percent
in 2014 and displaced the share of other suppliers, such as Saudi Arabia, in
the Chinese import market.[39] Russia began to treat China not as a bargaining chip in its energy dealings with Europe, as was mostly the case prior to
the Ukraine crisis, but as the top-priority market.

The central banks of the two countries signed a currency-swap agreement worth 150 billion yuan (around US$25 billion), enabling Russia to
draw on yuan in case of need, and Beijing officials announced China was
willing to help the Russian economy.[40] As leading Western agencies down-
graded Russia's ratings to junk or near-junk level, the Chinese credit-rating
agency Dagong Global gave Russia's Gazprom the highest rating, AAA,
which enabled the Russian energy giant to place shares in Hong Kong.[41]
While Western financial institutions drastically cut lending to Russian businesses, Chinese banks were expanding their presence in Russia, with many
of the loans denominated in the yuan.[42] Another sign of growing collaboration in finance was the growing share of Russia-China trade conducted in
the two countries' national currencies (mostly the yuan) rather than the US
dollar. By May 2015, this share grew to 7 percent, compared to almost zero
only a few years before.[43]

Russia has traditionally been wary of any Chinese presence in its Far East, which shares a four-thousand-kilometer border with China. However, over 2014 and 2015 Moscow lifted tacit restrictions on Chinese investments and began to actively court Chinese capital. In a landmark move, the Russian government agreed to sell Chinese companies stakes in the country's most lucrative oil field and the world's third-biggest copper field, both located in eastern Siberia.[44] Russia and China began construction of a railway bridge, the first-ever permanent link between the two countries across the Amur River that will connect the Russian Far East's hinterland to China's Heilongjiang Province. Russian and Chinese companies also agreed jointly to develop the port of Zarubino, strategically located at the junction of the Russian, Chinese, and North Korean borders. The port will provide China's landlocked provinces of Jilin and Heilongjiang with direct access to the Sea of Japan.

There are areas where Russia and China have competing interests, particularly in Central Asia, where China's growing economic presence has long worried Russia. However, since 2014, Moscow has become more accommodating toward China's presence there. In May 2015, Putin and Xi agreed to coordinate their flagship economic initiatives in Central Asia, the Russian-led Eurasian Economic Union (EEU) and China's Silk Road Economic Belt (SREB). In their joint declaration, the parties expressed willingness "to make coordinated efforts toward the integration of constructing EEU and SREB," with the Shanghai Cooperation Organization serving as the main platform for linking up the two initiatives. The document also mentions "a long-term goal of progressing toward a free trade zone between EEU and China."[45]

On the political-military front, Russia and China have been increasing the frequency and scale of their joint drills. In May 2015, in a move fraught with symbolism, they conducted their first naval exercise in the Mediterranean, NATO's maritime backyard. Perhaps even more important, Russia, in a departure from its previous policies, appears ready to sell China its most advanced weapons platforms, such as S-400 surface-to-air missile systems and Su-35 fighter jets.[46]

The Moscow-Beijing entente is also manifesting itself in the countries' narratives on World War II. The victory in World War II has always been considered in Russia to have been achieved primarily through the efforts and sacrifice of the Soviet Union, with the help of the American and British allies. Russia's official discourse is now palpably changing, with China replacing the Western allies as the second most important contributor to the outcome of the war: the Soviet Union made the decisive contribution to the defeat of the Nazi Germany in Europe, while China overcame imperial Japan in Asia. Xi Jinping's participation in the 2015 Victory Day celebrations in Moscow and Vladimir Putin's return visit to Beijing in early September 2015 for the commemoration of the end of the war in Asia have consolidated this new interpretation of history.

Moscow-Beijing Axis Redux?

The Russian-Chinese strategic partnership has been assessed in a variety of ways since its inception in the second half of the 1990s. Until recently the dominant view in the West was that it is "an inherently limited partnership," or "an axis of convenience," which is unbalanced and shaky because of cultural barriers and the two countries' significantly divergent interests, which are likely to diverge even more in the future.[47] Any idea of upgrading the partnership to the level of alliance has been rejected as unrealistic.[48]

From the beginning, however, there was also a dissenting view that saw Russian-Chinese collaboration as something much more durable and having great potential for further development. In 2001, Ariel Cohen characterized it as an "emerging alliance" that would require careful monitoring, predicting that "the degree to which the Sino-Russian alliance may become anti-Western in future depends on how deeply the two Eurasian powers feel that the United States threatens their interests."[49] In an article published in 2008, Thomas Wilkins concluded that the Moscow-Beijing partnership is "a highly efficacious vehicle for coordinating Russo-Chinese-SCO security policy. Those who doubt its capacities and durability may be in for a shock as it increasingly exercises dominance in Central Asia and begins to wield powerful influence on the global stage."[50]

The latter view, emphasizing the potency of Russian-Chinese collaboration, appears to be supported by developments since 2012, and especially in the wake of the Ukraine crisis, that amount to a steady increase in the depth and scope of the bilateral relationship. It may not yet be accurate to describe the Russian-Chinese strategic partnership as an alliance, but the relationship is certainly growing stronger. Indeed, the Russian-Chinese partnership, as it stands today, looks more solid and efficient than some of Washington's "treaty alliances" such as the one with Thailand.

China and Russia see their crucial national interests as mutually nonexclusive. As Dmitry Trenin observes, the Russia-China bond "is solid, for it is based on fundamental national interests regarding the world order as both the Russian and Chinese governments would prefer to see it."[51] Moscow is not inimical to China's rise as a great power, as this creates for Russia economic and political alternatives other than the West. For its part, China sees its security interests as generally compatible with those of Russia.[52] This convergence of basic interests constitutes the foundation for a strategic partnership. The existence of a common foe—the United States—may be transforming the partnership into an entente, or perhaps an alliance.[53] Russia's leading foreign policy experts increasingly characterize the Russian-Chinese relationship as a "de facto alliance."[54] A joint report by Russian and Chinese scholars sees "elements of a military-political alliance," albeit not legally binding, emerging between the two countries.[55] The report argues that, "if need be, the ties can be converted into an alliance relationship without long preparations."[56]

The consensus in the Russian ruling elite is that, in the foreseeable future, China will not pose a threat to Russia and can be a reliable partner. Retired General Leonid Reshetnikov, who heads the Russian Institute for Strategic Studies (the Kremlin's foreign policy think tank) describes the situation as follows:

> We are closely following the situation in China. Of course, this is a big country, where different factions exist, including expansionist ones. But we are confident that China is interested in good relations with Russia. China's main rival is the United States, not Russia. Therefore China needs a well-protected and quiet rear area. For the next 30–40 years Russia is unlikely to face any threat from China. Beijing is doing its best to avoid whatever might cause Russia's irritation and negative reaction. A serious conflict between Russia and China is possible only if grave mistakes are made by us or by the Chinese, or else if the American agents do a good job in China. The Western countries are keen to set Russia and China against each other. They keep forcing on us this China threat notion. Yet we will never buy that.[57]

Calculus of the Sino-Russian Entente

The interests and aspirations of China and Russia converge to a significant degree, providing the basis for their quasi alliance. Key issues on which their interests converge are summarized in the sections that follow.

BALANCE OF POWER AND GEOPOLITICS

First and foremost, Sino-Russian entente is predicated on shared hostility to US hegemony in world politics. Viewing themselves as great powers, both Moscow and Beijing loath the idea of a systemic hegemon that dictates and adjudicates global rules, particularly considering that Russia remembers itself as having been a superpower, and China preserves memories of Middle Kingdom glory. From the balance-of-power perspective, it is only natural that two lesser poles should join forces against the preponderant player. At the regional level of geopolitics, US hegemony prevents Russia and China from enjoying dominance in what they regard as their rightful domains. For Russia, this is the post-Soviet space; for China, East Asia.

To counterbalance the United States on the global stage, Russia and China coordinate their steps in the world governing bodies, particularly the UN Security Council, and promote new institutions, such as BRICS and its New Development Bank, designed to serve as alternatives to the Western-dominated international order. In their common regional neighborhood, Moscow and Beijing aim for what may be dubbed "Eurasian continentalism." What they envision would be based on the newly expanded Shanghai Cooperation Organization and, possibly, on the recently reinvigorated Conference on Interaction and Confidence-Building Measures in Asia. These are organizations in which Beijing and Moscow play prominent roles and the United States is conspicuously absent. China and Russia seek to act as the principal coleaders and shapers of the new economic and security architecture of continental Eurasia, with inputs from Delhi, Islamabad, and Tehran, while collaborating to exclude the United States. Finally, Moscow and Beijing seem ready to provide tacit diplomatic support to each other in the event of conflicts with their neighbors in Eastern Europe and East Asia, respectively. That means, for example, that China takes a position of benevolent neutrality regarding Russia's actions on Ukraine, and Moscow looks the other way when Beijing pushes its claims in the South China Sea.[58]

IDENTITY POLITICS

Moscow and Beijing both see the US-led West as the primary threat to their nations' civilizational identities as well as to the legitimacy of their political regimes. Gilbert Rozman makes a compelling case that what drives China and Russia close together are their national identities, which contain significant elements of the shared communist legacy (and also draw on significant commonalities in their precommunist histories). Despite the lack of cultural affinity and trust, the Russian-Chinese identity gap is likely to remain much narrower and less obtrusive than the two nations' respective gaps with the United States. For both states, the post–Cold War era is best characterized as a struggle between two civilizations, theirs and the West. Their fervent anti-US sentiments cement their partnership.[59]

Moscow and Beijing also share an interest in guarding their state-centric autocratic political systems against what they perceive as Western subversion. As emphasized by Feng Yujun, director of the Russian Studies Institute at China Institutes of Contemporary International Relations, Russia and China grow "increasingly close in their concepts of political governance," and the two countries "have a greater stake in mutual support to counter political pressure from the West."[60] One indicator of the cross-pollination taking place between Moscow and Beijing on domestic political issues is that the CCP seems to have taken a page from Putin's playbook by introducing a law, similar to Russia's legislation, crippling nongovernmental organization with foreign sponsors or partners.[61]

GEOECONOMICS

Economic calculations have been another powerful force in the Sino-Russian strategic partnership. On the face of it, commercial links between the two countries may not look very impressive. Sino-Russian trade is less than $90 billion, which is a fraction of the commercial relationships China has with the United States, Japan, or South Korea. China has been Russia's primary trade partner since 2009, accounting for 11 percent of Russia's exports and imports. Nevertheless, European Union countries collectively still account for almost half of Russia's trade turnover. For China, trade with Russia is even less significant if measured only in terms of statistics. Russia is responsible for a mere 2 percent of Chinese exports and imports, ranking ninth among China's trade partners, trailing Australia and Malaysia.

However, there may be more than meets the eye in the Sino-Russian economic relationship. Security calculations are as important as commercial considerations in driving economic collaboration between Moscow and Beijing. Since a hot war between contemporary great powers is becoming more and more unthinkable given the enormous destructive force of nuclear warheads and other modern arms, warfare is migrating into the domain of trade and finance. In the twenty-first century, economic sanctions are becoming weapons of choice in the conflicts between major powers. This is what Russia, penalized by the West, has experienced in the Ukraine crisis. And this is what China may face, if and when it clashes with the United States. Thus, mutual geoeconomic support becomes crucial for Moscow and Beijing. The bond with China will give Russia a considerable degree of economic independence from the sanctions-prone West, providing an alternative source of finance and capital goods. In return, China will enjoy secure overland access to Russia's vast reserves of natural resources, especially oil and gas, so that its voracious economy can continue functioning even in the event of a US-imposed naval blockade.[62] Chinese strategists take this scenario very seriously.[63]

Not wishing to put its faith in the freedom of navigation guaranteed by the United States and concerned about perennial instability in the Middle East, China seems to have emphasized overland supplies of vital commodities, even if it means higher costs.[64] Russia is the indispensable element in China's quest for energy and resource security. For security reasons, China will continue to be interested in Russian oil, even though that oil may be more expensive than the crude oil imported from the Middle East.[65] Interestingly, China's total imports and Russia's total exports of oil roughly correspond; China imports 6.2 million barrels per day of crude oil (as of 2014), while Russia exports approximately 7.4 million barrels per day of oil and petroleum products (as of 2012).[66] Theoretically, in the event of a conflict pitting the PRC against the United States and/or US allies that would disrupt China's maritime oil shipments, Russia would be able to replace China's oil (and natural gas) imports via terrestrial routes beyond the reach of the US forces (provided Moscow stops deliveries to European customers, which it may be willing to do if it attaches top priority to its relationship with Beijing).[67] Russia, being one of the world's top grain producers, also figures as a potentially important element in China's food security.[68] Strong relations with Moscow also guarantee China access to the resources of Central Asia, where Russia remains the most influential security and political player.

PERSONALITY POLITICS

The personalities of the Russian and Chinese leaders, Vladimir Putin and Xi Jinping, are a major factor in the contemporary Russian-Chinese alignment.

Each is an autocratic chief executive who has concentrated in his hands almost exclusive powers to make foreign policy decisions. In the case of Russia, there has never been much doubt that it is Putin who personally makes principal decisions on foreign policy and national security. In China, until recently strategic decision making had been done by the party-state collective leadership. But now Xi appears to be running the country's diplomatic and security policies on his own, with the Politburo's Standing Committee playing only a small role.[69]

Although Putin and Xi seem to get along quite well, and some experts point to "a clear personal affinity" between them, they do not even need to have good chemistry between themselves—as long as they see eye-to-eye politically. It appears that Xi and Putin understand each other perfectly well because they share the flair for hardball realpolitik in international affairs, coupled with a conservative and nationalistic authoritarianism in domestic affairs. Both leaders attach high priority to military force and the security apparatus as tools for defending national interests abroad and maintaining what they see as legitimate order at home.

Rozman writes of "striking parallels in the ways in which presidents Xi Jinping and Vladimir Putin envision the resurgence of their countries domestically and internationally."[70] Another strong conviction shared by the two is that the West poses the main obstacle to grand projects of "Sinocentrism" and "Russocentrism."[71] Thus, Putin and Xi are drawn together as natural allies against the US-led West. It is significant that Putin and Xi are likely to be in power for a long time; Putin is likely to seek, and win, reelection in 2018 and Xi's expected two-term tenure will keep him in office until 2022. Xi may continue to serve as China's paramount leader even beyond 2022.[72]

Conclusion

Sino-Russian relations are now at their highest point since the mid-1950s. Some would even argue that the two countries are on the verge of reinstating a full-blown alliance. In an eerie throwback to the early 1950s, it took a war to cement the partnership of Beijing and Moscow and turn it into a potent strategic axis. In 1950, the Korean War foreclosed possibilities for normalization between China and the United States. Stalin's Soviet Union became the only external option for Beijing. Before the Ukraine crisis Moscow had envisioned a single European space from Lisbon to Vladivostok that would be based on shared values, interests, and partnership with the European Union. In 2013–2014, the crisis and ensuing war in Ukraine caused a profound alienation between Russia and the US-led West. Today the Russian leadership talks of building a continental Eurasian "common economic space" in collaboration with China.[73]

The question is how durable this new edition of Sino-Russian entente will be. We may expect that the Moscow-Beijing axis will continue to exist, and possibly grow even stronger, as long as the leaders in the Kremlin and Zhongnanhai perceive a common overriding threat from the world's only superpower, Washington, which both see as opposing Russia's and China's legitimate geopolitical aspirations and as trying to undermine the two countries' political systems and social values.

To be sure, there is a possibility that the Sino-Russian quasi alliance will collapse, repeating the unfortunate trajectory of the Soviet-Chinese alliance. As in the 1950s, when the young People's Republic was a dependent and junior partner, there seems to be an inherent asymmetry in the current relationship. Russia, isolated and sanctioned by the West, apparently needs China more than China needs Russia. This might tempt Beijing to assert its dominance in the dyad, which would likely cause Russian backlash and rupture of the relationship. This scenario is theoretically possibly but unlikely. First, the current leaders in Moscow and Beijing have a strong sense of history, and no doubt keep in mind the lessons of the Sino-Soviet split, an experience neither party wants to repeat. And, in contrast to the toxic relationship between Khrushchev and Mao, Putin and Xi appear to be on the same page. Second, there is probably some underestimation of the degree to which China depends on Russia. As long as there is a real risk of China clashing with the United States (over the South China Sea, Taiwan, or the Senkakus), the strong bond with Russia—the only major power that can provide Beijing with diplomatic support, military technology, and secure access to vital commodities—will be crucial for the PRC.

Although there is a solid consensus within the two countries' governing circles that China and Russia must remain close, there is less agreement on that among the broader political, business, and intellectual elites. In Russia, there is a strong undercurrent of opinion, especially among liberal-leaning quarters, that questions the wisdom of moving closer to China. The same is true of China, where many liberals portray Russia in a negative light.[74]

If and when these groups, whose ideological sympathies lie with the West, begin to play a larger role in the policy making of either of the two countries (or in both), the Sino-Russian entente may be doomed. However, the triumph of liberalism is a very unlikely proposition for Russia and China, at least in the next seven to ten years. Absent changes in the countries' political regimes, and with the United States being viewed as the principal foe by both Moscow and Beijing, the Sino-Russian axis will only grow stronger.

Notes

1. See, for example, M. I. Sladkovskii, *History of Economic Relations Between Russia and China* (Jerusalem: Israel Program for Scientific Translations, 1966).

2. See, for example, Joseph Fletcher, "Sino-Russian Relations, 1800–1860," in *The Cambridge History of China*, vol. 11, *Late Ch'ing, 1800–1911, Part 1*, ed. John K. Fairbank (Cambridge: Cambridge University Press, 1968), chap. 7. On the century of humiliation, see Zheng Wang, *Never Forget National Humiliation: Historical Memory in Chinese Politics and Foreign Relations* (New York: Columbia University Press, 2012).

3. See Robert C. North, *Moscow and Chinese Communists*, 2nd ed. (Stanford, CA: Stanford University Press, 1963).

4. Economic calculations also played a role. China was a large potential market for Soviet industrial products and a source of some agricultural and mineral commodities that the Soviet Union lacked.

5. Alexei Volynets, "Kak Stalin v Kitay investiroval" [How Stalin Invested in China], *Russkyaya Planeta*, October 7, 2014, http://rusplt.ru/society/kak-stalin-v -kitay-investiroval-13386.html.

6. Interview with China historian Alexander Pantsov, *Echo Moskvy*, May 30, 2010, http://echo.msk.ru/programs/hrushev/683318-echo/#.

7. Moscow only provided air cover over North Korea and northeastern China, advisers, and military supplies. Underscoring Stalin's attitude toward Mao's China was the stark fact that the Soviet Union presented Beijing with a hefty ($2 billion) bill for the matériel provided during the Korean War. See Warren Cohen, *East Asia at the Center* (New York: Columbia University Press, 2000), 389.

8. Alexei Bogaturov, ed., *Sistemnaya Istoriya Mezhdunarodnyh Otnosheniy* [Systemic History of International Relations] (Moscow: Academic Educational Forum on International Relations, 2003), 3:152.

9. Alexei Borodavkin, "Rossiya i Kitay: Po puti dobrososedstva i sotrudnich-estva" [Russia and China: Moving Toward Good Neighborliness and Cooperation], Institute for Far Eastern Studies of the Russian Academy of Sciences, October 19,

2009, http://www.ifes-ras.ru/publications/pdv/120-aaieiaeaaeei-einney-e-eeoae-ii
-iooe-aeiaeininaaenoaa-e-nioeoaeiedanoaa.

10. See Lorenz M. Luthi, *The Sino-Soviet Split: Cold War in the Communist World* (Princeton, NJ: Princeton University Press, 2008).

11. This is not to say that Moscow did not care about China. When Khrushchev was ousted from office in 1964, one of the accusations leveled against him by other senior party leaders was that he had mishandled relations with Beijing. After Khrushchev's dismissal, Moscow made some, albeit rather weak, efforts to restart relations with the CCP, but the Chinese rebuffed those efforts.

12. M. Taylor Fravel, *Strong Borders, Secure Nation: Cooperation and Conflict in China's Territorial Disputes* (Princeton, NJ: Princeton University Press, 2008), 311.

13. In addition, any economic rationale for Sino-Soviet normalization was weakened by the fact that China, at that time, did not need the natural resources that its northern neighbor could provide. This was especially the case with respect to oil, because China was a net exporter of oil in the 1970s and 1980s. In this respect, the economies of Russia and China were competitive rather than complementary.

14. Bogaturov, *Sistemnaya Istoriya,* 445–446.

15. Ibid., 470.

16. China's main economic value was considered to be as a commercial partner for the border provinces of the Soviet Far East. In June 1988, Moscow and Beijing concluded an agreement on the development of trade and economic relations between their border provinces and enterprises. See Viktor Larin, *V teni prosnuvshegosya drakona* [In the Shadow of the Awakened Dragon] (Vladivostok: Dal'nauka, 2006), 25–31. China had similar considerations, expecting to boost the development of its northeastern provinces, particularly Heilongjiang, by expanding their commercial exchanges with the neighboring Soviet Far East.

17. Evgeny Bazhanov, "Soviet Policy Toward the Asia-Pacific Region," in *Russian Strategic Thought Toward Asia,* ed. Gilbert Rozman (New York: Palgrave Macmillan, 2006), 40.

18. See Harry Harding, *China and Northeast Asia: The Political Dimension* (New York: Asia Society, 1988).

19. Gilbert Rozman, "Overview," in Rozman, *Russian Strategic Thought,* 7.

20. Yuri Tavrovsky, *Kitay, Rossiya i Sosedi: Novoye Tysyacheletiye* [Russia, China and Neighbors: The New Millennium] (Moscow: Vostochnyaya Kniga, 2015), 119–121.

21. That said, there were moments in the early 1990s when the Kremlin's chaotic decision making put Russian-Chinese relations at risk. The most serious incident occurred in 1992, when one of Yeltsin's top aides persuaded him to sign a decree allowing the opening of Taiwan's de facto embassy in Moscow, which was

almost tantamount to recognizing Taipei. The decision was quickly reversed after protests from China and Russia's Ministry of Foreign Affairs.

22. See, for example, Jim Mann, "US Carrier Group Sails Near China as Tensions over Taiwan Mount," *Los Angeles Times*, January 27, 1996, http://articles .latimes.com/1996-01-27/news/mn-29246_1_taiwan-strait.

23. Alexander Lukin, "The Russian Approach to China Under Gorbachev, Yeltsin, and Putin," in Rozman, *Russian Strategic Thought*, 148.

24. Ibid.

25. "Declaration on a Multipolar World and Formation of a New International Order," *Zakony Rossii*, April 23, 1997, http://www.lawrussia.ru/texts/legal_743/ doc743a830x878.htm. An English version can be found at http://fas.org/news/ russia/1997/a52--153en.htm.

26. The Shanghai Five group was formed in 1996 during Yeltsin's visit to China and initially served as a confidence-building arrangement along the border areas.

27. The Treaty of Good Neighborly Friendship and Cooperation Between the Russian Federation and Chinese People's Republic, July 17, 2001, http://www .rg.ru/2009/03/20/russia-kitai-dok.html. An English version is available at http:// www.chinese-embassy.no/eng/dtxw/t110017.htm.

28. Lukin, "Russian Approach," 160.

29. Rex Li, *A Rising China and Security in East Asia* (New York: Routledge, 2009), 160.

30. See Neville Maxwell, "How the Sino-Russian Boundary Conflict Was Finally Settled: From Nerchinsk 1689 to Vladivostok 2005 via Zhenbao Island 1969," *Critical Asian Studies* 39, no. 2 (2007): 229–253, http://www.tandfonline .com/doi/full/10.1080/14672710701340079#abstract.

31. See Thom Shanker and Mark Landler, "Putin Says US Is Undermining Global Stability," *New York Times*, February 11, 2007, http://www.nytimes.com/ 2007/02/11/world/europe/11munich.html?pagewanted=all.

32. C. J. Chivers, "Central Asians Call on US to Set a Timetable for Closing Bases," *New York Times*, July 6, 2005, http://www.nytimes.com/2005/07/06/ world/asia/central-asians-call-on-us-to-set-a-timetable-for-closing-bases.html.

33. Vladimir Portyakov, "O nekotorykh aspektakh sovershenstvovaniya rossiysko-kitayskogo strategicheskogo partnerstva" [Some Improvements in the Russian-Chinese Strategic Partnership], *Problemy Dal'nego Vostoka*, no. 5 (2007): 24.

34. Beijing's reluctance to support Russia in its conflict with Georgia over Abkhazia and South Ossetia also reflected concern over a precedent their secession might create for Tibet and Xinjiang.

35. Shinji Hyodo, "Russia's Security Policy Towards East Asia," in *Russia and East Asia: Informal and Gradual Integration*, ed. Tsuneo Akaha and Anna Vassilieva (New York: Routledge, 2014), 44–53.

36. Paul Eckert, "Analysis: Tensions with Allies Rise, but U.S. Sees Improved China Ties," *Reuters*, November 3, 2014, http://www.reuters.com/article/ 2013/11/03/us-usa-china-xi-analysis-idUSBRE9A205B20131103. See also Zhang Baohui, "Xi Jinping, 'Pragmatic' Offensive Realism and China's Rise," *Global Asia*, 9, no. 2 (Summer 2014): http://www.globalasia.org/wp-content/uploads/ 2014/06/568.pdf.

37. "Security Council Fails to Adopt Draft Resolution on Syria as Russian Federation, China Veto Text Supporting Arab League's Proposed Peace Plan," *United Nations Meetings Coverage and Press Releases*, February 4, 2012, http://www.un.org/ press/en/2012/sc10536.doc.htm.

38. "Putin Confirms Plans to Meet Chinese President During APEC Summit in Beijing," *RIA Novosti*, October 14, 2014, http://sputniknews.com/politics/ 20141014/194060827.html.

39. Press statements following Russian-Chinese talks from May 8, 2015, http:// en.kremlin.ru/events/president/transcripts/49433; and "Russia, OPEC Jostle to Meet China Oil Demand," *Wall Street Journal*, January 23, 2015, http://www.wsj .com/articles/russia-opec-jostle-to-meet-china-oil-demand-1421987738.

40. "Russia May Seek China Help to Deal with Crisis," *South China Morning Post*, December 18, 2014, http://www.scmp.com/business/banking-finance/ article/1664567/russia-may-seek-china-help-deal-crisis. See also "Beijing Ready to Help Russia's Rattled Economy, Chinese Foreign Minister Says," *South China Morning Post*, December 22, 2014, http://www.scmp.com/news/china/article/ 1667633/beijing-ready-help-russias-rattled-economy-chinese-foreign-minister-says.

41. Jerin Mathew, "China's Dagong Undermines Western Sanctions on Russia, Rates Gazprom's Debt at Top AAA," *International Business Times*, February 2, 2015, http://www.ibtimes.co.uk/chinas-dagong-undermines-western-sanctions -russia-rates-gazproms-debt-top-aaa-148621.

42. "K zaemnoi vygode stroron," *Kommersant*, June 4, 2015, http://kommer sant.ru/doc/2740551. See also Alexander Gabuev, "Smiles and Waves: What Xi Jinping Took Away from Moscow," *Carnegie Moscow Center*, May 29, 2015, http:// carnegie.ru/eurasiaoutlook/?fa=60248.

43. Press statements following Russian-Chinese talks, *Website of the President of Russia*, May 8, 2015, http://en.kremlin.ru/events/president/transcripts/49433.

44. Alexei Lossan, "Rosneft to Sell 10 Percent Stake in Largest Oil Field to Chinese Company," *Russia Beyond the Headlines*, September 8, 2014, http://rbth .com/business/2014/09/08/rosneft_to_sell_10_percent_stake_in_largest_oil_field _to_chinese_com_39607.html; and "Russia, China to Jointly Develop Udokan Copper Field in Transbaikalia," *ITAR-TASS*, May 20, 2014, http://www.bgk-udo kan.ru/en/press-center/31/4252/.

45. Joint Declaration by the Russian Federation and the People's Republic of China on the Coordination of the Construction of the Eurasian Economic Union and the Silk Road Economic Belt, May 8, 2015, http://kremlin.ru/supplement/4971.

46. Catherine Putz, "Sold: Russian S-400 Missile Defense Systems to China," *The Diplomat*, April 14, 2015, http://thediplomat.com/2015/04/sold-russian-s-400-missile-defense-systems-to-china/; and Nikolai Novichkov and James Hardy, "Russia Ready to Supply 'Standard' Su-35s to China, Says Official," *HIS Jane's 360*, November 25, 2014, http://www.janes.com/article/46273/russia-ready-to-supply-standard-su-35s-to-china-says-official.

47. Bobo Lo, *Axis of Convenience: Moscow, Beijing, and the New Geopolitics* (Washington, DC: Brookings Institution, 2008). See also Stephen Kotkin, "The Unbalanced Triangle," *Foreign Affairs* 88, no. 5 (September–October 2009): 130–138.

48. See, for example, Natasha Kuhrt, "Russia and China: Strategic Partnership or Asymmetrical Dependence?," in *Russia and East Asia: Informal and Gradual Integration*, ed. Tsuneo Akaha and Anna Vassilieva (New York: Routledge, 2014), 91–107.

49. Ariel Cohen, "The Russia-China Friendship and Cooperation Treaty: A Strategic Shift in Eurasia?" Heritage Foundation, July 18, 2001, http://www.heritage.org/research/reports/2001/07/the-russia-china-friendship-and-cooperation-treaty.

50. Thomas Wilkins, "Russo-Chinese Strategic Partnership: A New Form of Security Cooperation?," *Contemporary Security Policy* 29, no. 2 (August 2008): 378.

51. Dmitri Trenin, *Russia and the Rise of Asia* (Moscow: Carnegie Moscow Center, 2013), 6.

52. Rex Li, *A Rising China and Security in East Asia* (New York: Routledge, 2009).

53. Dmitri Trenin, *From Greater Europe to Greater Asia: The Sino-Russian Entente* (Moscow: Carnegie Moscow Center, 2015).

54. See, for example, Sergey Karaganov, "Mezhdunarodny krizis: Izbezhat' Afghanistana-2" [International Crisis: Avoid "Afghanistan 2"], *Vedomosti*, July 28, 2014, http://www.vedomosti.ru/opinion/news/29501801/izbezhat-afganistana-2.

55. Igor Ivanov, ed., *Rossiysko-Kitayskiy Dialog: model' 2015* [Russia-China Dialogue: 2015 Model] (Moscow: Russian International Affairs Council, 2015), 6.

56. Ibid., 8.

57. Remarks by Leonid Reshetnikov, director, Russian Institute of Strategic Studies, roundtable at Far Eastern Federal University, Vladivostok, February 2014 (author's personal notes).

58. For example, Russia's head representative at the *Shangri La Dialogue* on Asian security, Deputy Defense Minister Anatoly Antonov, did not even mention the South China Sea controversy. See "Main Points of Speech by Deputy Minister of Defense of the Russian Federation Dr. Anatoly Antonov at the 14th Asia Security Summit 'The Shangri-La Dialogue,'" Singapore, May 30, 2015, http://www .iiss.org/en/events/shangri%20la%20dialogue/archive/shangri-la-dialogue -2015-862b/special-sessions-315c/antonov-da7d.

59. Gilbert Rozman, *The Sino-Russian Challenge to the World Order* (Stanford, CA: Stanford University Press, 2014).

60. Feng Yujun, "Razdumya ob ukreplenii kitaysko-rossiyskih otnosheniy vsestoronnego strategicheskogo vzaimodeiystviya i partnerstva na fone bolshoi turbulentnosti v mezhdunarodnyh otnosheniyah" [Reflections on the Strengthening of Sino-Russian Relations of Comprehensive Strategic Interaction and Partnership Against the Background of High Turbulence in International Relations], in *Rossiysko-kitayskiye otnosheniya: Sostoyaniye i perspectivy razvitiya*, ed. Konstantin Kokorev and Boris Volkhonsky (Moscow: Russian Institute of Strategic Studies, 2014), 51–53.

61. Julia Famularo, "The China-Russia NGO Crackdown," *The Diplomat*, February 23, 2015, http://thediplomat.com/2015/02/the-china-russia-ngo-crackdown/.

62. Judging from the debate among US security specialists, economic strangulation of China by means of a naval blockade is emerging as the optimal strategy for dealing with China in a major conflict. See, for example, Sean Mirski, "Stranglehold: The Context, Conduct and Consequences of an American Naval Blockade of China," *Journal of Strategic Studies* 36, no. 3 (2013): 10–11. See also T. X. Hammes, "Offshore Control Is the Answer," *US Naval Institute*, December 2012, http://www.usni.org/magazines/proceedings/2012-12/offshore-control-answer.

63. Andrew Erickson and Gabriel Collins, "China's Oil Security Pipe Dream," *Naval War College Review* 63, no. 2 (Spring 2010): 90. See also Kenji Horiuchi, "Russia and Energy Cooperation in East Asia," in *Russia and East Asia: Informal and Gradual Integration*, ed. Tsuneo Akaha and Anna Vassilieva (New York: Routledge, 2014), 165.

64. Erickson and Collins, "China's Oil Security Pipe Dream," 90.

65. Interview with Mikhail Dmitriev (prominent Russian economist), *Novaya Gazeta*, February 6, 2015, http://www.novayagazeta.ru/politics/67153.html.

66. "China: Crude Oil Imports," *US Energy Information Administration*, http://www.eia.gov/beta/international/analysis.cfm?iso=CHN; and "Russia: Oil Exports," *US Energy Information Administration*, http://www.eia.gov/beta/inter national/analysis.cfm?iso=RUS.

67. Of course, there is a problem of transportation capacity to ship increased amount of Russian oil and gas to China in case of such an emergency. China may already be thinking about that. See Feng Yujun, *Razdumya*, 56.

68. Zhang Hongzhou, "China Is Marching West for Food," S. Rajaratnam School of International Studies, Singapore, February 4, 2014, http://www.rsis.edu .sg/rsis-publication/rsis/2148-china-is-marching-west-for-foo/#.VVqlg5PmUqM. See also Ariel Cohen, "How Russia Could Become a Food Superpower," *Wall Street Journal*, July 15, 2015, http://blogs.wsj.com/experts/2015/07/15/how-russia -could-become-a-food-superpower/.

69. Jane Perlez, "Chinese Leader's One-Man Show Complicates Diplomacy," *New York Times*, July 8, 2014, http://www.nytimes.com/2014/07/09/world/asia/ china-us-xi-jinpeng-washington-kerry-lew.html?ref=asia&_r=0.

70. Rozman, *Sino-Russian Challenge to the World Order*, 1.

71. Terms used by Rozman in ibid.

72. Willy Lam, "Xi Jinping Forever," *Foreign Policy*, April 1, 2015, http://foreign policy.com/2015/04/01/xi-jinping-forever-china-president-term-limits/.

73. "Press Statement by Vladimir Putin Following Russian-Chinese Talks," President of Russia website, May 8, 2015, http://en.kremlin.ru/events/president/ transcripts/49433.

74. Andrey Karneev, "Rossiysko-kitayskiye otnosheniya v kontekste ideyno-politicheskih techeniy sovremennogo Kitaya" [Russia-China Relations Within the Context of Ideological-Political Camps of Modern China], in *Rossiysko-kitayskiye otnosheniya: Sostoyaniye i perspectivy razvitiya*, ed. Konstantin Kokorev and Boris Volkhonsky (Moscow: Russian Institute of Strategic Studies, 2014), 38–39.

TEN

China's Engagement with Northeast Asia
Patterns, Trends, and Themes

Thomas Fingar

A primary objective of this book is to describe and explain the evolution of China's interactions with key countries in Northeast Asia during the era of reform and opening that began in 1979. China's aspirations, priorities, perception of what was necessary and possible at different times during the decades examined here, and policies to achieve its objectives, are central to the analysis presented in each chapter, but they are not the only focus. The book, especially the chapters by Takagi, Yu, Fingar and Straub, and Lukin, also examines the concerns, goals, and policies of others in the region, and how pursuit of their own objectives shaped their interactions with China and the impact of Chinese policies. In most cases, outcomes were shaped by the efficacy and interaction of policies pursued by all the regional players, and the cumulative impact of multiple interactions transformed both the region and relationships among countries. The result is both a snapshot that captures key elements of China's relationship with the region in the second decade of the twenty-first century and a collection of case studies that facilitate comparisons and identification of patterns and learning curves.

In addition to providing a snapshot of current forms of engagement and analyses of how relationships and interactions evolved from what they were forty years ago to what they are today, the book is intended to facilitate comparisons among regions and over time. The first book in this series, *The New Great Game: China and South and Central Asia in the Era of Reform and Opening*, employed a similar approach and identified a number of patterns and trends in the way China engaged with countries in that region.[1] Some of the patterns identified in that study (e.g., the importance of geography and geopolitics, the role of major countries, and the growing importance of economic goals in the policy calculus of decision makers) are evident in this study as well. Many of the trends identified in South and Central Asia have much less salience or relevance in Northeast Asia (e.g., China's role as a balancer, hedging factor, and driver of economic change in the region).[2]

Primacy of Security and Development Goals

The centrality and primacy of concerns about security and the quest for economic growth or development that emerges in this compendium is consistent with both the findings of *The New Great Game* and the hypothesis developed in the first chapter of that volume. That hypothesis asserts that China accords highest priority to security (i.e., deterring or defeating external aggression, and maintaining internal stability) and development (i.e., growth and modernization of the economy). These goals are intertwined. Security and stability are necessary for sustained economic growth and modernization of the country, and modernization and economic growth are necessary for security and stability. Both must be pursued simultaneously, but the relative salience of each varies over time. How and why their relative salience varied is discussed later in this chapter. Here I want to focus on the finding that the way each of the chapter authors describe China's perceptions, priorities, and policies toward other states in the region is consistent with the hypothesis that what Beijing seeks to achieve is predicated on prior judgments about what the country in question can do *to* China (i.e., whether and how it threatens China's security and other interests) and what it can do *for* China (what it can contribute to China's quest for modernity, wealth, and power).

As demonstrated in the previous chapters, Beijing has pursued a five-part strategy in Northeast Asia to enhance China's external and internal security. One strand of the strategy is the classic balance of power ploy of aligning with one partner (in this case, the United States) to counterbalance the perceived threat from the Soviet Union. Both the initial phase of US-China rapprochement in 1971–1978 and full normalization on January 1, 1979, were predicated on shared concern about a common enemy. The United States was delighted to be able to use China to complicate Moscow's security calculus, but Beijing was at least as pleased to be able to use the United States to deter China's most dangerous adversary. This strand of the strategy became much less viable in Northeast Asia after the demise of the Soviet Union because there was no longer a common enemy in the region, and the threat of international terrorism, which gained salience after 2001, was a very poor substitute.

Improving relations with the United States also served to reduce the imputed direct threat from the United States and the indirect threat from American allies Japan and the Republic of Korea. This is the second strand of the strategy. Despite four decades of US assistance to China's drive for modernity, officials and official media still maintain that the United States is attempting to "contain," "surround," and "threaten" the People's Republic of China (PRC).[3] To deal with this imputed threat, Beijing has sought to maintain reasonably good relations with the United States and to avoid moves (e.g., sales of missiles and nuclear technologies) likely to anger Washington.

The third strand of Beijing's security strategy is to improve relations with China's neighbors, including, but not exclusively, those in Northeast Asia. China has many reasons for wanting good relations with its neighbors; the one I want to focus on here is to use a mixture of charm, opportunity, and economic dependence to diminish the willingness of US allies to act in concert with the United States. The most egregious example of this behavior is Beijing's attempt to use economic leverage to persuade Seoul not to accept installation of the US Terminal High Altitude Area Defense (THAAD) missile defense system.[4] Beijing has misplayed its hand with respect to this strand, especially so with Japan and more assertive tactics in the East and South China Seas that have caused others in the region to see renewed value in using the United States to hedge against China's uncertain intentions. However, developing its own ties to US allies remains a part of Beijing's security strategy.[5]

The fourth strand is military modernization: the acquisition of more capable nuclear and conventional forces to deter real and imagined enemies. During the decades since the end of the Cold War when other regional states, except the Democratic People's Republic of Korea (DPRK), have reduced or made limited enhancements to their own military capabilities, China's military budget has grown by double digits and it has acquired capabilities targeted at assessed US and allied vulnerabilities.[6] This military buildup is primarily a hedge against uncertainty, but it is also a response to what at least some in Beijing regard as a direct threat from the United States and its allies.[7] In recent years, however, Chinese actions vis-à-vis Japan have caused others in the region to worry more about China's ability and willingness to use military as well as economic power to intimidate its neighbors.[8]

The final strand of Beijing's security strategy is to press ahead on its drive to modernize China's economy and achieve sustained high rates of growth in order to meet rising expectations from ever-more-demanding citizens.[9] China's leaders worry more about the threat of internal instability and domestic challenges to the regime than about foreign aggression and appear determined to do whatever is necessary to retain legitimacy by providing concrete benefits to their citizens. Repressive measures of control are part of the strategy to maintain order, as are appeals to nationalism that emphasize party and government resolve to defend China's sovereignty and "core interests" against all real and imagined challenges; but economic performance is the principal pillar of regime legitimacy, and that fact contributes to the high priority accorded to economic development.[10]

Economic performance is the most frequently cited indicator of China's rise to what some characterize as "superpower" status. Displacing Japan to become the world's second-largest economy is a major achievement, and the lot of literally hundreds of millions of Chinese citizens has improved significantly in the past forty years. But China's nominal per capita gross domestic product ranked only seventy-ninth on the International Monetary Fund's 2014 list of 186 countries, distribution is highly inequitable, and gains from efficiency are much less significant than those from increased capacity.[11] The economy is huge and still growing, but it remains more imitative than innovative, heavily dependent on external markets and technologies, and highly vulnerable to corporate and governmental decisions made in other countries.

The fact that China still has a long way to go to meet its developmental goals is a primary shaper of the country's foreign policies. Stated another way, the primary objectives and tasks of Beijing's foreign policy are to ensure security and facilitate development and economic growth. To achieve both these goals, Beijing must maintain reasonably good relations with the United States and the other advanced economies by being attentive to their concerns (e.g., countering the proliferation of weapons of mass destruction, showing greater respect for human rights, conforming to the rules and norms of the international system), prevent or limit violent instability anywhere that could jeopardize China's access to resources, markets, or other factors critical for sustained growth, and cultivate opportunities for inward and outward investment.

These tasks are global in scope but have particular salience in Northeast Asia because Japan and the Republic of Korea (ROK) are especially important to the attainment of China's developmental objectives and both are closely allied to the United States. China needs their investments, markets, and other contributions to the quest for modernity and would like to weaken their ties to the United States, but its own military build up and the actions of its North Korean ally make that a complicated task. Pyongyang's greatest leverage over Beijing is its capacity to endanger regional security and stability in ways that jeopardize China's security and economic future. The ROK wants China to do more to constrain the DPRK and to facilitate reunification, but finding a way to do so that does not jeopardize China's interests has proved all but impossible.

The high priority China assigns to security and development is a primary driver and shaper of PRC policy toward other countries in Northeast Asia. It is also an important determinant of the way other countries perceive China, respond to its policy initiatives, and pursue their own security and economic objectives. But these are not the only factors shaping perceptions, priorities, and policies. Individual chapters of this book have identified or implied other shaping variables, and reading the chapters together reveals patterns and trends that transcend individual countries. The rest of this chapter describes some of the overarching trends and patterns and compares the way they are manifest in Northeast Asia to the findings of our companion volume on China and South and Central Asia.[12]

The Importance of Changes in the International System and the Policies of Regional States

The most important change in the international system during the era of reform and opening, the demise of the Soviet Union, had a much smaller impact on relationships in Northeast Asia than it did in South Asia, Central Asia, and Europe.[13] Korea and China remained divided, alliances remained intact, and the United States maintained the policy of support for China's quest for modernization and economic growth that it had adopted in 1978 to make the PRC a stronger partner in the Cold War competition with the Soviet Union. Beijing seems to have been surprised by the constancy of US policy despite the profoundly negative American reaction to Deng Xiaoping's use of military force to remove protesting students from Tiananmen Square in 1989 and harsh criticism of China during the 1992 presidential campaign. Worried that Washington might curtail support to China's drive to modernize, Beijing took steps to firm up relations with the United States by becoming more attentive to US concerns about proliferation and other transnational issues, and to solidify ties with Japan and the ROK.

The Chinese were not and are not the only ones baffled by the constancy of US policy toward the PRC. Many inside and outside the region interpret almost everything that Washington says or does (e.g., the Obama administration's rebalance to Asia) as part of a strategy to contain or constrain China's rise and seem to think it only a matter of time until the inevitable military clash between the United States and the PRC.[14]

The chapters by Zhao, Fingar, Takagi, and Yu describe the efforts by China, Japan, and Korea to protect still new and fragile relationships. Russia's security and economic situations were obviously very different. Decisions and actions during the Gorbachev era had substantially reduced the military threat to China and Pyongyang's ability to use Moscow to counterbalance Beijing and Washington, but the collapse of the Soviet Union dramatically curtailed Moscow's interest in and ability to influence developments in Northeast Asia. As described in the chapter by Lukin, Russia became a much less important player in the region except as a potential supplier of energy and other raw materials to the booming economies of China, Japan, and South Korea.

In Northeast Asia, the policies of individual states had greater impact than did changes in the global order. The most important of the national policy changes were the complementary decisions of China to adopt a model of export-led growth requiring access to the US-led group of developed democracies, and the decision of the United States to assist China's efforts to do so. The first phase of US-China normalization initiated by Mao Zedong and Richard Nixon cleared the way for Japan to expand economic ties with China. The second phase, beginning with Jimmy Carter's decision to assist China's quest for modernity and symbolized by the establishment of diplomatic relations on January 1, 1979, paved the way for increased cooperation between Japan and China and, a decade later, between China and the ROK.

Arguably the change in the international system that has had the greatest impact on China's relations with Japan, the ROK, Taiwan, and many other places is the spread of computer-based information and production technologies and the development of production and supply chains reflecting comparative advantage at each stage of the production process. Japanese and Korean firms are able to move portions of their manufacturing operations to China to take advantage of abundant and cheaper labor than can be found at home. Moving only portions of the production chain takes advantage of relative efficiencies without risk of putting all eggs in one basket. China did not invent or make possible globalized production chains, but it—and its regional partners—has benefited greatly from the ability to capitalize on the possibilities those production chains create.[15]

The Importance of Geography and Geopolitics

Geographic proximity and few natural barriers to the movement of people, goods, and ideas among the nations of Northeast Asia make this arena of China's interaction with other countries unique in many ways. Ease of movement across relatively level terrain and narrow seas facilitated trade, cultural interchange, and military conquest. Interaction was always a two-way process, but China's vastly greater size and population enabled the Middle Kingdom to dominate its smaller neighbors (Korea and Japan) during much of the premodern era. Chinese through the centuries tended to see this state of affairs as natural and appropriate; China's neighbors, however, viewed its preeminence as dangerous, problematic, and impossible to ignore. Centuries of interaction produced a mixed history of friendly and mutually beneficial relations, mutual understanding, and deep-seated antipathy.

Historical memory, or more accurately, different memories of their shared histories continue to shape the perceptions and policies of China and its neighbors. The chapters by Takagi, Yu, and Fingar and Straub underscore the mixed character of historical memories and their influence on policies. The mixture of positive and negative memories and perceptions of one another complicates the policy calculus in all capitals, but proximity and economic complementarities are at least as important in shaping interactions among state and private-sector players.[16] The net assessment that emerges from the chapters in this volume is that geography facilitates contemporary interaction and helps to explain China's relationships with countries in Northeast Asia. But the chapters also make clear that memories resulting from historical interactions strongly influence the way Chinese and others in the region perceive one another and the policies they adopt to protect their interests while pursuing perceived opportunities.

The geography-centered dynamic revealed in this book is considerably different from the one described in my edited volume on China and South and Central Asia. Rather than a facilitator of interaction between China and its neighbors in that region, geography was a major inhibiter until the 1990s.[17] But geopolitics, specifically the character of relationships between countries in each region and third-country actors (the United States and the Soviet Union) had a major impact on China's security concerns and calculations with respect to both regions. The demise of the Soviet Union had a much bigger impact on China's interactions with South and Central Asia than it did on Beijing's perception of the security challenges resulting from the Japanese and ROK alliances with the United States.

In Northeast Asia, the willingness of Japan and South Korea to assist China's quest for modernization and to tie their own economic fates to the PRC was also affected by their relationship with the United States. As the chapters by Takagi and Yu make clear, Japan and the ROK both felt that they needed US acquiescence to deepen economic ties with China, and that they could accept a perhaps otherwise uncomfortable level of economic dependence on China because of their security relationship with the United States.

The Importance of Major Countries

Among the characteristics that make Northeast Asia unique is the fact that most states in the region warrant classification as "major" countries by virtue of the size of their economies and military capabilities. China, Japan, Russia, and South Korea have the second-, third-, tenth-, and thirteenth-largest economies; including the United States as a regional power adds the largest economy to the mix. Measured in terms of military personnel, regional states rank number 1 (China), 2 (United States), 5 (North Korea), 6 (South Korea) and 23 (Japan). Four have nuclear weapons (United States, Russia, China, North Korea), and four are among the top-seven trading nations (China, United States, Japan, South Korea).[18] Much the same is true if one considers many other dimensions of national power. All (except for Mongolia and Taiwan) can be considered major players, on at least some important dimensions. This both complicates and makes more consequential the management of relationships between and among them.

In international relations, size still matters. A central argument in this book is that China's relationships with other nations are shaped primarily by calculations about whether and how the other country threatens or might contribute to China's security, and by what a country can contribute to China's quest for modernization and economic growth. The primacy of these considerations has special significance in this region because the countries China considers to be actual or potential adversaries (the United States, Russia, and Japan) have substantial independent military (and economic) capabilities that China feels compelled to counterbalance, in part by building up its own military forces.[19] China's security calculus is made even more demanding by the fact that US alliances in the region unite the capabilities of three of the most powerful and economically dominant countries in the world (United States, Japan, South Korea). Beijing's only ally—in the region and in the world—is the DPRK. As the chapters by Fingar and Fingar and Straub (Chapters 6 and 8) demonstrate, Beijing seems to consider its relationship with the DPRK to be more a dangerous liability than source of additional strength.

The chapters in this book present important insights into the calculations and impact of a country with much less influence and impact than one might expect from its size and capabilities (Russia), and one that has greater centrality in Chinese thinking than one would expect from its size and limited economic strength (North Korea).[20] During most of the era of reform and opening, the Soviet Union/Russia played only a small role in China's security calculations and drive for economic growth. Gorbachev's policies significantly reduced the direct military threat from the Soviet Union, but concerns about China played little role in Moscow's decision to scale back the size of the Red Army and reduce deployments along the Chinese border. Gorbachev did what he did as part of an attempt to address the Soviet Union's severe economic weaknesses, not to improve relations with a fellow Communist Party–led state. Moreover, in the initial decade of reform when Moscow had the ability to assist China's modernization, it did not do so for ideological reasons. By the time the Soviet Union had been transformed into Russia and the other Newly Independent States, China's needs, except for energy and raw materials, had outgrown Russia's ability to be helpful.

Perhaps the most interesting Chinese foreign policy challenge in the region is that posed by North Korea, the weakest and least capable actor on the regional stage. Beijing opposes the North's possession of nuclear weapons and disapproves of much that the regime says and does, but it is constrained by knowledge that Pyongyang has the capacity to jeopardize China's own security and economic development by provoking military retaliation by the ROK and/or the United States. The DPRK can contribute little at the high end of requirements for Chinese development, but it has coal and other resources needed to sustain economic growth in the PRC. It is willing, however, to make them available to China only if Beijing continues to provide economic assistance and at least minimal political cover for the North. Thus far Beijing appears to have calculated that it has more to lose from alienating the DPRK than it stands to gain by breaking with the regime.[21] Although he does not draw explicit comparisons, Lukin's description of how Moscow's perceptions of China changed over time evinces many parallels with the evolution of Beijing's view of the DPRK.

The Importance of China's Rise to Balancing and Hedging in the Region

China's rise and the end of the Cold War greatly altered the way China and other countries in the region think about the need to counterbalance potential threats to security and hedge against uncertainty. The demise of the Soviet Union dramatically reduced the perceived threat from the north that gave rise to the US-Japan alliance and US-China rapprochement. Russia's very different perception of and relationship with the DPRK reduced Pyongyang's ability to play Moscow and Beijing against each other for its own benefit, but the North's acquisition of nuclear weapons and China's military buildup changed the strategic situation in the region in ways that compelled Japan, South Korea, and the United States to respond.

Efforts by Japan and the ROK to elicit reassurances from the United States and US responses intended to provide them and to prevent attempts by either ally to seek an independent nuclear weapons capability were interpreted by Beijing as threatening to its own security. For a combination of reasons, the security assessments and arrangements that had undergirded peace and prosperity in the region for decades began to seem less relevant and less reliable. China's rise was only one of the factors contributing to reassessments and partial realignments across the region, but it frequently headed the list of factors identified as triggering or requiring new ways to preserve peace and hedge against threats to economic and military security.[22] As the chapter by Liru Cui demonstrates, Chinese leaders and geostrategic thinkers are well aware of the spotlight on China's actions and aspirations and have made a concerted effort to reassure others that China's rise will be beneficial to all and threatening to none.[23]

Balance-of-power thinking has a very long history in Northeast Asia, and much of what has occurred in the past decade can be understood as the natural and predicable response of smaller neighbors to the increased capabilities and more assertive posture of the PRC. To counterbalance China, Japan and the ROK, and for a while the DPRK as well, sought to bolster their relationships with the United States as a hedge against PRC threats to their interests and independence.[24] The same is true of their response to North Korea's acquisition of nuclear weapons—the first step was to obtain reaffirmation of the US extended deterrence commitment.

But China's rise has affected hedging calculations in other ways as well. Until quite recently, Japan and the ROK depended heavily on the United States for both security and prosperity. Now, however, pursuit of economic opportunities and reduced dependence on the US market has made both countries significantly more dependent on the health of their economic ties with China and has caused them to feel increasingly conflicted about their new state of dual dependency in which they rely on the United States for protection and on China for prosperity. This would make them uncomfortable under any circumstances, but their discomfort is magnified by the widespread conviction that rivalry between a rising China and a status quo or declining United States is inevitable and will leave them trapped between giants and forced to make an unpalatable choice. Perhaps the most graphic illustration of how such thinking is affecting politics is the short-lived, but nonetheless important, decision by Japanese prime minister Yukio Hatoyama to seek a more balanced relationship with China and the United States.[25]

As the weakest player in the region, North Korea was the most active seeker of new ways to counterbalance what it perceived as security threats from China, the United States, the ROK, and Japan, and to reduce its economic dependence on China by improving relations with Russia, Japan, and the ROK. None of these efforts achieved more than partial or temporary success, but Pyongyang sees no alternative except to try harder, maintain its nuclear weapons, and hope that fear of what it might do will elicit cooperation from countries that do not and will not work with the North to achieve other shared objectives. This calculus is central to the chapter by Fingar and Straub.

Other Similarities and Differences Between Northeast Asia and South and Central Asia

The overarching framework for this volume and the previous one on China and South and Central Asia argued that Beijing's highest foreign policy priorities in the era of reform that began in 1979 have been security (defined to include domestic stability as well as security from foreign military threats) and economic development (modernization).[26] These goals are interdependent—a peaceful international environment is necessary to achieve export-led growth and development facilitated by foreign investment, imported technologies, advanced training from abroad, and access to foreign markets, and comprehensive modernization is required to strengthen the nation, build a powerful military, and satisfy the needs and demands of the public. The case studies focused on Chinese policy in these volumes are consistent with the posited framework and support the hypothesis that Beijing formulates policies toward particular states on the basis of judgments about the threat they pose to China and what they might contribute to China's quest for modernity, prosperity, power, and influence.

The United States held the key to the success of the reform and opening strategy because it was better able—and seemingly more willing—to assist China's pursuit of peace and development than were other nations, but also, and as important, because at the time the strategy was adopted, all countries with the capacity to provide the kinds of assistance China desired were part of the US-led "free world" system. Without US approval, China could not gain access to the markets, firms, technologies, schools, and capital of the world's most advanced nations. As the second-largest economy and arguably the second most advanced country, Japan had the potential to play a major role in China's development—if Washington approved, Beijing could overcome deep-seated antipathies toward Japan, and Tokyo could be persuaded to strengthen a past and potential rival. All three conditions were met and, from the beginning, Japan has played a crucial role in China's rise.

But the partnership is an uneasy one, and public opinion in both countries challenges economic interdependence and mutual benefit for priority in the decision calculus of Tokyo and Beijing.

South Korea was more developed than China in 1979, but it took another decade for the ROK to reach the stage at which its firms were eager and able to build ties with China, and China was prepared to make the political adjustments necessary to establish a new type of relationship with the ROK. To make the shift from unqualified support for Pyongyang to deepening engagement with the ROK, Beijing had to rework its security calculus to downgrade the importance of having the DPRK as a buffer against United States troops in South Korea, and to recalibrate the threat from the United States and its allies. It did so in order to sustain high rates of economic growth and access to technologies and markets in nearby countries with long and strong historical ties to China.

No country in South or Central Asia had what China most needed in the initial phases of reform and opening and security considerations, principally India's relationship with the Soviet Union, remained a formidable barrier to cooperation. As a result, China's engagement with both subregions was delayed even longer than it was with the ROK. It was only after the demise of the Soviet Union reduced the indirect threat from India and China had developed to a point that it needed raw materials and intermediate inputs from the region and desired access to internal markets that China began a more concerted effort to build ties with South and Central Asia.

There are interesting but incomplete parallels between China's perception of and policies toward its long-standing special partners in each region: the DPRK in Northeast Asia and Pakistan in South Asia. The two special partners are very different—culturally, politically, and in terms of their relationships with other countries—but both had the capacity to assist China's pursuit of security objectives. As Beijing assessed that it needed them less for security reasons and had more to gain by expanding economic ties with the principal rival of each special partner, namely the ROK and India, it began to shift attention and priority to the enemy of their erstwhile special friends. The DPRK saw this coming and has attempted to compensate (see Chapter 8); Pakistan thus far has remained confident that China's friendship is unqualified and enduring.[27]

China's economic rise has been important to developments in both regions, but the character and impact have been very different in Northeast

Asia than in South and Central Asia. In Northeast Asia, China has become the leading trade partner of Japan and South Korea, but much of this trade is the result of the positions that each country holds in global production and supply chains. To a considerable extent, Japanese and Korean firms have tapped China's abundant and, until recently, cheap supply of workers willing to perform repetitive assembly jobs fabricating products designed elsewhere and often including components and subassemblies made in third countries. Most of the products assembled in China are destined for markets in North America, Europe, Japan, and the ROK. In exchange, China provides raw materials needed by Japanese and Korean firms.

The situation in South and Central Asia is considerably different. In both subregions, Chinese firms and investment are a major driver and shaper of local economies, and the infrastructure that China has built to overcome natural barriers and centuries of practices intended to limit trans-border interchange has changed relationships among regional states. China's beneficent role is more obvious and arguably a more important driver and shaper of economic and social change in South and Central Asia than is the case in Northeast Asia. In other words, China plays important roles in both regions, but the nature of those roles is quite different.

Another significant difference is the role played by public opinion. In South and Central Asia, limited historical contact and the relative unimportance of nationalism as a factor in relationships between China and its regional partners give national leaders a relatively free hand to devise and implement engagement policies. That is much less the case in Northeast Asia, especially so with respect to the relationship between China and Japan. In both of those countries, public opinion both drives and constrains leadership efforts to manage the bilateral relationship and sometimes seems to trump economic self-interest as the most important shaper of perceptions and policies.

The final observation on patterns and trends in the two regions concerns the impact on perceptions and attitudes in China and its partner countries. That observation is that while citizens and officials in all dyads like the benefits of increased interaction with China, they do not appear to have gained greater appreciation or affection for China, the Chinese system, or the Chinese people. Interaction has brought economic benefits to people in both countries and created interdependencies that should enhance the stability of relationships, but it does not appear to have increased empathy, affection, or mutual understanding. Indeed, especially in Northeast Asia, greater interchange seems to have increased suspicion of Chinese ambitions and intentions, discomfort with perceived vulnerabilities to pressure and demands from Beijing, and worry about being forced to choose between Beijing and Washington. All parties seem to be aware of this, but none has yet devised a successful way to address the problem. Though important to all parties, their partnerships are uneasy at best and often deeply troubled.

Notes

1. Thomas Fingar, ed., *The New Great Game: China and South and Central Asia in the Era of Reform and Opening* (Stanford, CA: Stanford University Press, 2016).

2. The patterns and themes in South and Central Asia are described in ibid., chap. 13.

3. See, for example, John Hemmings, "Hedging: The Real US Policy Towards China?" *The Diplomat*, May 13, 2013, http://thediplomat.com/2013/05/hedging-the-real-u-s-policy-towards-china/.

4. Choe Sang-Hun, "South Korea Tells China Not to Meddle in Decision over Missile System," *New York Times*, March 17, 2015, http://www.nytimes.com/2015/03/18/world/asia/south-korea-tells-china-not-to-meddle-in-decision-over-missile-system.html?_r=0.

5. See, for example, Tom Vanden Brook, "Former Enemy Vietnam Seeks US Help to Counter China," *USA Today*, August 18, 2014, http://www.usatoday.com/story/news/world/2014/08/17/vietnam-war-dempsey-visit-counter-china/14185033/; and Jonathan D. Pollack, "The Strategic Meaning of China-ROK Relations: How Far Will the Rapprochement Go and with What Implications?," *Asan Forum*, September 29, 2014, http://www.brookings.edu/research/articles/2014/09/strategic-meaning-china-south-korea-relations-pollack.

6. Data on country military budgets can be found at the Stockholm International Peace Research Institute's *SIPRI Military Expenditure Database*, http://www.sipri.org/research/armaments/milex/milex_database.

7. See, for example, Andrew J. Nathan and Andrew Scobell, "How China Sees America: The Sum of Beijing's Fears," *Foreign Affairs* 91, no. 5 (September–October 2012): 32–47. For analyses of China's military modernization, see Ashley J. Tellis and Travis Tanner, eds., *Strategic Asia 2012–13: China's Military* Challenge (Seattle: National Bureau of Asian Research, 2012); Richard D. Fisher Jr., *China's Military Modernization: Building for Regional and Global Reach* (Stanford, CA: Stanford University Press, 2010); and Anthony H. Cordesman, Ashley Hess, and

Nicholas S. Yarosh, *Chinese Military Modernization and Force Development* (Washington, DC: Center for Strategic and International Studies, 2013).

8. See, for example, Michael Schuman, "Why Do We Fear a Rising China?," *Time*, June 7, 2011, http://business.time.com/2011/06/07/why-do-we-fear-a-rising -china/.

9. See, for example, Jamil Anderlini, "China's Ever Greater Expectations," *Financial Times*, November 8, 2012, http://www.ft.com/intl/cms/s/2/1fb9441a -2998-11e2-a5ca-00144feabdc0.html#axzz3gZZO6eMQ.

10. Erica Strecker Downs and Phillip C. Saunders, "Legitimacy and the Limits of Nationalism: China and the Diaoyu Islands," *International Security* 23, no. 3 (Winter 1998–1999): 114–146.

11. Rankings based on per capita gross domestic product are from International Monetary Fund, *World Economic Outlook Database*, April 2015.

12. Thomas Fingar, "Patterns, Trends, and Themes," in *The New Great Game: China and South and Central Asia in the Era of Reform and Opening*, ed. Thomas Fingar (Stanford, CA: Stanford University Press, 2016), chap. 13.

13. Ibid.; and Robert O. Keohane, Joseph S. Nye, and Stanley Hoffman, eds., *After the Cold War: International Institutions and State Strategies in Europe, 1989– 1991* (Cambridge, MA: Center for International Affairs, 1993).

14. See, for example, Jae Ho Chung, *Between Ally and Partner: Korea-China Relations and the United States* (New York: Columbia University Press, 2007); Kevin J. Cooney and Hoichiro Sato, ed., *The Rise of China and International Security: America and Asia Respond* (New York: Routledge, 2009); and Aaron L. Friedberg, *A Contest for Supremacy: China, America, and the Struggle for Mastery in Asia* (New York: W. W. Norton, 2011).

15. See, for example, Leonard K. Cheng and Henryk Kierzkowski, eds., *Global Production and Trade in East Asia* (New York: Springer Science + Business Media, 2001).

16. For more on the impact of geography and geographic proximity, see Robert D. Kaplan, *The Revenge of Geography* (New York: Random House, 2012); and Richard C. Bush, *The Perils of Proximity: China-Japan Security Relations* (Washington, DC: Brookings Institution, 2010).

17. Fingar, *New Great Game*, chap. 13.

18. Rankings are from International Monetary Fund, *World Economic Outlook Database*, April 2015, https://www.imf.org/external/pubs/ft/weo/2015/01/weodata/ index.aspx; and Institute of International Strategic Studies, *The Military Balance 2015* (New York: Routledge, 2015).

19. See Ben Blanchard, "China's Military Build Up Aims to Prevent Repeat of WW2 Disaster," *Reuters*, May 7, 2015, http://www.reuters.com/article/2015/05/08/ us-china-defence-idUSKBN0NT07P20150508.

20. See Chapter 9; and Charles K. Armstrong, *Tyranny of the Weak: North Korea and the World, 1950–1992* (Ithaca, NY: Cornell University Press, 2013).

21. See Eleanor Albert and Beina Xu, "The China-North Korea Relationship" (backgrounder), Council on Foreign Relations, February 8, 2016, http://www.cfr.org/china/china-north-korea-relationship/p11097.

22. See, for example, Ming Xia, "'China Threat' or a 'Peaceful Rise of China'?," *New York Times*, n.d., http://www.nytimes.com/ref/college/coll-china-politics-007.html.

23. Bonnie S. Glaser and Evan S. Medeiros, "The Changing Ecology of Foreign Policy-Making in China: The Ascension and Demise of the Theory of 'Peaceful Rise,'" *China Quarterly* 190 (June 2007): 291–310.

24. See Evan S. Medeiros, "Strategic Hedging and the Future of Asia-Pacific Stability," *Washington Quarterly* 21, no. 1 (2005): 145–167.

25. See, for example, Michael J. Green, "The Japan-US-China Triangle Under New Management," Freeman Report, Center for Strategic and International Studies, October 2009, http://csis.org/files/publication/fr09n10.pdf. For a more general assessment of South Korea's perceived dilemma, see Jae Ho Chung, *Between Ally and Partner: Korea-China Relations and the United States* (New York: Columbia University Press, 2007).

26. Chapter 1 of this volume; and Fingar, *New Great Game*, chap. 1.

27. Syed Rifaat Hussain, "Sino-Pakistan Ties: Trust, Cooperation, and Consolidation," in *The New Great Game: China and South and Central Asia in the Era of Reform and Opening*, ed. Thomas Fingar (Stanford, CA: Stanford University Press, 2016), chap. 6.

Index

Lightning Source UK Ltd.
Milton Keynes UK
UKOW04f0302131117
312504UK00002B/173/P